"Brilliant! *Climb the Green Ladder* can help you move from idea to action. The practical 'how to' guide and real world case studies will send you along a path of real change and success – for your company and yourself."

Seth Farbman, Senior Partner,
Worldwide Managing Director,
Ogilvy & Mather

"Packed with personal accounts on what it takes to provide leadership for sustainability, and the sorts of results you can expect to see for your career, your company and the planet."

Dr Victoria Hands, Environmental and Sustainability Manager,
London School of Economics & Political Science

"Key to climbing any green ladder is effective communication: Fetzer and Aaron do an excellent job in describing the myriad approaches to greening a company, and provide meaningful insights in an easy to read, informative style. The book provides golden nuggets of information about all aspects of greening your company. Read them and think about how they can be applied to your company!"

Paul Toyne, Head of Sustainability, Bovis Lend Lease UK

"No-one wants to check their principles at the office door; this book explains how to take them in with you and how to put them to good commercial use."

Anthony Kleanthous, Senior Policy Adviser,
Sustainable Business and Economics, WWF-UK

"This is a remarkable book written in a language that is accessible and direct. It is a must read for every office manager, corporate responsibility leader, and even CEOs of companies. They will find plenty of inspiring examples and well-developed tools to move their businesses along a smart and ethical pathway."

Yacob Mulugetta, Deputy Director,
Centre for Environmental Strategy, University of Surrey

"This is book needed to be written. Most books written on environmental topics focus on *what* we need to do or *why*. *Climb The Green Ladder* focuses on *who* and *how*. It has the power to inspire any individual to integrate more environmental thinking and action into their role – whatever their function or level; and it helps those in charge of environmental strategy to better understand the nuances and best practices for driving internal change.

It recognizes that the old way to drive environmental change – being preachy, using guilt and pressure is not sustainable; and puts forth a new green approach to help people deliver environmental improvements in their organizations using the power of human psychology and business logic."

Yalmaz Siddiqui, Director, Environmental Strategy, Office Depot

"There is no doubt that climate change is the greatest challenge mankind has faced. We can adapt to that change, but it is as people where the key lies. Yes, we can develop new technologies, rules and regulations, but wastage is all around us and in our daily lives we take energy for granted, like the air we breathe. Until now that is. This book is an inspiring cornucopia of what people and organisations have done to meet these new challenges and develop new approaches, collectively to achieve significant energy savings and sustainable practices.

We need top talent to inspire us and there are certainly many career opportunities today and even more tomorrow. We can and must stay ahead in the move to the low carbon world. This well-considered publication will help to steer us in the right direction whilst still maintaining twenty-first century businesses and lifestyles."

Professor Martin Fry, City University, London

"*Climb the Green Ladder* provides a refreshing outlook at how being green in today's business world is not only good for the environment, it's good for business."

Melissa Perlman, Manager of Public Relations, Office Depot

CLIMB THE GREEN LADDER

CLIMB THE GREEN LADDER

Make Your Company and Career More Sustainable

AMY V FETZER and SHARI AARON

A John Wiley & Sons, Ltd., Publication

To our amazing husbands, Will and Steve, and Shari's wonderful sons, Jake and Michael.

We would not have been able to walk this journey without your love, support and encouragement, nor survive the late nights and lack of sleep.

You have given us the strength and motivation to aim for a more sustainable and successful world.

CONTENTS

PREFACE

THE STORY OF CLIMB THE GREEN LADDER

Everywhere we go – conferences, talks, events, even parties – everyone is asking the same question: 'What can I do to help save the planet?' However, the answers coming back feel either inadequate (such as 'Change your light bulbs') or extreme (such as 'Superglue yourself to an oil refinery!').

There also seems to be a circular argument about responsibility. Do governments need to legislate, corporations change their practices or individuals alter their behaviour? The solutions will come from all these places, but everyone seems to be ignoring one key source of influence. Governments and corporations are made up of *people*. That gives individuals like us the power to change organisations from within, to set them on more sustainable, more successful paths and, in the process, future-proof our careers.

There are many talented, passionate and creative people using their individual power to make companies or organisations more sustainable, while getting ahead in their careers. The knowledge is out there, but it is under the covers and hard to find. There certainly isn't much evidence of it in newspapers. When we do find valuable advice, it is often couched in jargon or described in abstract terms that makes it hard to translate into our own working lives.

We want to make a difference, to uncover this knowledge and share it so that we can work together towards a more successful, sustainable future. We know that 'more sustainable' means 'more successful' – both for the company you work for and for you personally.

Climb the Green Ladder shows the myriad ways that people are using resources more wisely, reducing emissions, pollution and waste and alleviating social injustice and poverty just by helping their organisation change their business practices. All successful sustainability strategies are underpinned by the same basic principles. We have detailed them here to provide a framework for others to follow; adding the personal stories behind the business successes makes them real.

People are trying to live responsibly in their home lives, for example by recycling, composting, buying fair trade and organic, and flying, driving or buying less. It can be uncomfortable and distressing to feel that, during our work lives, we are contributing to wasteful, disrespectful, dangerous or environmentally damaging behaviour – often on a scale that dwarfs our personal efforts.

Many people want to do something about their company or organisation's unsustainable practices, but don't know where to start. By bringing all this information together, by collaborating and sharing solutions, this book is a ladder to a more successful future – both for yourself and your career, your company and, ultimately, our beautiful planet.

Based in the UK and the US, and with an ocean between us, we relied on the wonderful communications tool Skype (www.skype.com) to write this book, and spent hours each day discussing it via video chat. Many times we wanted to jump on a plane to meet and be together, to be able to work on one document around the kitchen table or to pop the champagne when we submitted our final manuscript. But this compromise is one way we are trying to walk our talk.

We're not perfect. We still fly, and drive, and buy. But we're doing it less and less, and continuing to look for greener, more socially responsible solutions. Sustainability means looking for ways to achieve goals without sacrificing people, planet or profit. Sometimes, that means reassessing the goals themselves, but together we are finding new ways and new habits.

No company or organisation is perfect either. Sustainability is evolving all the time as new solutions, information and ways of thinking come to light. However, the principles described in this book will remain the same.

We're not making a judgement on whether the companies or individuals within them described in this book are sustainable. We are hoping to share the *successes* they have had. We want to show that everyone – in any industry and with any job title – can make a difference and stand up for what they know is right for their workplaces.

You'll read about people who are personally making a difference and about interesting, innovative and effective initiatives that are making business practices more sustainable. Our readers work for, or run, a wide range of companies and organisations – from multinationals to nongovernmental organisations (NGOs) and public sector organisations. To reflect this, we've used 'company' and 'organisation' interchangeably. All these strategies should apply wherever you work, whether it's a school, a charity, a small or multinational company, a government, a farm, a hospital or your own business.

We hope you enjoy this book and find it helpful. We wish you a fulfilling and inspiring journey as you *Climb the Green Ladder*. Please tell us of your progress, and we'll share updates via our website: www.climbthegreenladder.com. We look forward to meeting you on the way up.

Amy and Shari

ACKNOWLEDGEMENTS

A special thank you goes to those who participated in our survey and in-depth interviews. Your words and insights can be found throughout our work. We applaud your inspirational work and thank you for allowing us to share your stories with our readers.

The international experts, champions and sustainability leaders we interviewed and called upon include:

Camilla Flatt	Africapractice
Ian Barnes	Alliance Boots
Richard Ellis	Alliance Boots
Michael Passoff	As You Sow
Gwyn Jones	Association of Sustainability Professionals
Mark Parker	Aztec
Peggy Connolly	Boston Center for Corporate Citizenship
Dr Paul Toyne	Bovis Lend Lease
Bob Gordon	British Retail Consortium (BRC)
Doug Shaw	BT Global Services
Maria Figueroa Kupcu	Brunswick Group

David Stangis	Campbell Soup Company
David Vincent	The Carbon Trust
Matthew Hawtin	Careers Development Services
Veena Ramani	Ceres
Erika Vandenbrande	City of Redmond
Martin Fry	City University
Wood Turner	Climate Counts
Katherine Allison	CMS Cameron McKenna
Alastair Fuad-Luke	Co-design Services for Sustainability Transition
J. B. Schramm	College Summit
Simon Graham	Commercial
Ryan Mickle	Companiesandme.com
Sara Ellis Conant	Deloitte Consulting, LLP
Tom Fogden	Deloitte Consulting, LLP
Coral Rose	Eco Innovations
Julie Chang	Ecology and Environment
Tony Gale	Ecology and Environment
Amy Hall	Eileen Fisher
Sophie Hanim	Energy Saving Trust
Sara Parkin, OBE	Forum for the Future
Kathee Rebernak	Framework:CR
Ed Gillespie	Futerra
Jeff Melnyk	Futerra
Jo Confino	The Guardian
Scott Davidson	Global Action Plan
Trewin Restorick	Global Action Plan
Frank Dixon	Global Systems Change
Roger East	Green Futures Magazine
Michael Dupee	Green Mountain Coffee Roasters
Sandy Yusen	Green Mountain Coffee Roasters
Helen Trevorrow	Green Row PR
Joel Makower	GreenBiz.com
Sarah Daly	Heath Avery Architects
Randy Boeller	Hewlett Packard (HP)

Ken Bosley	Hewlett Packard (HP)
Debbie Ledbetter	Hewlett Packard (HP)
Bonnie Nixon	Hewlett Packard (HP)
Erin Simon	Hewlett Packard (HP)
Charlie Browne	IKEA
Don Carli	Institute for Sustainable Communication
Rich Liroff	Investor Environmental Health Network (IEHN)
Martin Smith	JustMeans
Martin Horwood, MP	Liberal Democrats
Stephanie Chesters	London Borough of Brent
Dr Victoria Hands	London School of Economics and Political Science
Birgitte Rasine	Lucita
Richard Gillies	Marks & Spencer
Steven Lanou	Massachusetts Institute of Technology (MIT)
Lynn Frosch	Microsoft
Benjamin Jones	Monodraught
Will Rowberry	Monitor
Gil Friend	Natural Logic
Natalia Oberti Noguera	New York Social Women Entrepreneurs
Melissa Perlman	Office Depot
Yalmaz Siddiqui	Office Depot
Freya Williams	Ogilvy & Mather, OgilvyEarth
Mike Jones	Open Minds Consulting
Chantal Cooke	Passion for the Planet Radio
Anne Roos-Weil	Pesinet
Kristen Thomas	The Phelps Group
Abby Ray	Rainforest Alliance
Tensie Whelan	Rainforest Alliance
Mark Gough	Reed Elsevier
Neil Turner	RES
Guy Watson	Riverford Organic Vegetables
Dr Martin Blake	Royal Mail

Vicky Forster	Sherborne School for Girls
Bruce Lowry	Skoll Foundation
Jennifer Schramm	Society of Human Resource Management
Holly Fowler	Sodexo
Thomas Jelley	Sodexo
Shelley Rowley	Speechly Bircham, LLP
Jennifer Woofter	Strategic Sustainability Consulting
Ann Finlayson	Sustainable Development Commission
KoAnn Skrzyniarz	Sustainable Life Media
Sofia Bustamante	Turn up the Courage
Lisa Landone	United States Postal Service
Dr Keith Pitcher	University of Leeds
Ian Christie	University of Surrey
Tim Jackson	University of Surrey
Yacob Mulugetta	University of Surrey
Alex Salzman	VizCapital
Perry Abbenante	Whole Foods
Libba Letton	Whole Foods
Anthony Kleanthous	World Wildlife Fund (WWF)

For more information on our research, see Appendix 2.

Special thanks to our research interns, without whom we would have had no sleep: Tara Quinn (especially for her hard work on Appendix 1) and Katie MacKichan who transcribed interviews, obtained permissions and so much more. Thanks also to Brian Murken for designing our wonderful cover and logo.

Additional thanks to our helping hands who provided guidance and support throughout the development of this book. These include our commissioning editor Claire Plimmer at John Wiley & Sons, Ltd, Bruno MacDonald (who edited every chapter), Natalia Oberti Noguera, Don Carli, Carrie Young, Lauren Young and David Young.

We would also like to acknowledge those who inspired and supported our efforts, pointed us to resources and helped us on our journeys. These include Amy's parents, Sharie and Rodney Fetzer, whose love, support and encouragement have always been a source of confidence and strength. Amy's sister, Rosie 'the great' Seldon, also gave us great marketing advice which helped the survey achieve such high response rates.

Other people to whom we are indebted include Danny Wells, Annabel Gibson, George Rowberry, Martin Smith, Jo Opot, Stelios Loizides, Peter Kelley, Patricia Charles, Danielle Changala, Carolyn Parrs, April Fraulo, Patti Ivry, Randy Deskin and the University of Connecticut Writers Group led by Professor Suzanne Davis, and Shari's fellow writers, Jenny Meyburg, Kathy Medbery, Ginny Bitting and Lisa Mcadam Donegan.

Chapter 1

WHY WE NEED THAT GREEN LADDER

> Do you want to make your workplace more sustainable but feel unsure where to start?
>
> Do you want to get ahead in your career and develop a reputation as a dynamic, creative achiever?
>
> Would you like to help your company save money, boost profits and improve its brand?
>
> Would you like to know how to persuade colleagues that sustainability is good for business?

If you answered 'yes' to any of the questions above, you are not alone. All over the world, people are looking for answers. Their numbers are growing as more become concerned about climate change, the unsustainable use of resources and social injustice. Yet only 1 in 10 people feel they have the training or knowledge they need to make their company or organisation more sustainable.[1]

However, many individuals *have* used their power to make their company more sustainable, while getting ahead in their careers too. You may be one of them. Yet these success stories are often 'under the radar', and valuable advice can be couched in jargon that makes it hard to understand or apply to your own situation.

Not any more. In plain English, and with case studies and examples, *Climb the Green Ladder* will give you the tools to make your company and career more sustainable *and* successful.

You may already have made great inroads in bringing sustainability into your workplace, or you may feel frustrated and unsure where to start. Whatever your level or industry, and whether you'd like to transform your entire company or just get colleagues recycling, this book will show you how to maximise your impact.

Corporations and governments are made up of individuals. Those individuals have the power to change an organisation from within. Don't believe us? This book is filled with stories of people who have done just that. Freya Williams helped Ogilvy & Mather launch a green consulting arm (see box **A new way of working**). Dr Victoria Hands from the London School of Economics and Political Science started by getting her university recycling, before rolling out recycling programmes at every

London university. At The Phelps Group, Kristen Thomas' idea to swap disposable lunch dishes for reusable ones started a green tidal wave that led to her company becoming the largest private solar power installation in Santa Monica.

Climate change and the global financial crisis of 2008 have shown we need to find a new way to do business. We *must* think differently to survive and thrive, and that means thinking sustainably. Businesses are like battleships. They take time to change direction but, when they do, they bring enormous power with them. *You* can harness it to make sure that businesses are using their power to meet the demands of a changing world and a changing climate.

We already have the technology and knowledge to solve many of these challenges. By thinking sustainably, we can harness our extraordinary imagination and expertise to implement solutions. If we all work to tackle the issues that we can influence, the challenges can be conquered together.

It can be demanding to get colleagues on board and to show them why thinking sustainably is good for business. Yet the right approach can get them on your side. Simple things like taking photos to show colleagues exactly how much waste your department throws away will *engage* them in your recycling initiative. Working out the money you'd save on materials and transport costs by designing products more efficiently demonstrates the *business case* for sustainability. Understanding which strategies work will allow you to bring about incredible changes that benefit the 'bottom line', the environment, communities and your career.

Climb the Green Ladder will reveal these key sustainability strategies, bringing them to life with the stories of people who have made change happen. This will help you apply the same principles in your workplace.

The key principles are: **mindset**, **business case**, **engagement**, **communication**, **collaboration** and **culture**. Each will be discussed in its own chapter:

- Get the mindset
- Make the business case
- Get your colleagues on side
- Have two-way conversations

- Work together
- Make it part of the culture

First, though, this chapter will put sustainability in context, to explain why tackling issues like climate change and social injustice are crucial for business, society and the planet's survival. The purpose of this book is not to explain climate change and why it is happening. You probably know that. Its purpose is to help you help companies change their behaviour, and innovate, so business isn't contributing to the problems but solving them.

Next, it will give you a summary of why green is good for business and how sustainability can future-proof your career, before diving into more detail in the rest of the book.

◢ A new way of working

Freya Williams came back from maternity leave to her job at Ogilvy & Mather determined to make a difference:

'I am a strategic planner at a global ad agency in New York so you might ask, "What has sustainability got to do with my job?" But having time out made me realise I didn't want to go back to business as usual. I had two choices: stay home and "live green" or use the position and access I have to multinational corporations to change them from the inside. I chose the latter!

'I spoke to my planning director about setting up a sustainability practice which could speak to consumers, clients and employees about the need to go green, and help clients understand how to move their sustainability agenda forward.

'I started by speaking to the head of procurement who gave me a load of old invoices. I added up the amount spent on things like paper and bottled water. We spent a huge amount on paper; I knew we could cut it in half by printing double-sided and being less wasteful. I helped ensure that every employee received a reusable (SIGG) water bottle, and that we used "green" cleaning and paper products in our bathrooms. I also spoke to my COO about switching to renewable energy. He agreed and we now purchase 100% renewable energy through our local utility. With it being a creative agency, it was easy to do a fun campaign to engage employees. And that was just the start!

'All companies are moving in this direction. They need agencies to work with them to communicate their messages authentically, so embracing sustainability ourselves and launching OgilvyEarth has enabled us to better serve our existing clients and even win new ones.

'Sustainability is also great for your career: it makes you stand out in your organisation. But the best thing is I am helping to make a difference. I always wanted to find more meaning in my work, and having a child encouraged me to elevate my priorities.'

THE NEED FOR ACTION: PUTTING SUSTAINABILITY IN CONTEXT

The planet is in peril. The decadent use of fossil fuels has pumped vast amounts of greenhouse gases into the atmosphere, gases that were laid down in the Earth over millennia. This has wildly upset the balance of the Earth's atmosphere and is slowly but surely leading to the warming of the planet. A few degrees doesn't sound like much but it is significant. The warming is not spread evenly across the globe; some places will change by only a fraction of a degree, others will change by several.

However, even a fraction of a degree can make a difference. The world's ecosystems exist in delicate balance. For example, small but prolonged rises in sea temperature cause coral colonies to expel the food-producing algae on which they depend. This process is known as bleaching. Many cannot recover and, as coral is crucial to much sea life, this is having a devastating effect on global fish populations. Overfishing is also decimating global fish stocks. When you consider that 2.6 billion people, or nearly 40% of the world's population, rely on fish as a major source of protein, this is alarming,[2] and this is only one of many examples of how the changing climate is putting us all in danger.

Small changes caused by an increase in greenhouse gases lead to further warming effects. One of these is the melting of the ice caps. As they shrink, there is less white mass to reflect the sun's heat from the Earth and so the planet heats further. These effects are called positive feedback loops. Scientists are worried that these loops will cause the planet to reach a tipping point where several systems combine to create runaway climate change that cannot be controlled.[3]

The Intergovernmental Panel on Climate Change (IPCC) concluded that climate change poses a severe threat to water, food and land.[4] It predicted the spread of disease; that millions will be affected by drought, famine and extreme weather; that there will be vast numbers of environmental refugees; and that the biggest impact will be on the poorest people on the planet. We will also lose an estimated one-third of all species by the end of the century.

Even if we stop putting greenhouse gases into the atmosphere today, it is too late to prevent the world warming. We are already feeling the effects of a changed climate, and events are accelerating even faster than scientists predicted.

THE SOLUTION: LEARN TO CHANGE

IPCC scientists agree that limiting global temperature rises to 1–2 °C won't stop far-reaching and dramatic effects. However, life on Earth would still be possible, albeit with significant species and habitat loss. Higher temperatures of 4–5 °C are likely to prompt much more extreme weather. Droughts, fires and floods will lead to serious food shortages and mass extinction, while rising sea levels will submerge cities like London, New York and Shanghai.

If we carry on with 'business as usual', we're heading for a 4–5 °C rise. However, if we change our behaviour, we have a much better chance of limiting increases to 1–2 °C. We just have to take on the challenge.

RESOURCES AT RISK

Unfortunately, climate change isn't the only problem the planet faces. Even climate sceptics can't deny we are living beyond the means of the Earth.

Historically, businesses have exploited resources to make profit. Any social or environmental fallout was deemed to be an unfortunate by-product. Some businesses tried to mitigate negative outcomes by engaging in philanthropy or corporate social responsibility programmes, but this tended to be a luxury that fell by the wayside when profits were under pressure.

Now, in the 21st century, as pressure on resources mounts, there is an increasing realisation that the Earth's balance sheet just doesn't add up.

The plunder for profit approach might work for a few more years, but it can't carry on indefinitely. Environments, resources, societies and species have been damaged or destroyed, and there may not be any way to replace them. This will leave businesses and people struggling to survive. With only one planet Earth, we need to start using our resources responsibly.

PEOPLE IN PERIL

A third problem is one of social justice. Access to the world's resources is not spread equally between nations, or between people within those nations. In fact, 20% of the population in developed nations consume 86% of the world's resources.[5] The US, Japan, Germany, Canada, France, Italy and the UK – that's less than 12% of the world's population – consume 43% of fossil fuel production, 64% of paper and 55% of all aluminium, copper, lead, nickel and tin.[6]

Wealth is also unevenly distributed. The richest 20% of the world's population receive nearly 50 times the average income of the poorest 20%.[7] At the same time, the *poorest* 20% of the population receive 1.5% of world income.[8] That is less than $1 a day. Almost half of the world's population lives on less than $2 a day.[9] The average American is 61 times richer than the average Tanzanian,[10] and more than 850 million people, including one in three children under five, are in a vicious cycle of malnutrition.[11]

Much of this injustice could be alleviated by changes in the way we do business. This includes ensuring that farmers and producers are paid a fair, living wage, and that responsibility is taken for products and processes to protect workers' rights and reduce or eliminate pollution that damages communities and ecosystems.

SUSTAINABILITY AS A SOLUTION

Sustainability addresses all these challenges, but what does 'sustainability' actually mean? To be sustainable, an action must be able to continue, or be sustained, indefinitely. For this to be possible, you have to consider the social, environmental and economic dimensions of every action (see Figure 1.1).

The *social dimension* means the human element of your actions, issues such as health, wellbeing and social expectations. The *environmental*

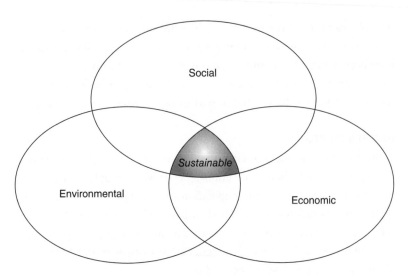

Figure 1.1. The three dimensions of sustainability

dimension means making sure your behaviour doesn't have a negative impact on the ability of natural resources and ecosystems to sustain themselves. The *economic dimension* means the technological and financial systems and issues that underpin most political and business thinking to ensure an action is financially viable in the long term.

People and organisations sometimes use the term 'sustainable' when a business activity is sustainable *in one area*, such as being financially sustainable, when the activity is not socially or environmentally sustainable. Using the term in this context is misleading because the three dimensions of sustainability are like the legs of a stool. Allow one to suffer and it will fall over. An action cannot continue indefinitely if the resources, finance or ability of people to perform that action are compromised by the process.

Similar Idea, Different Jargon

Corporate social responsibility (CSR) is the name often given to socially responsible thinking in business. It can also be called corporate citizenship, or corporate social and environmental responsibility (CSER).

Traditionally, CSR tended to focus more on social issues such as workers' rights or charitable activities, and was considered a discrete part of business that didn't impact on day-to-day operations. Although CSR and CSER are integral to sustainability, and are often used interchangeably with the term, their scope can be more limited.

CLIMB THE GREEN LADDER

The scale of the issues means it is easy to feel overwhelmed. However, you don't have to tackle them alone.

Changing attitudes and moving towards new ways of doing business takes time, patience and knowledge, but, with the right strategies and tools, you can shift your work and your company towards more sustainable practices. You may have already changed your lifestyle to reflect your concern about climate change, resource constraints and social injustice. By bringing those values to work, you can *Climb the Green Ladder* and work towards a brighter future.

Try adopting a *sustainability mindset*: an open, optimistic and practical mindset that incorporates the social, environmental and economic impacts into all of your thinking. This means seeing a bigger picture and taking your values to work each day. Just as you learned to speak the business language of budgeting and time management, so sustainability can become part of your, and your company's, everyday thinking.

◖ A green revolution

'I'd been recycling at home, so I thought, "We should be doing this in the office!"' explains Mark Parker, commercial director the UK-based Aztec Event Services. The idea kick-started a green revolution that has revamped company practices and saved money too.

'I brought in an auditing company called Go Green which advises small businesses, like our 30-person company. Together, we worked out a strategy for things like switching from bottled water to chilled tap water and fitting a device to plugs so anything that's left on standby gets automatically turned off. Simple things like that helped us reduce our electricity consumption by 15% in just six months.

'Our CO_2 footprint was calculated and we found the biggest carbon emitter was our fleet of vans. So we converted to biofuel straight away.

'We also partnered with an advisor from Transport for London who helped us set up a travel plan. This included encouraging people to cycle more and putting speed limiters on the vans. This saves mileage and fuel, which cuts costs and ensures safer driving. We got 50% funding for laptops so we could work from home and be flexible. This improved everyone's quality of life immensely, as it helped work fit in with family life. It's a great example of the wider lifestyle benefits that sustainability can bring.

'My colleagues embraced the ideas. It has taken time but, the more feedback we've given people, the more *they've* given back. In a year, we've reduced our carbon footprint by 20%, been nominated for the Go Green awards and been invited to communicate to other businesses how it can be done. It has also won us business and had a really positive response from local communities, industry and customers.'

DOING WELL WHILE DOING GOOD

Major businesses from Wal-Mart and Kraft to Hewlett Packard and Marks & Spencer have realised that embracing sustainability and taking a leadership role makes excellent business sense.

Increasing climate change regulation and customer expectations mean that being knowledgeable about these issues is crucial to survival. Meanwhile, scarce resources and new scenarios lead to new opportunities. However, you don't have to take our word for it. Research by the Aberdeen Group found sustainability strategies reduce risk, increase brand loyalty and give companies a competitive advantage.[12] The survey of 4500 companies found that globalisation, increasing compliance requirements and supply cost pressures were driving companies towards improved sustainability and CSR. Key issues were the desire to be viewed as sustainability leaders; the rising cost of energy, supplies, material and transport; the search for competitive advantages and product differentiators; and growing pressure from customers.

Can sustainability really do all of these things? It can, and throughout *Climb the Green Ladder*, we'll demonstrate exactly *how* it does, with examples from the people and companies who have seen these benefits in action.

✤ Sustainable by design

The Hewlett Packard TouchSmart PC doesn't *look* green, with its sleek, touch-screen technology designed to tempt style-conscious consumers looking for cutting-edge gadgets. Yet because it was made with sustainability in mind, it's been designed to reduce PC energy use by up to 45%. It arrives in 100% recyclable packaging with more paper and less plastic foam for easier recycling and the machine itself uses 55% less metal and 37% less plastic than standard PCs and monitors.

Ken Bosley, the brand manager on the TouchSmart project, explains why adopting a sustainability mindset was crucial to the success of the project: 'By taking sustainability issues to heart, we were able to produce something that was a lot less material, and that used a lot less power and a lot less packaging. Each benefit just fed back into each other!'

The desire for a slender, sexy product increased consumer appeal. The reductions in material use, packaging materials and increased transport efficiencies proved good for the environment *and* the bottom line as costs were lower. Viewing the green goals as a team challenge meant that everyone was stimulated and motivated by the goal of creating a product with the greenest possible credentials. ✤

STRENGTHENING THE BRAND

The brand reputation element of sustainability is vital for companies. A McKinsey survey found that 95% of CEOs said society now has higher expectations of business taking on public responsibilities than it did five years ago.[13]

Our own survey indicated that 9 out of 10 employees link brand reputation to environmental and social impacts.[14] The negative press associated with poor corporate behaviour shows that mistreating workers and bad environmental management lead directly to reduced sales.

In a digital age with powerful nongovernmental organisations (NGOs) and socially conscious consumers, companies are under increasing scrutiny. Protecting their reputation is vital. Implementing strong sustainability and corporate responsibility policies is an effective way to do this.

'The business and social environment is changing as climate concerns and resource constraints become more real to people,' says Professor Tim Jackson of the University of Surrey. 'There is much more pressure on organisations to take action. Organisations are also much more ready to make pledges because they feel the need to be *seen* to be doing something. This is a real force that individuals can harness to create change.'

♪ Coffee beans and business opportunities

A good example of how sustainability helps companies to 'do well while doing good' is Kraft coffee and McDonalds. In 2003, Kraft started buying coffee beans from Rainforest Alliance certified farms. It now integrates millions of pounds of these beans into mass market brands such as Kenco (UK) and Yuban (US).

Kraft's support accelerated a programme that brought 252,000 hectares under sustainable management practices and improved the lives of 1,260,000 farmers, workers and their families. The programme costs money, but it was shown to make good business sense when Kraft landed a major contract with McDonalds to sell certified sustainable coffee in outlets across Europe. It also increased sales and brand perception. Unit sales went up 15%, coffee sales went up 23% and 40% of customers said the Rainforest Alliance certification was important to them.

Kraft views sustainable coffee as an investment in brand equity and consumer loyalty because it helps assure the long-term consistency, quality and viability of its supplier farms. ♪

ATTRACT AND KEEP TOP TALENT

Sustainability promotes employee engagement. Firms are facing such a strong demand for CSR from their employees that it has become a serious part of the competition for talent.[15] Employers rank the biggest benefit of CSR in the workplace as staff retention, followed by attracting talent and increasing motivation and engagement.

Many large companies say the business rationale for their CSR efforts is that they help to motivate, attract and retain staff. People want to work at a company whose values they share. Featuring in lists such as *The Sunday Times* Green List has become an important recruitment tool, as has appearing in sustainability indices such as the Dow Jones Sustainability Index and the FTSE4Good (see **Appendix 1: Who can help** for more details). These are crucial instruments for building reputation and trust with consumers and investors alike.

By providing the tools to make your organisation a force for good and by helping you to align company values with your own, *Climb the Green Ladder* will help you and your co-workers to feel engaged and involved.

❧ Talent contest

Amy Hall, director of social consciousness at award-winning US ethical women's clothing company Eileen Fisher, believes strong values attract and retain staff: 'Our success demonstrates how strong principles strengthen employee engagement. We have over 800 employees, but we only have a 5.5% employee turnover rate, and we receive more than 10,000 resumés every year. We're certain this is a result of our value-driven stance.'

FUTURE-PROOF YOUR CAREER

Thinking sustainably is a smart career move. Helping your company save money, reduce environmental and social impacts, and gain a competitive edge, will help you meet targets and get promoted.

Being an innovator will raise your profile within the company and give you a reputation as a dynamic, creative achiever. It brings the positive attention of management and identifies you as a smart employee. The satisfaction of living your values and helping to make a difference will ramp up your motivation and make work more enjoyable (see box **Falling in love with work again**).

◗ Falling in love with work again

'Greening the mail and getting involved in sustainability has increased my passion for my job,' says Lisa Landone, customer relations coordinator at the United States Postal Service (USPS). 'Sometimes, if you do the same job for a long time, it becomes a job you do without purpose. But when you are able to take what is in your heart and find a way to bring it to your everyday work, people are more receptive and doors open to help you increase your passion. This makes life more fulfilling.'

Lisa didn't work in sustainability, but she wanted to ensure the mailing community was engaged in the substantial green initiatives USPS had undertaken to reduce their impact. These included the use of soy inks on stamps, sustainable design on Priority Mail packaging and fleets that run partly on bio-diesel.

Lisa presented an idea to develop an employee and customer education programme to showcase USPS environmental initiatives. Management loved the idea and gave her the go-ahead. Now, thanks to Lisa and the Postal Customer Council, postal employees and business mailers across the US have been educated about USPS's sustainable initiatives to help the mailing community 'green' its practices.

Originally concerned that her colleagues would see her as an environmental nut, Lisa found quite the opposite: 'Management feels positively about my efforts because they recognise it as an important issue.'

Lisa is certain the initiative she demonstrated by thinking beyond her job title has increased her standing. It also led to a new role as a sustainability champion. She has now been asked to focus on sustainability issues and to investigate what the organisation can do to save energy, increase recycling and continue on its quest to be greener. ◗

TAKING CARE OF BUSINESS

Business is facing a massive need to transform. Employees and executives must actively engage in the process. Those who believe the world will fix itself and that individuals play a small, insignificant role stand to be victims of our times rather than passionate leaders who can shape our shared future.

Gandhi said, 'You have to be the change you want to see.' Your power, energy, creativity, innovation and intelligence are powerful resources. If you *want* the change, you will find the solutions.

Your aim may be to achieve one small but meaningful act, such as getting fair trade coffee stocked in the office kitchen. You may want to transform your workplace more fundamentally, by reducing energy use across your supply chain or re-engineering your product to use more sustainable materials. However big or small your ambitions, the tools and strategies in *Climb the Green Ladder* will give you a comprehensive toolkit for action.

The solutions can be as individual as your thumbprint. There is no one 'right' way or formula for achieving sustainability, but what we have discovered is that all successful sustainability initiatives, however varied they may appear, are underpinned by the same themes.

We surveyed 430 people and interviewed over 80 experts, as well as inspirational people who had personally contributed to making their organisation more sustainable, from the inside out. During our research, almost everyone we interviewed, surveyed and encountered, and the literature we reviewed, returned to these same themes. We have distilled this knowledge and information into six themes:

● Get the mindset
● Make the business case
● Get your colleagues on side
● Have two-way conversations
● Work together
● Make it part of the culture.

Your influence may lead to the one lasting programme or idea that secures your company's successful future. It can also play a vital part in conserving the planet. Bringing your passions and beliefs into the office, and having the skills and knowledge to persuade your colleagues and management, can help elevate your status, advance your career and make you fall in love with your work.

So, are you ready to *Climb the Green Ladder*?

Chapter 2
GET THE MINDSET

‘Human beings, by changing the inner attitudes of their minds, can change the outer aspects of their lives. ’ William James[1]

Does the huge pile of disposable plates and cups in the office trash drive you mad? Would you love your company or organisation to have its own source of solar power, or to offer sustainable products to clients? Do you wish your colleagues would set their computers to sleep mode so they power down when they're not using them? That co-workers would save and re-use packaging materials? Or that your workplace had bike storage and showering facilities so more people could cycle to work?

You've probably had some of these thoughts, but you'd have to be the CEO or someone pretty senior to begin to change things – right? Wrong.

Kristen Thomas, a PR specialist from the Los Angeles-based marketing agency, the Phelps Group, is proof that one employee can be the catalyst to change a whole company for the better. Frustrated every day by piles of Styrofoam plates and cups in the trash, Kristen decided to speak up and voice her values. She struck a chord, and people responded.

What started as an initiative to eliminate disposable dishes in the office kitchen has led to a whole range of sustainable innovations – from the installation of solar panels to offering clients marketing materials made from recycled materials.

Kristen's decision to live her values at work started a snowball effect (see box **PR specialist and dumpster diver**). It revamped company operations, saved money and waste, and engaged and motivated her colleagues. It attracted new clients and reinforced relationships with existing ones. It also ramped up Kristen's leadership role within her company while increasing her commitment to the company and her passion for her work.

This is an example of the incredible things that can happen when you decide to take action. It takes creativity, determination, courage and positivity, but it can be done. From the biggest multinational organisation to the smallest charity; from schools, manufacturing plants, government offices, restaurants and farmers to self-employed plumbers, journalists, auditors, designers and marketing consultants – everywhere you look, individuals just like you are starting ripple effects that reverberate throughout the working world.

PEOPLE CAN BE THE SOLUTION

To cope in a world of limited resources and an altered climate, we have to change our mindset. 'Business as usual' is not an option. Clients, employers, employees and consumers – citizens – want a new way of working.

They are demanding that the companies and organisations which serve them – and us, the people who work within them – become the solution, not the problem. The result is that people in companies world-wide are finding ways to become more efficient, to provide better services, to save money, trade fairly, invest in and protect natural resources, inspire and motivate employees, improve their brand and win more business – all the while contributing to the creation of a more sustainable, more socially just world.

This global shift in mood towards more active citizenship and respon-sibility and the deep sense of reward it can offer was reflected in Barack Obama's 2009 inauguration speech. 'What is required of us now is a new era of responsibility,' declared the newly sworn-in President. 'A recogni-tion … that we have duties to ourselves, our nation, and the world, duties that we do not grudgingly accept but rather seize gladly, firm in the knowledge that there is nothing so satisfying to the spirit, so defining of our character, than giving our all to a difficult task.'[2]

You may think about sustainability in your personal life, but it can be difficult to know how to live these values at work. It needn't be. The path to becoming more sustainable is a journey and it starts with just one step. It's a new and exciting path on which each victory should be savoured and celebrated. As Kristen's experience shows, from small begin-nings – such as switching to reusable dishes or persuading a stubborn colleague to use recycling facilities – to huge leaps such as cutting emis-sions across a global supply chain, you can kick-start a revolution. It will transform your workplace for the better and make you feel proud and fulfilled to work in an environment that reflects your values.

GET THE MINDSET

One individual can make a difference. Coral Rose helped retail giant Wal-Mart introduce organic cotton clothing ranges. Jo Confino at *The*

Guardian helped the UK newspaper and media group revamp its whole operations. These are just two of the people whose stories you'll read in this chapter. They represent a tiny proportion of the people from around the globe who are making change happen. Their experience teaches us one vital lesson: to believe in your own power. With the right mindset, even the impossible is possible.

Nine ways to get the mindset:

1. Think sustainably
2. Believe in your own power
3. Live your values at work
4. Think positive
5. Don't be overwhelmed
6. Be determined and tenacious
7. Question the system
8. Be creative in looking for solutions
9. Plan for a sustainable future.

This chapter will explain how each of these elements can inspire you to find sustainable solutions that wow colleagues, impress customers and make you feel good about going to work.

♪ PR specialist and dumpster diver

'I am a PR specialist, copywriter, proofreader and dumpster diver,' laughs Kristen Thomas at the Phelps Group. As someone who tried to live green in her home life, Kristen's decision to stay true to her values at work was the impetus behind company-wide change. This ranged from installing solar panels to offering clients marketing materials made out of recycled materials. And it all started with Styrofoam plates.

'I thought it was great my company bought us lunch twice a week,' Kristen explains, 'but seeing all the Styrofoam being thrown away really got to me. One day, at a company party, I started talking to my CEO's wife and I realised I could do something about it.

'An intern found Sustainable Works – a free service which helps businesses in Santa Monica green up. They were amazing – they helped, and once things started rolling, it just snowballed.

'At first you get push back as people change their habits but we've achieved great things. It started small. We just bought a few plates and said: "Let's teach people that, yes, you have to scrape your plate off and put it in the dishwasher after lunch. Let's try it for a month and see how it goes." And it was such a success! So next, instead of paper cups, we invested in mugs with everyone's name on them so people knew which was theirs.

'It took some time, some getting used to and some grumbling – but it wasn't nearly as hard as I thought it was going to be. Having Suzie at Sustainable Works was wonderful. You want to do things, but figuring out how to change is hard and they made it easier. For example, through Suzie, we realized the city would take our recycling for free. So we informed the cleaning crew, and installed saddlebags in each desk bin so the main pail became recycling and the garbage went into the saddlebag. It was simple once people knew what to do. And it led to us reducing our waste bills and trash output.

'The running joke now is that I am dumpster diver. I go around each day and check things are getting recycled. Everyone says: "Here comes Kristen – it's three o'clock!" And when I go on vacation, my colleagues even do the dumpster diving for me!

'It's incredible seeing ideas become a reality. When the CEO told me we were installing solar panels, I almost fell out of my chair. When we first discussed it, his reaction was "too expensive". Then, two months later, he told me we were going to be the largest private solar installation in Santa Monica. We are the first private company to take that kind of initiative, which is incredibly exciting.

'The whole experience has made me much more committed to my company. I take pride in the fact that my home away from home is a better place and that colleagues and clients have been attracted to our company because we have gone green. We also have a really good employee retention rate.

'I have received recognition for it too, which feels good. It has also enabled me to take more of a leadership role within the company so it's been fantastic for my career too.'

I. THINK SUSTAINABLY

'If unsustainable development is the result of millions of unknowingly wrong decisions and actions,' says Forum for the Future founder Sara Parkin, 'then sustainable development can be the result of millions of knowingly right ones.'

Once you've trained your brain to consider the social, environmental and economic impact of every action, success is never far behind. Ordinary people all around the world have achieved extraordinary things by adopting a sustainability mindset. For every action, they have learned to ask, 'Can I do this in a way that I and my company or organisation can continue to do it indefinitely?' That is all being sustainable means – doing something in a way that you can continue to do it indefinitely.

These inspirational people have trained themselves to consider automatically the social, environmental and economic impacts of every action in order to try and find a better, more balanced way to work. You can do it too by adopting a sustainability mindset.

2. BELIEVE IN YOUR OWN POWER

With the right attitude and the right approach, you can create a one-person ripple effect. In his book, *The Tipping Point*, Malcolm Gladwell calls this 'the law of the few'. One person, or a minority, can wield enormous power to change the behaviour of those around them. In the right circumstances, little changes can have big effects.

'When I graduated,' explains Dr Martin Blake from the UK's Royal Mail, 'I realised there are two ways you can change organisations. One is by being on the outside, being an activist. But I never saw myself that way. I thought I could make a greater difference on the inside. So I went to work for an oil company and became the conscience of the corporate from within.

'My job as head of sustainability is to make companies recognise what their impacts are. I am constantly challenging them to think differently. If we are building a new building, I ask, "How much would it be worth in 10 years time if it was carbon neutral? And how much would it be worth as it has been designed now?" In this way I can show the benefits by pointing out that we are writing off something like £100,000 of savings in 10 years time for the cost of £10 000 now.'

Even without such clear business benefits, the growing realisation that we are living beyond the capacity of the planet, and the heartfelt desire of many of your co-workers to do good, means there is likely to be a groundswell of support behind you. This means your actions have the potential to be the tipping point that transforms your business for the better, while elevating your career to a new level.

'I felt like a cartoon character,' explains Jo Confino, head of sustainable development and executive editor of the UK newspaper *The Guardian* (see box **No sex please, we're *The Guardian***). He helped the famous British paper and website revamp its whole operation to reflect its values of social and environmental justice. 'I felt like a character repeatedly racing at a closed door, trying to knock it down. Then, suddenly, at the last moment, someone opens the door and I go flying through, tumbling to the ground. I look up and the boss says, "Well, go on, do it then."'

'There are real champions at the right place in organisations who can move things forward, even though it may seem like they're going against the tide,' says Professor Tim Jackson of the University of Surrey. 'The ones who are most successful are often the ones who have a mixture of influence, they're motivated to take action on the issues, and they can access resources to help them do it. These people might not have set out to be a champion of sustainability but they find themselves in a position where they can change things, and because they care about it, they embrace the challenge to make a positive difference.'

◗ No sex please, we're *The Guardian*

How could *The Guardian*, a newspaper that champions women's rights, make money from advertisements for sex phone lines in the pages of the weekly *Guide* supplement? This was the question Jo Confino, head of sustainable development and executive editor, asked himself in frustration.

'You can't pick and mix ethics,' he says. 'It has to be across the board. For me, the motivation was about creating change. It was important to use the same skills as a journalist within my own organisation, looking at problems and challenging people about things that didn't stack up.

'When I started nine years ago, we had sex line ads in the paper. I questioned it. I said, "*The Guardian* has a long tradition of leading the way in championing women's rights but we are receiving revenue of hundreds of thousands of pounds a year from sex ads, which are often linked to the illegal trafficking of women. It doesn't add up." Movement tends to come from challenging the status quo and I kept at it until there was a recognition that the ads were incompatible with our values. So we stopped publishing them.'

Jo then applied the same principles to sustainability.

'We've always been a paper with strong values of social justice, which puts people and the planet first. But while the board knew these were the paper's core values, they weren't filtering down through the organisation. By creating a sustainability strategy, producing an independently audited annual report and doing lots of high profile events – such as getting involved with our local community, cutting waste and changing everything from our paper to our printing processes to reduce their impacts – I've worked to make our values explicit. This helps ensure they are being communicated to, and understood by, everyone.

'We have 1700 people here at *The Guardian*. That's a huge pool of intelligence and I'm trying to harness that energy to wield it as a force for good. My experience is that when you are really clear about something, the energy comes in to support it. If there is confusion about what to do, the energy short circuits. That's why it was so important to have a real understanding of what our values and responsibilities are – because, once you recognise them, you act on them.

'We also recognised that it's possible to do good and also to be commercially successful. By becoming a world leader in environmental coverage, we gain a crucial business differentiator. Beyond our journalism and commercial activities, we also looked at our supply chain and ways to reduce our carbon footprint. These weren't on the agenda when I started but they're now at the heart of strategy across the company. We have people in place, right across the business, who are delivering change – and it has happened rapidly. Only 18 months ago there was me and a colleague doing this on our own. Now there are around 40 people within the company who exclusively or primarily concentrate on sustainability issues, including a team of nearly 15 journalists.'

3. LIVE YOUR VALUES AT WORK

Perhaps you've managed to cut your company's waste by changing the packaging design of your products. Maybe your lunch-break volunteering initiative is helping children keep up in school. Doing 'good' and staying true to your values is one of the simplest ways to feel satisfied at work.

More people are trying to live responsibly in their home lives, for example by recycling, composting, buying fair trade and organic, and flying, driving or buying less. So, it can be uncomfortable and distressing to feel that, during our work lives, we are contributing to wasteful, disrespectful, dangerous or environmentally damaging behaviour, often on a scale that dwarfs our personal efforts. This has led many people to find ways to connect their values to their jobs (see box **Eat organic, wear organic**).

Making it easier for employees to live their values at work is beneficial for the company. It ignites people's passion for their employer, making them feel more committed and motivated, while inspiring them to come up with sustainable solutions that usually benefit the brand and the bottom line.

'Our notion of how we choose to live our lives, or what makes us truly happy in our lives, is shifting,' explains Mike Dupee, head of corporate social responsibility at Green Mountain Coffee Roasters in Vermont. 'We know that our employees want to live their values at work, so we help them, for example, by facilitating volunteering and ridesharing, providing recycling services, and involving them in the work we are doing to support coffee-growing communities. We also offer financial incentives to help them assess and reduce their personal carbon footprint, a matching donations program, educational sessions, and other similar engagement opportunities. Raising awareness and getting employees engaged is major part of our strategy.'

Start with yourself

'As we seek to impact our workplace, we need to first understand that change at an institutional level must start with examining and changing individuals – ourselves,' says Dr Victoria Hands from the London School of Economics and Political Science. This one-woman force-for-change got every London university recycling and has been credited with diverting hundreds of tonnes of rubbish from landfill.

Change can start by rephrasing a common question. Instead of asking 'What am I doing in the world?', try 'Who am I being in the world?'

'You only truly control who you are being,' explains Victoria. 'So when I reached a plateau, I started to change who I was being to who I wanted to be. When you start to live your values, you become a trusted and authentic employee and you stop feeling frustrated, because you're acting on the things that you believe in. If you think about sustainability not as a mountain that will be too steep to climb, but rather as a system that can be transformed, then you become more open, and able to achieve a transformation at your workplace. Living your values is immensely satisfying!'

The way we behave at work affects our dignity and self-respect. Leaving our values at the door just leads to frustration and discomfort. Holding back or not speaking up usually ends up being more tiring than trying to be a positive advocate for change.

Leading by example

Your colleagues won't expect you to be an eco saint who is sustainable in every area of your life, but it is important to be honest about the choices you make, or you may end up giving your critics ammunition. If you're open, people will accept that everyone, faced with the practicalities of everyday life, has to make compromises, but they'll still respect the efforts you do make.

'If you are firm in your convictions, you will be successful in influencing others,' explains Sofia Bustamante from the UK-based leadership coaching firm, Turn up the Courage. 'By bringing up the issues, they rub off on others, whether they seem to care about sustainability or not.'

Kristen Thomas at the Phelps Group has seen first hand how living your values at work can affect those around you. 'It was really interesting. Once people knew I cared about the issues, I started getting questions about all sorts of things I do at home, such as composting. I was also the only vegetarian in the office, but that seemed to get people thinking and now other people are saying they want to cut back on meat because of the massive environmental impact of intensive livestock farming. It's amazing how living your values can change the behaviour of those around you.'

Another unexpected benefit is that the company's sustainable policy has rubbed off on clients. 'Clients have asked us to share what we've been doing and asked to see our business plan. We didn't push them to go green – they came to us. This was partly because we encourage our clients to come in and have lunch with us at our weekly "brain bangers" meetings, and they saw the changes first hand. They saw we had real plates and cups instead of disposables and they started asking questions. Leading by example has been much more effective than saying, "Hey look, we did this, don't you want to do this too?" '

Eat organic, wear organic

Coral Rose discovered that bringing her values to work at Sam's Club and Wal-Mart created a new revenue stream, inspired colleagues and led to the formation of her own company.

'I'd embraced sustainability in my personal life for decades,' explains Coral, 'for example, by eating locally and organically. So when, in 2003, I learned about the stunning negative impacts that result from pesticide use on cotton, my social consciousness kicked in.'

Coral couldn't leave her concerns at the company door. As a senior ladies apparel buyer for Sam's Club, the impact and scale of her daily decisions was enormous. She decided to incorporate her social consciousness into her business decisions by developing organic cotton clothing lines for Sam's Club. Initially this was a challenge. While Sam's Club and Wal-Mart buyers understood the benefits of organic foods because of the reduced use of pesticides and chemical fertilisers entering the food chain, they couldn't understand the need for organic cotton.

So Coral explained that, after cotton is processed, 40% of the cotton that remains is fibre, while the remaining 60% is cotton seed. Cotton seed winds up in the food chain as cotton seed oil and is used in many foods, such as baked goods, while the cotton seed itself is used as animal feed. The meat from these animals often ends up on the dinner table. This helped her colleagues to understand why Sam's Club and Wal-Mart's use of organic cotton in clothing mattered – it could help reduce the levels of pesticides and toxic chemicals entering the environment and the food chain.

The organic cotton yoga sets that were initially developed by Coral clearly struck a chord with customers, and the first 190 000 units flew off the shelves in just ten weeks. 'Just as we were preparing to present our new business model for organic cotton,' says Coral, 'my yoga sets hit the floor and began outselling every other item. We were able to present our vision to the executive committee with the economic business case in hand. The sales figures proved that organic cotton was more than just a good idea; it was also a potentially profit-making one.'

Coral's influence didn't stop there. She and a colleague, Andrew Fraser, created and co-led the Wal-Mart Organic Cotton and Sustainable Fibers Value Network. Their team influenced other divisions across Wal-Mart and Sam's Club to source, develop and create organic and sustainable textiles. The process they used to bring together a team on sustainability and educate their colleagues has been used as a best practice throughout Wal-Mart. Coral's success – and the overwhelming, positive response to sustainable textiles – led her to launch Eco Innovations, a consultancy that works with leading companies to source, develop and procure sustainable textiles. ◢

4. THINK POSITIVE

Step outside the realm of what's predictable and into the realm of what's possible.

'It's not about changing people's organisations,' agrees sustainable design consultant and author Alastair Fuad-Luke, 'but about changing people's heads. It's about showing them the benefits of thinking more holistically. One of my favourite quotes is from the French Dada artist and poet Francis Picabia. He said "Our heads [are] round, so that our thinking can change direction." We only have to turn our heads to see things differently. That act itself is a catalyst to raising people's awareness. The people who are aware of sustainability are connectors; they connect climate change and carbon emissions to new business opportunities.'

In practice, this just means opening your eyes, taking a step back and seeing whatever you're doing as part of a bigger system. For example, if you're designing packaging, this means checking it fits within the existing recycling system. So it would not be enough to use a material like EPA foam, which, although theoretically recyclable, is rarely recycled because most customers don't have easy access to facilities.

◗ Words of wisdom

'Forget that this task of planet-saving is not possible in the time required,' advises Paul Hawken, environmentalist, entrepreneur, journalist and author of many books, including *Blessed Unrest*.[3] 'Don't be put off by people who know what is not possible. Do what needs to be done, and check to see if it was impossible only after you are done.

'When asked if I am pessimistic or optimistic about the future, my answer is always the same: if you look at the science about what is happening on Earth and aren't pessimistic, you don't understand the data. But if you meet the people who are working to restore this Earth and the lives of the poor, and you aren't optimistic, you haven't got a pulse. What I see everywhere in the world [is] ordinary people willing to confront despair, power, and incalculable odds in order to restore some semblance of grace, justice, and beauty …

'No one knows how many groups and organisations are working on the most salient issues of our day: climate change, poverty, deforestation, peace, water, hunger, conservation, human rights, and more. This is the largest movement the world has ever seen. Rather than control, it seeks connection. Rather than dominance, it strives to disperse concentrations of power. Like Mercy Corps, it works behind the scenes and gets the job done. Large as it is, no one knows the true size of this movement. It provides hope, support, and meaning to billions of people in the world.'[4]

Success will come more easily if you stay positive. Enjoy the journey, picture yourself succeeding and see challenges, not obstacles.

In *The Power of Positive Thinking*,[5] Vincent Peale advocates that we all have power to choose our outlook. 'If you think constantly of the forces that seem to be against us we will build them up to a power far beyond that which is justified. But, if on the contrary, you mentally visualize and affirm and reaffirm your assets and keep your thoughts on them, you will rise out of any difficulty regardless of what it might be.'

Replace 'I can't' with 'I'll try' and 'I'll succeed'. This might take you out of your comfort zone and feel uncomfortable at first, but these feelings will quickly give way to a glorious feeling of empowerment and energy that will motivate you to take on challenges.

❧ The psychology of success

Ken Bosley and the team behind Hewlett Packard's TouchSmart PC were able to think outside the box to create a product that broke new ground both in cutting edge functionality and environmental performance.

'We asked: "What's the best way, what's the obstacle, why aren't we doing it?"', Ken explains. 'Usually the answer to "Why aren't we doing this?" was "We're not sure!" so we decided to find out. The key is not to say we can't do X because of Y. But to say, if the impediment to X is Y, what can we do to eliminate Y? We might need to think about that one for a while, but we can usually find a solution in the end!

'We asked questions like, "Why do we have an accessory box and cushions? Why can't the cushions be the accessory boxes?" We started to question why we weren't using more cardboard in the packaging, which is easy for customers to recycle, instead of foam, which usually isn't. We discovered it was because we didn't know if it would pass all of our drop tests which we do to check packaging can protect products in transit. So we did all the drop tests. And it failed first time. But so did the foam first time, so we didn't let that put us off. We went back to the drawing board and tried and tried again until we succeeded.'

The hard work and positive approach paid off with 100% recyclable packaging with more paper and less plastic foam for easier recycling; a sleek, customer-friendly, all-in-one design that uses 55% less metal and 37% less plastic than standard PCs and monitors; and technology that can reduce energy use by up to 45%.

'The gains made on the TouchSmart are now being fed back into the mainstream HP production line,' says Ken. 'For example, we're now trying to incorporate more cardboard usage into the packaging of our mainstream products and looking at ways we can utilise energy efficiencies.'

Setting the bar high – aiming for the ideal rather than the practical, while embracing a challenge – motivated the team and unleashed their creativity. This allowed them to find innovative solutions with multiple benefits, which fed back into each other to save materials, energy, resources, money and the environment – while creating an attractive, market-leading product.

5. DON'T BE OVERWHELMED

We can't all be Al Gore, and you don't have to solve climate change single-handedly. We're all different pieces of the jigsaw, and by each working in our own area, we can help address our common goals of tackling climate change, the unsustainable use of resources and social injustice. We can also change our workplaces in ways that improve the world and make good business sense.

'It's important to have faith in the process,' says Jo Confino from *The Guardian*. 'When you truly believe in something, you tend to fight for it. It's like having a guiding star at night and saying, "I don't know what I will come across, or what blocks I may face, but that's the direction I'm going in."'

♦ Paper trail

Frustrated by the paper waste at Monodraught, a UK company specialising in energy-saving products, research engineer Benjamin Jones carried out a paper audit while on a university placement. 'I calculated that the company spent thousands of pounds on paper and skips to take their rubbish away,' he explains. 'When I fed this back, the company looked into the issue, and steps were taken to reduce use.

> This included encouraging the re-use of paper, and placing requests at the bottom of emails asking recipients to consider the environment before printing. It's nice to know my actions contributed to a few small steps in the right direction.'

'If you start with small steps, you will see quantum leaps,' says Yalmaz Siddiqui, director of environmental strategy for Office Depot, 'but if you push for quantum leaps, you may fail. This is because you will be perceived as someone who is not in the same camp as the rest of the company, someone who doesn't understand the business world. A good philosophy is to accept small steps and to recognise there is always more that a function or department can do, without getting upset or feeling defeated when you cannot get everything you want.

'One way to start is by making small changes to your everyday purchases and practices. For example, buy green by seeking products with recycled content or be green by turning off your light each time you leave your office. By starting small, you can start to go green without feeling overwhelmed. Once these few small steps become habits, you can think about bigger things.'

This approach works well for your colleagues too. As the concept of sustainability is unfamiliar to many people in business, it gives your colleagues and clients time to adjust to the idea that sustainability is not only good for business but integral to it.

'You cannot say to your suppliers, "You must change the way you source your products, I want this paper to be 100% recycled, I don't care what it costs!"' Yalmaz explains. 'That would not have gone very far – that was the old environmental way. The way to approach things is to persuade the company that this is really about business; that it really is relevant to operational cost savings, top line, bottom line, customer experience and employee engagement.

'All this information needs to be communicated and brought in slowly. It's not going to happen overnight. Especially when you have to get these ideas through to a huge organisation; for example, a $14.5 billion company such as Office Depot which has 42,000 associates across the world. You have to reach out to other departments and make them ambassadors to help drive change.'

🌢 Sacked!

Mark Gough was not particularly interested in the environment, but when he started doing research at Reed Elsevier one day a week, he was shocked to see the amount being thrown away at the publisher and information provider. So he bagged it up and took it away to be recycled. This simple act started a chain of events that led to Mark being promoted to the company's global environment and health and safety manager, and to a position as a teaching fellow.

'I started carrying out so much I was called before management who wanted to know what I was doing. I found out afterwards they thought I had been stealing electronic equipment!

'They let me carry on taking stuff to be recycled. That got the attention of my colleagues, and they started to do it with me. I still only worked one day a week, but I would go in every day to get the recycling. This gathered momentum.

'Next, I went away and researched how a company like ours in central London could recycle for no cost, and what products could be collected. I took my findings to management and they agreed to do a little investigating. I'd also started studying for an environmental degree in the evenings. When I went to the global headquarters to make suggestions, they had just appointed a CR manager. They were able to create the necessary structure while I could bring the groundswell of support from employees.

'I suggested they hire me to run the environmental network. It was initially a part-time role – now it's full-time. Later on, when I recommended health and safety improvements, that was added onto my title. And it all started because I couldn't stand to see how much was being thrown away!' 🌢

Tailor your approach

Every organisation and industry has its own culture and operating systems. Each has a slightly different range of reasons for, and benefits from, becoming more sustainable. You'll achieve greater success if you tailor your efforts to those things that are most in line with the goals and aims of your industry or organisation.

If cost-cutting is your organisation's priority, choosing green products and practices that deliver immediate savings will be the most readily accepted, for example switching to double-sided printing or ensuring lights and equipment are turned off when not in use. If you work in an industry that has a large logistical component, your focus could be on products and practices that reduce fuel, energy and related greenhouse gases. You may work in an industry where increasingly strict compliance laws mean that it would be beneficial – in terms of reducing costs and risks, while protecting employee and customer health and the environment – to source nontoxic alternatives to hazardous components.

Being able to present the business case to your colleagues, clients and suppliers is also invaluable. This is discussed fully in **Chapter 3: Make the business case**.

6. BE DETERMINED AND TENACIOUS

The road to sustainability doesn't always run smooth. There will be times when you feel like you're knocking at a locked door, or that change is happening at a snail's pace. This is perfectly natural.

Change will come if you keep faith, stay determined and keep thinking of creative solutions. The door can fly open when you least expect it – and, when it does, sailing through will feel glorious.

In the meantime, try not to get embroiled in office politics and keep your eye on the bigger picture. What you're working towards is worth it. Securing a strong network or support system will also ease your journey.

Sometimes, you run out of time, energy, budget or room to compromise and it stops you solving every challenge. Accept it and keep trying. Persistence is crucial.

'For us and the TouchSmart,' says Ken Bosley (see box **The psychology of success**), 'I wish we could have figured out a way to make the plastic components of the PC from recycled plastic. It's the same with the cardboard packaging. Unfortunately, with our global supply chain, at the time, it just wasn't possible to guarantee a recycled supply of materials. But we took the attitude to make it another thing we'd keep working on. Our attitude is: just because you can't solve it right upfront, doesn't mean you should stop working on it. Keep it on the list for the next project, because the world changes. And in fact, since the TouchSmart, we've kept working on it. And we have found some more solutions. So now, for the HP Pavilion All-in-One MS200, we've managed to create packaging made with a minimum of 60% recycled material.'

American president Theodore Roosevelt said: 'It is hard to fail, but it is worse never to have tried to succeed.' It's natural to fear failure or to worry you may look a fool in your colleagues' eyes, but most people's experience is actually the opposite. Their colleagues respect their efforts and they feel the journey to find workable solutions is an enjoyable, challenging one.

'As we prepare to be successful, so must we prepare too for roadblocks,' explains Debbie Ledbetter, marketing manager at HP, US. 'They're just part of the process. Not everyone is interested in sustainability and you cannot influence everyone at first, but you must continue and be prepared for resistance and setbacks, at least once. When I listen to the opportunities and lessons that I've learned through the process, I become more successful.'

Failure can even be a signal that you're getting close to your goal. 'Once you fail,' says Dr Victoria Hands at the London School of Economics and Political Science, 'you know what to improve to succeed.' Most of the great inventors and successful people today have lost everything at some stage.

Fear of failure may be tied to moments in the past when standing out made us so embarrassed that we decided subconsciously never to do it again (see box **Leaving the inner eight-year-old behind**). Work out what's holding you back so you can rationalise it, because fears from the past (when you were younger) can be combated with the skills and talents you have now developed.

◖ Leaving the inner eight-year-old behind

'There is no way I can stand up and talk in front of a crowd of people, including former London Mayor, Ken Livingstone.' This was the thought haunting Dr Victoria Hands from the London School of Economics and Political Science. Her recycling project was being presented at the prestigious City Hall in London and someone would have to give the welcome speech.

'Everyone I asked said, "Victoria, this is your passion and your project: you should do the speech." But I wouldn't listen. I was petrified of standing up in front of all those people. When I thought about it, I realised it stemmed from when I was about eight years old. I'd made a mistake at school and everyone stared at me as my teacher told me off. Standing there, going bright red, I'd decided I was never going to stand up in front of people again.

'That's how the human brain develops. Your brain makes a connection and any time something similar happens, you think, "I don't want to make a fool of myself. I don't want that terrible feeling." I realised I was letting an eight-year-old child's reaction stop me doing what I wanted. So, I chose to create new possibilities. I decided to be a leader. And I asked, "What would a leader do now?" I realised, this is my project. I should give the speech!

'In front of that crowd and Ken Livingstone, I started to feel those child-like feelings again. But after a few words, I realised I was being a leader. It was so rewarding. There wasn't anybody in that room who I didn't think was 100% behind the project. And Ken Livingstone came and thanked me and gave the most moving speech on how we can work together to face the challenges of climate change. As he was putting his cup down, I noticed his hand was shaking. It might have been nothing, but I thought, "Perhaps he gets nervous too!" And if other people overcome nerves and their own barriers to be amazing leaders in life, then I can, and others can, too.

'Now, I'm pleased to be a leader. Because sustainability is an area where we really do need leaders!'

7. QUESTION THE SYSTEM

Be a positive deviant

'Positive deviance,' explains Sara Parkin, Forum for the Future founder and originator of the phrase, 'means doing the right thing despite institutional and policy barriers and uncooperative colleagues ... it also means doing it in a way that helps to bring about change in all of them. This means questioning assumptions, challenging the status quo and searching for different ways of doing things. For example, this could mean looking at your supply chain and working out how to ask for sustainable goods and services, then working with your supplier to help them provide it. You will benefit and so will they as they become preferred suppliers to others on the same sustainability quest as you.'

Companies, like people, become accustomed to established systems that aren't always the most efficient or effective. The way to drive innovation and improve efficiency is to question everything. Ask:

- Why has it always been done this way?
- Is it for a good reason?
- Can I change it for the better?
- What's really necessary to achieve this goal?
- Is there another, better way to get the same result?

Often systems become ingrained out of habit rather than sense. We have heard stories of constantly flushing urinals that ran day and night, until one person installed a flush-on-demand system, of hotel boilers that were kept on permanently to provide hot water for restroom taps that no one ever used in the Middle Eastern heat, until one cool-headed spark turned them off and of licensing certificates being sent out in cardboard boxes instead of envelopes until someone thought to question why.

Very few new products or creative ideas come from standing in the same spot, looking at the same things in the same way. Visionaries are those who have taken bold steps and found new profits or brand benefits.

Take mobile phones, the internet, iPods or Google. Who would have believed 20 years ago that mobiles would be commonplace across the globe, that businesses would survive and thrive on the world wide web, that you could have all the songs you've ever loved on a music player smaller than a pack of cards or that you could type any question into your computer and get an answer in seconds? Curiosity and creativity are the heart of the solutions to a more successful future.

'Business as usual' is a formula for disaster. William Taylor, author and founder of *Fast Company* magazine, suggests we need to develop a sense of *vuja dé* (a term coined by the comedian George Carlin). *Déjà vu* describes the feeling when an unfamiliar situation feels like it has happened before. *Vuja dé* means looking at a familiar situation with fresh eyes, as if you have never seen it before, and using that to develop a new line of sight into the future.

'Transforming and questioning things is actually really energising and liberating,' says Dr Victoria Hands. 'It's like in *The Matrix* when people didn't realise they were plugged in. It feels tiring initially as you are out of your comfort zone, but it's actually waking up. You're brought up not to question the "small" things. Your family and your teachers mean well, but it is rare that we critically examine everyday things. It's not the norm to pick up a shampoo bottle and question the ingredients.'

You should be questioning everything about it – from the bottle it's made from (is it plastic, recycled plastic or compostable?) to the ingredients (are they toxic or biodegradable, do they pollute waterways, harm wildlife or people and what impacts result from their production processes?). These are all questions that forward-thinking shampoo designers at companies like Boots and Marks & Spencer consider every day. They may not have solved the issues yet but, by asking the questions, they're getting closer (see box **Supply and demand**).

♪ Supply and demand

'We wanted to introduce a 100% recycled expanded polystyrene cushion to package a line of HP products,' explains Randy Boeller, a packaging engineer manager for HP. 'So we got directly involved with packaging material suppliers and the chemical company who supplied the raw materials. We told them what we wanted and made the commitment to them that, if they made a product from 100% recycled content, we'd buy it. That really motivated them.

'We discovered the chemical company couldn't get their hands on enough waste expanded polystyrene as the recycling stream isn't well developed yet. So we went to our large commercial customers in North America and said: "We know you guys get a lot of expanded polystyrene, from our products and other people's – let us help you get rid of it."

'We connected our raw material suppliers with our customers. Now the chemical company have the supply they need while they are helping our clients recycle their waste. The whole process took about a year, but because we told them what we wanted and put some skin in the game and worked with them, we managed to get our 100% recycled expanded polystyrene cushion. We have a track record of working with suppliers because it's the best way to make things happen.' ♪

8. BE CREATIVE IN LOOKING FOR SOLUTIONS

When you hit a brick wall, try to think of creative ways around the problem. If you're trying to cut down on packaging, unpack all the packaging pieces so you can see them in front of you while you're thinking up solutions. Use software to model new products, so you can play around with virtual material and energy-saving designs. Invite a local cook to provide you and your colleagues with healthy lunches to improve your health and to cut down on the takeaway cartons and Styrofoam containers that clutter up office waste.

Often, great progress can be made by aiming for the ideal and imagining how you'd approach an issue if you didn't have any limitations, such as budget or size constraints. It was this out-of-the-box approach that Hewlett Packard brand manager Ken Bosley took with his research team when designing the TouchSmart (see box **The psychology of success**). 'We sat down and said if we had a clean sheet of paper, what would we do?' explains Ken. 'We said, forget any constraints, let's look at this on an ideal basis. What would we do if we could do anything?'

Approaching new products, new systems or new business opportunities in this way allows you to innovate, unhampered by habit or protocol. Rather than being constrained by established systems, you can come up with innovative solutions that often have multiple benefits.

'Think again about different routes in,' says Trewin Restorick, a behaviour change expert at Global Action Plan. 'Are there different ways to do what you're trying to achieve? It's also useful to play the "yes, but" game. Basically, you have fun coming up with all the "yes, but" responses people will give to your suggestions. This gives you the chance to get all the answers prepared, so when you get those "yes, buts" in reality, you've got the answers.'

Creativity is the heart of our shared future. 'Technology and legislation exist because we engineer and influence them,' says Sofia Busamante from Turn Up the Courage. 'Using our ingenuity and imagination to engage in more conversations with designers, inventors, government officials and others, we can have a tremendous impact – because sustainability is about finding human solutions.'

Advertisements, the media and many modern social norms tell us that we need to *have* goods to be happy. The perverse thing is that while disposable income and gross domestic product (often accepted as a standard of wellbeing) increased dramatically throughout the 20th century, people in industrial economies such as the United States and much of Europe don't report being any happier. In fact, research suggests people are unhappier. An enormous body of research demonstrates how our contemporary culture of consumerism and materialism negatively affects everyday happiness and psychological health.[6]

The desire to acquire, and the negative impact it has on our planet as well as our happiness, is described brilliantly in Annie Leonard's short film *The Story of Stuff* (see box ***The Story of Stuff***). The growing realisation of the absurdity of consumer culture has led many people to reject the quest to consume. Instead, they focus on the things that are ultimately more satisfying, such as investing in relationships and working in a way that is respectful of people and the planet.

◗ The Story of Stuff

Annie Leonard is living proof of the power of one person. Her short film, *The Story of Stuff*, has inspired many around the world to change their behaviour to work towards a brighter future.

In the first 18 months after its launch, *The Story of Stuff* website (www.thestoryofstuff.com) was viewed by six million people in 228 countries. It's likely that millions more watched it in classrooms, conferences, offices, churches and community meetings, and on public access TV.

Annie's short film clearly, cleverly and comically describes the absurdity of plundering the planet in a never-ending quest for more profit and more stuff, which leaves us unhappy and unfulfilled. It's an excellent tool to show sceptical colleagues, illustrating the need for urgent action, as well as the need for optimism.

'There are so many points of intervention,' Annie explains in the film. 'There are people working here on saving forests and here on clean production. People working on labour rights and fair trade and conscious consuming and blocking landfills and incinerators and, very importantly, on taking back our government so it really is by the people for the people. All this work is critically important – but things are really gonna start moving when we see the connections, when we see the big picture. When people along this system get united, we can reclaim and transform this linear system into something new, a system that doesn't waste resources or people …

'Some people say it's unrealistic, idealistic, that it can't happen. But I say the ones who are unrealistic are those that want to continue on the old path. *That's* dreaming. Remember that old way didn't just happen by itself. It's not like gravity, that we just gotta live with. People created it. And we're people too. So let's create something new.'

9. PLAN FOR A SUSTAINABLE FUTURE

'Sustainability is about thinking forward and imagining what a good future would be like 20 or 30 years from now,' says Sara Parkin, from Forum for the Future. 'We possess the technology, skills and capacity to envision a new future, but we must put our extraordinary imaginations and expertise to use to advocate and collaborate for change.'

As you engage with a global, interconnected world, it's possible to see how many elements of social and environmental responsibility you can have an impact on. It's hard to imagine fully how the challenges we are facing today can be turned into long-term solutions, but believing we will get there takes us one step closer.

Adopt the mindset

Sustainability is a personal journey that can feel transformational and intense as you start examining every action with fresh eyes – eyes that consider the social, environmental and economic impacts of everything you see and do, from the materials used, the production process, logistics and procurement, to marketing and energy use.

This fresh appraisal of everything from printing to production lines and the way you get to work is likely to causes shifts in your habits and in your view of the world. You will become familiar with concepts such as life cycle assessment (where the impact of a product or process is considered from its creation to its end of life and disposal), carbon and water footprinting, energy management and industrial symbiosis (where organisations work together to share resources, such as waste heat from a sugar beet processing plant heating greenhouses for growing tomatoes), and fair trade (where you guarantee to pay suppliers a fair price for their products, which allows them to live sustainably).

These ideas may seem foreign at first but, with understanding, they seem obvious and a logical component and consideration for business. The ways they can be used to help **Make the business case** are discussed in the next chapter.

These are exciting times to champion social and environmental responsibility at your workplace. When it comes to showing leadership and making change happen, Forum for the Future founder, Sara Parkin is fond of asking, 'If not you, then who?'

Just as budgets, marketing and time management have become part of our everyday, unconscious business thinking, so too should sustainability. Once you have decided to take on the challenge, the mindset will come naturally. You'll find yourself energised and empowered by the decision to make sustainability an everyday part of your business.

The next chapter, **Make the business case**, will reveal how to translate sustainability into business speak. This will allow you to demonstrate categorically to your colleagues that taking the social, environmental and economic impacts of your company or organisation into account will lead to a stronger business and a happier workforce while propelling you and your career forward.

Chapter 3
MAKE THE BUSINESS CASE

‘Sustainability will only continue to grow in importance as an opportunity for forward-thinking firms, and a threat to competitors that fail to act.’ Ernst & Young report, Green for Go, Supply Chain Sustainability[1]

How do you persuade an organisation that processes 85 million pieces of mail each day, via 180,000 staff and 35,000 trucks, that sustainability is good for business?

You show them the business case. Dr Martin Blake persuaded the UK's Royal Mail that cutting carbon wasn't just good for the planet but good for the company's bottom line and the rest of the business. For example, Martin estimated that inefficiency in Royal Mail buildings alone was wasting 30 to 40% of fuel – waste that was costing the company £20 million a year and adding 50,000–100,000 tonnes of carbon to its footprint.

Being sustainable can generate income. Your company or organisation can gain a competitive edge, enhance its public image, qualify for tax breaks, be eligible for 'green' loans or ethical investment, increase its tendering opportunities and potentially add green credentials and premiums to its products.

Being unsustainable costs money. This includes the day-to-day expense of wasted energy, unnecessary transport miles, compliance, carbon offsets, fiscal penalties, waste disposal, absenteeism and high staff turnover. There are the huge bills that can result from civil lawsuits when disgruntled workers or communities take you to task over unsustainable practices or when profits are hit by lost sales. There is the reputational damage that ensues when toxics turn up in your products or workers' rights issues hit the headlines. Unsustainable practices cost money at virtually every level – and it's getting more expensive.

This chapter will illustrate how and why sustainability generates income and saves money. It will also give you the tools to present the business case for sustainability to others.

You may already have an idea of the issues you want to tackle in your workplace or you may feel unsure where to start. The section headed **Making your workplace more sustainable** will outline ways to assess and improve your organisation. This will give you ideas of where you can start or give you inspiration to expand your existing activities.

Then, once you know what you'd like to achieve, the section headed **Presenting the business case** will explain how to present your argument powerfully so you can make your idea a reality.

Some background: a changing business landscape

As political, social and commercial concern about climate change – and the unsustainable use of resources – grows, new practices and regulations are coming thick and fast. Businesses need to transform just to keep up and must take sustainability to heart if they want to lead in the marketplace.

The landscape is changing all the time. The US is shifting towards carbon regulation. The European Union has ever-increasing environmental regulations. South Korea has invested an incredible $38 billion into a green fiscal stimulus package.[2] The UK has the Carbon Reduction Commitment. Meanwhile, nongovernmental organisations (NGOs) are fighting for human rights and to improve labour laws.

As governments, corporations and NGOs work to tackle these issues, there is not yet agreement on exactly which systems should be adopted. Nor is there one shared set of definitions or a common language to describe the issues surrounding sustainability. These will come in time and there are concepts that are becoming standards – such as life cycle assessment (LCA), carbon footprinting, carbon trading, ethical sourcing and fair trade.

Thinking about resources and efficiency can save money *and* lessen your footprint on an already stretched environment. The most effective sustainability initiatives strengthen business and brand, inspire and motivate the workforce, create goodwill, improve relations with stakeholders and ensure that your organisation flourishes. This chapter will give you the tools to demonstrate how.

Turbocharge your career

Thinking sustainably is also a clever career move. However, to persuade your colleagues, and especially management, that sustainability should be a priority – you need to show you understand the *business* of business. In many organisations, sustainability or corporate social responsibility is seen as a regulatory function or something soft and vague that doesn't understand what the business is about.

Being able to present the business case will demonstrate that you understand the fundamentals of the business world and that you're not a hemp-wearing idealist with your head in the clouds, but a forward-thinking realist. It will also do wonders for your career.

The ability to understand sustainability and how to apply it to business is a skill employers are looking for. According to a survey by the National Environment Education Foundation, 78% of respondents believe the value of a job candidate's environmental and sustainability knowledge will increase as a hiring factor within five years.[3] Therefore, the more you understand and know about sustainability, the more attractive an employee you'll be, pushing you ahead of your peers.

◖ Delivering the goods

'I showed them figures and the penny dropped – carbon costs money!' That's how Dr Martin Blake, head of sustainability for Royal Mail, persuaded Britain's largest nongovernment employer that sustainability is good for business. 'I showed them the business case and management had an epiphany. They recognised if you reduce fuel, you reduce carbon and fuel costs. I don't care whether people are dedicated to preventing dangerous climate change or if they want to decarbonise because of money saving. The end result is what's important.'

By presenting the business case for cutting carbon, Martin has helped Royal Mail commit to reducing emissions by 25% by 2010 and 50% by 2015. The rest will be offset to make Royal Mail carbon neutral. With an annual footprint of 990,000 tonnes across its business, from buildings and waste to fleet emissions, that equals considerable savings, and a considerable challenge.

'We've got 180,000 employees – almost one percent of the UK's working population – working for us!' explains Martin. 'In every tiny village and hamlet there's a postman and a post van. It's a massive logistics operation to deliver to 27 million letterboxes every day. We do two million miles every night. So our footprint is huge, and we need to look at lots of different ways to mitigate it. So I established ARRO: Avoid, Reduce, Replace and Offset.'

First the company aims to **avoid** emitting carbon, for example by eliminating unnecessary journeys and avoiding leaving doors open or

---

lights on. Then it aims to **reduce** the amount of fossil fuel it uses and carbon it emits. For example, introducing double-decker trailers into the heavy fleet has reduced their carbon footprint by 20%.

Next, unavoidable fuel or energy used will be **replaced** with low or zero carbon equivalents, such as the hydrogen vehicles currently on trial. Once that's been done, and it can't eliminate any more emissions from its operations, it will **offset**. The company is also auditing suppliers, to protect workers to ensure those who make items such as Royal Mail uniforms are well treated.

Martin concludes: 'You can say to someone, "The reason we need to reduce our carbon emissions is because it will reduce energy costs and stop us buying energy we don't need, reduce exposure for carbon taxation schemes and mitigate the amount we have to offset. It will also improve our brand and enable us to obtain and attract customers – and of course, we won't be releasing that carbon into the atmosphere, which helps the planet." Each point on its own would probably elicit a "We should do that" but, if we can show them how they can do all these things at once, it's a compelling argument. Management get to a point where they say, "Why weren't we doing it before?" They don't need to be convinced of each individual point – they just want you to get on with it.'

MAKING YOUR WORKPLACE MORE SUSTAINABLE

This section will explain the steps you can take to assess and improve your organisation.

1. Work out where to start

If you're looking for ways to make your company or organisation more sustainable, ask yourself the following questions:

- What and where are the most significant environmental impacts of your operations?
- Does your company have a sustainability policy or commitment – and is it living up to them?

- Which environmental impacts can you reduce most easily, for example waste, energy, greenhouse gas, toxic chemicals or procurement?
- Can processes be streamlined to use less energy and resources, or create less waste?
- Does your organisation invest in people by paying fair wages, looking after workers and trading fairly?

2. Understand your impacts

Another good way to understand the impact your business has on the environment and society is by starting with your personal day-to-day activities, and then working your way outwards with an eye towards how your workplace operates.

● Look at what you do day-to-day

You may want to start by looking at your day-to-day environment. Look around and assess whether lights, equipment, heating or air conditioning are left on when they're not needed, or whether these could be changed to energy saving equivalents. What about the things you do or use every day – such as how you get to work, the coffee you drink, the cup you drink it in, the way you throw away your rubbish or the type and amount of paper you use for printing? Can these be made greener or more socially responsible by switching to reusable, recycled or fair trade products? Or changing your systems to use less?

● Think about the services you sell

Ask how your organisation makes the products or services it sells. Are there impacts such as pollution, transport emissions and energy or water used to power the production process? Can these impacts be lessened? What about transport? From transporting materials to factories, to delivering products or services to consumers, logistics can be a huge chunk of your carbon footprint. What happens to products once they reach the end of their life? Can they be reused, recycled or made in a different way?

● *And the services you source*

Get to know your suppliers and their practices. Are they sustainable and do they protect workers' rights? Question what products are made of, how they are produced, where they come from, who made them and how they are disposed of. Think about whether a purchase is actually necessary or whether you could obtain the same resource in a different way – for example from recycled goods and materials or from a sustainable supplier.

What types of energy or fuel do you use? Can you switch to renewable energy or generate your own? What about support services from cleaners to event planners, distribution and office supply stores. Check whether your suppliers operate sustainably and that workers are well treated.

● *Review legal requirements and compliance*

Make sure you are complying with legal obligations; regulations cover issues from carbon emissions to pollution and waste. These can be as specific as the ratio of packaging size to product or how often staff are entitled to a break.

● *Consider socially responsible financing options*

What about the way your company invests and borrows money? Does it bank with an ethical organisation or could the company be inadvertently supporting unsustainable practices?

Sustainable initiatives can also help you qualify for funding, loan schemes or tax breaks, such as interest-free loans to install energy-efficiency equipment.

● *Look at how you impact your community*

Think about how your business interacts with the local community – as an employer and as a neighbour. Do you employ local people or purchase from local suppliers? These can make a huge difference to your community.

What about other ways you support the local community, from donations to charity to staff volunteering? Consider the amount of traffic you add to the roads and how you can reduce this. Do you create noise and, if so, what can you do to mitigate it?

- *Assess the treatment of your fellow employees*

Think about staff. Does your organisation make it easier for people to be healthy – for example by providing good quality food in the canteen? Does it help employees live their values at work and make them feel valued in return? Are people paid wages they can live on?

Other ways to make a difference

You could also think about:

- developing sustainable products and services;
- designing products and packaging that can be reused or recycled;
- minimising or eliminating hazardous chemicals and processes that produce harmful by-products;
- working with suppliers to assess and improve their sustainability or switching to more sustainable suppliers;
- installing energy-efficient equipment or using renewable sources of energy;
- collaborating with other businesses that can use your waste products;
- eliminating unnecessary activities – for example replacing travel with conference calls.

The important thing to remember is that you don't have to take on everything at once. Choose something you feel comfortable with. Then move from one issue, one process, one brand or one department to the next. Bit by bit, you can make incredible progress.

♪ Cheers!

'Replacing disposable cups is one of the most successful initiatives I've done,' says Shelley Rowley, CSR coordinator from UK law firm Speechly Bircham. 'It raised awareness of what we're doing and why we're doing it; how a small thing can trickle down to have a wider effect on environment and society. It elicited a lot of good responses and now it's just part of life here.

'Disposable cups were costing the company £11,500 a year. I couldn't believe it! It was quite simple to work out. I just looked around the office to

---

see how many cups were on people's desks at the end of the day, totted it up, and it was just under 250,000! Then I asked procurement how much a pack of cups cost, and worked it out.

'I took the figures to the CSR committee, then to the managing partner and director of finance. Everyone was really surprised, so they gave me the go-ahead to take it forward. At first, we weren't sure whether we'd need to buy mugs and a dishwasher, but we asked everyone to bring in their own cup, and everyone got used to washing theirs at the end of the day. I expected a barrage of complaints but everyone was supportive, saying they were so pleased it had finally happened, and that it was a great initiative.'

Shelley's efforts have also won her recognition within the firm and plaudits from the senior partners.

3. Take measurements – then act on them

'Measuring the right things, and communicating those results across your organization is the key,' explains Gil Friend, founder and CEO of Natural Logic in the US, 'because knowing where you are – and where you are headed – gives you a far better chance of getting there.'

Six key areas to examine are energy, water, waste, toxins, pollution and people. There are lots of tools you can use to assess your impact. One of these is life cycle assessment (LCA). This looks at the different stages of a product, from the raw material acquisition, through to manufacture, distribution, use and disposal. Looking at your product in this way might make you realise that it contains a toxic material, so you can seek a substitute. Organisations such as the European Ecolabel or Green Seal can help you get started as they provide information about life cycle considerations (see **Appendix 1: Who can help**).

Benchmarking – checking your company's performance, say on energy or water use, against the norm for your industry or your building – can also help identify places where savings can be made.

The Carbon Trust website has great tools and guides for walk-around surveys, developing action plans, carbon surveys and design advice, wherever you are in the world.[4] Also check out the work Climate Counts is doing to rate corporations on their efforts.[5] The Carbon Disclosure

Project holds the world's largest database of corporate climate change information.[6]

Measurement as a must

With increasing legislation and carbon regulation, it will become mandatory to report many environmental impacts. If you start to work out how to measure your emissions now you will be ready. Business experts, from HP to Marks & Spencer and Wal-Mart, agree that pre-empting these changes can be a competitive advantage. Being behind on the issue will make your business fall behind too.

'Measurement has grown exponentially over the past ten years or so,' says Kathee Rebernak, chief executive officer of Framework:CR, Connecticut. 'When we started working in this area, measurement was minimal and was confined mainly to environmental, health and safety data, mostly for compliance purposes. Now more than 80% of the Fortune 250 (America's 250 largest companies) publish information on their environmental, governance, and social performance.'

Developing measurement and metrics also makes you well placed to spot business opportunities, for example by selling the measurement systems you've developed to others. Measuring the impacts will also help you to find ways to reduce them or even products you can make and sell, which should lead to savings.

This means looking at things like energy, fuel and water use or the materials you use, the waste and pollution you create, both in your own premises and along the supply chain. Utility bills, waste disposal costs, material costs, procurement receipts, insurance and health care premiums can help you calculate how much your initiative can save.

The Global Reporting Initiative is seen as the world's standard in sustainability reporting guidelines.[7] Many companies use it, as it allows environmental performance to be measured and compared. Their mission is to make sustainability reporting as routine as financial reporting and, as more and more companies adopt them, this is becoming closer to reality. Their guidelines outline what should measured, who should be consulted, what should be reported, how it should be reported and what performance indicators should be used.

You can also use established key performance indicators (KPIs) to measure your environmental performance. These include systems for measuring emissions to air, water, land and resource use.[8]

Often there are creative ways to measure what seem like intangibles, such as customer loyalty, repeat business, absenteeism or staff turnover. For example, you can benchmark your business against others, or past performance, to see whether your strategy has made a difference. There are also frameworks that can help you measure things like community involvement, such as the UK's CommunityMark.[9]

PRESENTING THE BUSINESS CASE

Once you have an idea of where you are and what issues you want to tackle, presenting the business case will help you get the go-ahead. This section will show you how to make that case.

1. Keep pace with new market realities

In a volatile marketplace, business must think strategically to survive. This means asking questions such as:

- What long-term environmental or social pressures could disrupt your business?
- What if oil prices skyrocket?
- What if you have to factor the cost of carbon into the balance sheet?
- What can you tell investors, staff and customers when they ask how you are addressing your social and environmental impacts?
- What if your competitors can demonstrate that they're more sustainable?
- What if consumers start demanding fair trade for all mainstream brands?
- What would happen if your producers don't receive a living wage?
- What would happen if a human rights issue causes bad press?
- What would happen if intensive production depletes soil or resources or causes pollution?
- What if water shortages restrict the amount you have access to?

- Are your operations secure as extreme weather events become more common and as flooding or desertification make areas uninhabitable?

By thinking about these issues and raising them with management, you will be able to show how sustainability can help your company stay strong, while also gaining respect from your colleagues.

Use peer pressure

Management will also be motivated by their peers taking sustainability seriously. Research shows that executives are increasingly incorporating environmental, social and governance issues into core strategies. McKinsey found 60% of global executives said climate change is an important element to consider in corporate strategy.[10] Nearly 70% said climate change is important in managing corporate reputation and brands.

Executives are relatively optimistic about the business prospects that climate change could present. About one-third view climate change as representing an equal balance of opportunities and risks, while 61% view the issues associated with climate change as having a positive effect on profits if managed well.

Use this type of research to back up your case to management – to show them they can either lead or lag behind. Many will jump at the chance to be a trailblazer.

You can also draw management's attention to contemporaries who are being proactive. This means they get the same message about sustainability from *outside* the organisation as they do from their employees within.

'This is a pre-competitive space,' says Tensie Whelan, president of Rainforest Alliance. 'Most companies want to get everyone to a certain level, and big companies in particular find comfort in knowing their peers are engaged.'

Stop fighting fires

Taking control of your company can help you head off problems before they occur. It also prevents the need to react quickly when a competitor announces something that gives them the lead.

'At Marks & Spencer,' explains Richard Gillies, director of Plan A, 'we had been trying to tackle climate change and other social and environmental issues for a long time. However, as efforts weren't co-ordinated, there was a lack of understanding around what we stood for and we found ourselves responding to media or NGO pressure on a number of initiatives, rather than taking a lead.

'Our solution was a company-wide eco strategy called Plan A which could communicate our values clearly. It identified five issues the company would tackle: climate change, waste, sustainable raw materials, health and being a fair partner, and it set out a 100 point plan of targets. This included making our UK and Irish operations carbon neutral by 2012, and converting 20 million clothing garments, including £5 T-shirts, to 'fair trade' cotton. That's 10% of all Marks & Spencer cotton use.

'Having a strategy allowed us to bring all of our efforts together to make a much greater impact at every level, and within two years, the programme was cost neutral too.'

Sustainable spells success

'As a rule, being a greener company means being a better company,' says Joel Makower, executive editor of GreenBiz.com. 'And who wouldn't want to be a part of making their company better? At the very least, it's going to help you advance your career goals.

'Green is good because companies that adhere to environmental practices and principles are less wasteful and tend to be better managed and better run. They have a higher degree of employee engagement and involvement, are better respected by their customers, employees and the communities in which they operate, and sometimes are even more profitable.

'Every company has a different set of drivers for trying to become more sustainable. For some, their customers may be demanding it, as many now have ethical or environmental procurement guidelines.

'For others, it's what their competitors are doing and they have to do the same to keep up, or more in order to lead. Others do it to comply with regulation. Or they fear impending regulation and would rather design solutions than have the government do it for them. Sometimes activists make it a priority, or shareholders. Sometimes the boss wakes up one day and realises this is the legacy they want to leave behind. Usually it is some combination of these.

'Business is going through a fundamental shift in how it is operating and what it needs to be more efficient. We have looked at increasing the efficiency of people, we have looked at the efficiency of machines and automation and at the efficiency of outsourcing. Now we've finally started to look at the efficiency of energy, materials, water, toxic materials and the like – those have never really been optimized. There have been huge amounts of waste. Now that energy has a significant price, and carbon is starting to cost, it's time to start looking at this waste.'

Sell it on logic

'To create real momentum for change,' says Jennifer Woofter of Strategic Sustainability Consulting, 'it's not usually enough to just say "it is the right thing to do" or "it makes good business sense". You have to be able to articulate it clearly within the context of your business strategy.'

Thomas Jelley, corporate citizenship manager at food and facilities management company Sodexo UK & Ireland agrees:

'The way I try and communicate sustainability is by saying: "If you're looking at the environmental, social and economic factors that affect your business, then you are likely to understand your business better. This means you'll have more information at your finger-tips and fuller information drives better business decisions."

'It's just a simple matter of looking at what's going in and what's going out – you should do the same with every aspect of business. We get the buy-in by keeping it relevant, being balanced, professional and appreciating that we are sowing the seeds – helping change to happen.'

'I've found for most companies, the business case is simple,' says Tensie Whelan of the Rainforest Alliance. 'If your company is working with natural resources, or if your supply chain relies on them, you have an issue for the long term. Climate change, water scarcity, pollution, deforestation, child labour, poor working conditions – all these things are negatively impacting your supply chain. We provide the solutions to help companies help producers to grow products sustainably. This helps producers improve their yields and quality, which helps them make more money and makes them more sustainable as businesses. They also then provide you, the company, with a higher quality product.

'There are costs – but companies feel these are compensated by increased sales, brand benefits and staff benefits. People get overwhelmed and feel they cannot do anything – because it seems so complicated. But for me the success is that here we are, a relatively small organisation, and we are changing how tea is grown by working with Lipton – one of the world's largest producers of teas.

'For most cases, companies know they need to invest in their suppliers. They're already feeling the effects. Mars held a conference in Ghana because there is such a crisis in the cocoa industry in West Africa because there has been such massive land degradation, deforestation, soil erosion, and water scarcity. As a result, they are very concerned about the environmental impact of the cocoa industry.

'It's the same with coffee. For a while, people believed the way to grow coffee was to cut down all the trees and throw lots of chemicals on the steep slopes that were left. People didn't care about soil degradation, chemical leaching, loss of habitat and loss of trees. Now that dialogue is changing – everyone in the coffee industry understands this approach doesn't work if you want to carry on producing coffee in the long term. Consumers might not care yet, but everyone in the coffee industry does.'

◗ Looking for the win-win-wins

'Sustainable solutions are economically sustainable too,' says Richard Ellis, head of corporate social responsibility (CSR) at UK retailer Alliance Boots. 'So we're always thinking: "Can we find activities with social, environmental and economic benefits?" If there doesn't appear to be a commercial benefit the question is, "Can we look at the project differently so that there is one?" As a business, we have to be sustainable, but, if we're not making profits, our longevity as a business is thrown into question.

'For example, taking away desk bins and introducing recycling set the team who make our in-store promotional stands thinking. So they set themselves a challenge: to make all freestanding shelves from recyclable materials. That initiative has saved over 256 tonnes of waste to landfill and £156,000 in cost. It's a win-win-win so everyone feels good.

'Sometimes it's a question of looking at projects to see if they can be reframed to make them more commercially viable. Or I'll look at them to see if we can squeeze some more carbon savings. It's a balance – but if you don't have balance, people in business will see you as tree huggers and won't take you seriously. They won't see that you're making a valuable contribution to the long-term future of the company.'

◗

---

2. Show them the money

'You might have thought you were hiring a tree hugger,' Dave Stangis, vice president of corporate social responsibility, told his managers when he arrived at Campbell Soup Company in the US. 'But I'm here for the same reason you are. I'm here to make this a better company, and to make it more profitable.'

His words echo a truth about business – that if you can demonstrate a bottom line benefit, you're more likely to get the go-ahead. Fortunately, investments in sustainability often come with a financial incentive (e.g. tax breaks or energy efficiency savings).

The Stern Report's analysis of the cost of not acting on climate change proved that it's better to take action now. The cost of cutting emissions of greenhouse gases can be limited to about 1% of the world's gross domestic product. However, doing nothing will ultimately cost anything from five to 20 times more.[11] This means that every £1 spent now would save £5 in the future.

These savings require governments and industry to work together to spark a global shift to low carbon practices. Research by the Carbon Trust and McKinsey has found that tackling climate change has concrete benefits for individual businesses.[12] The opportunities and threats that the study analysed (in the automotive, aluminium, oil and gas, building insulation, consumer electronics and beer sectors) totalled approximately $7 trillion in market value – a figure that even the most die-hard climate sceptic can't ignore.

'The great thing about sustainability is that it makes sense,' explains David Vincent, director of projects at the Carbon Trust. 'Our research showed that up to 65% of capitalisation (market value) could be at risk if companies don't respond to climate change. As policy and legislative requirements send stronger signals to the market, those companies and sectors that haven't taken action will be exposed. Conversely, those companies which respond positively to climate change and take advantage of the opportunities presented could increase their value by up to 80%.'

To make your company one of those who benefits, the report recommends:

- looking at the opportunities for growth and the risks that climate change presents to your business;
- implementing strategies that will help your business move towards a low carbon economy;
- investigating new technology and revenue streams;
- working closely with regulators to help identify regulations that achieve reductions in emissions while creating value for your company.

Show the bottom line benefits

'An idea that doesn't make business sense, isn't the right idea,' says Dave Stangis of Campbell Soup Company. 'It has to make business sense for the company to get involved. This is why it's crucial to communicate your idea in a way that shows it is good business. You may not be able to demonstrate a 20% cost saving from the first two years – but if you can show it makes sense in the long term, you'll be in with a good chance.'

Debbie Ledbetter, marketing manager at HP in the US, agrees: 'There are regulations worldwide and, if we don't ensure that we are making products that meet them, we won't be able to sell our products worldwide. So there is a huge business case which it is often easy to demonstrate in terms of profit and loss and return on investment.'

Putting together a financial case is often easier than you think. Treat it as if you were asking for backing for any normal business activity, such as new equipment, marketing spend or legal services. Use the same types of balance sheets, adding appropriate columns to show outlay and benefit.

Calculating savings is often simpler than you'd expect. Resources such as the Carbon Trust website have figures for typical savings for different industries, buildings and business processes that you can use to bolster your argument. If you're in the UK, they can also help you design a programme.

Otherwise, it's often straightforward to make a simple calculation. For example, if you want to make the case for printing double-sided, ask procurement how many reams of paper you get through a month. Halve that, and you've got your estimated cost saving.

🌱 Thinking commercially

'We have saved £100,000 in two years and won new business because of our decision to go carbon neutral,' explains Simon Graham, environmental strategist at UK-based office services company Commercial.

In 2006 ambitious targets were set to achieve a 75% reduction of the company's carbon emission levels by 2010. By 2009, levels had already been reduced by 60% and waste to landfill reduced by 88%. These changes led to savings of over £100,000 in two years; the programme will break even within three. In addition, the company's strong environmental credentials have attracted new clients who have themselves saved typically £60,000 a year through the environmental savings that working with Commercial brought. These can come through initiatives such as the efficient use of IT or the use of environmentally friendly products, which can be cheaper than alternatives.

Commercial's own savings were made through innovations such as installing its own energy-efficient data centre, a dynamic routing system which considers factors such as road works and school holidays when planning routes for the fleet and a pioneering realtime blending system for sustainable biodiesel. What's more, over 40% of staff are engaged as green ambassadors, making personal commitments to reduce their own emissions and taking the environmental message to their local communities.

'One of the best ways to make your idea happen is to go to the board with financial figures,' recommends Simon, 'and a project plan for your whole strategy. Longer-term targets should be put forward with the shorter-term ones and the whole thing should be presented as one package, ensuring that funding and flexibility will continue for the more complex and time consuming projects.'

3. Gain competitive advantage

'We see environmental strategy as a competitive differentiator,' says Yalmaz Siddiqui, global director of environmental strategy at Office Depot. 'We have created a wide range of green solutions that differentiate our company and help our customers go green.

'Working on being green ourselves goes hand in hand with using green as a differentiator. Its important to be able to tell customers, "We can take the lessons we learned and help you go greener too." It's best to identify solutions that matter most to customers and that are not offered by competitors. For example, we learned in 2003 that customers wanted a simple way to find greener products, so we created a Green Book catalogue. Our competitors created their first green catalogues in 2008. By then we had already captured some of the greenest customers in the office supply marketplace.'

Dr Paul Toyne, head of sustainability at Bovis Lend Lease UK, agrees that thinking about sustainability can help you lead the market:

'As a construction company, the sourcing of sustainable materials is key. We decided to focus on responsible sourcing for some of the big ticket items we use like concrete and steel. Once we can source them, we can go on to other materials like insulation, plastic products and so on. We can build on our success and, bit by bit, turn the industry around.

'We are trying to demonstrate leadership and show how things are changing. There is a tremendous amount of goodwill – as well as some resistance along the lines of "We've always done it this way, why do you want to change?" But we've been clear, transparent, and ambitious about targets – that our key materials are both sustainably produced and responsibly sourced; and opened up conversations with people who want to help.

'To get the work off the ground, we had to demonstrate the business benefit to our company. The responsible sourcing of sustainable materials is important because it helps manage our risk by helping protect us from illegal materials or materials containing pollutants that have negative impacts. Responsible sourcing also helps us gain credits when using green building rating tools like BREEAM, and getting an excellent BREEAM rating is often a client requirement. It therefore gives us the opportunity to use sustainability to win business.'

4. Minimise compliance risks

Compliance costs money, especially if you're caught off guard and have to scramble to comply. However, if you can keep ahead of the curve, you can turn compliance into a competitive advantage. Changing systems or procedures, especially in multinational firms, can take months. It's imperative to have sustainability as part of the planning stages so that shifts don't disrupt business and cost as little as possible.

As John Viera from Ford Motor Company says: '[With] the rising cost of carbon… it will be the companies that have sustainability as part of their core strategies who succeed financially.'[13]

'We've found that staying ahead of compliance can give us a real competitive advantage,' says Randy Boeller, packaging engineer manager at Hewlett Packard US. 'Within the packaging field, there is significant growth in legislation. We work to influence laws. And if we're successful, we would hope that, as governments craft and finalise those laws, they create something similar to what we have in place because we can show we have created a system that works.

'We did this with PVC. Four years ago we started to design PVC out of our packaging, but we did it gradually so that we were able to keep the process cost neutral. We spread it out rather than waiting for a law to be passed and having to do it in an expensive rush. I watched a lot of competitors playing catch up!'

5. Reduce business risk

From headline-grabbing stories of toxic elements in toys to massive legal payouts over human rights, weak supply chain standards, or badly managed energy and waste systems, can leave you exposed. Being socially or environmentally irresponsible can cost serious money.

KPMG reviewed 50 studies addressing the business risks and economic impacts of climate change. They concluded that companies should be paying attention to physical, regulatory and reputational risks as well as litigation. Yet the scope and potential impact of these risks appears to be underestimated across all sectors.[14]

To demonstrate how your initiative reduces risk, do research. Ask around to see whether the issue you're addressing, such as worker rights for your suppliers, has caused problems in the past or dig out some news stories about where others, ideally competitors, have experienced damaging press, dented sales or withdrawn investment over the issue.

6. Social conscience matters

For some, the business case is all that matters but, often, organisations have defined values. This means that the moral case, if well presented and not preached, can be a powerful persuader.

For example, the company may boast that they're an 'investor in people'. You could show them how this translates to having a good ethical procurement policy that ensures suppliers have a good human rights record or how fair trade tea and coffee help to demonstrate the company's commitment to social justice.

The other method is to appeal to people's human side. Many big companies have changed direction because someone at a senior level has had that 'a-ha' moment. The penny drops, as the individual realises the scale of the problem and asks, 'What will be my legacy?' Suddenly, they decide they don't want a compromised planet to be their bequest. They want to be someone who changed business practices for the better. If you can be the person who sparks this realisation, and offers a solution, you will make good and grateful friends in high places. Even those who see themselves as mainly motivated by profit or the bottom line are having 'a-ha' moments when they realise that bad management of resources or a lackadaisical approach to human rights will seriously damage their business.

Big corporations have realised the way they manage and share resources, like water, with the communities who depend on them can be the difference between having operating licenses revoked or renewed. Both PepsiCo and Coca-Cola understand how these issues can make an impact as they have faced intense opposition from nongovernmental organizations (NGOs) as well as courts and communities in India over their use of water resources.[15] Again, if you're the person who sparks this realisation, and you help to offer a solution, your career will become more sustainable too!

🌿 Down to earth

'Like a spear to the chest.' This is the way Ray Anderson, of US-based carpet company Interface, describes the moment he realised that the planet was being plundered by business. Since founding his company decades before, Ray had not given any thought to its impact on the Earth, but when customers started asking questions about the environmental impacts of Interface products, he picked up Paul Hawken's book *The Ecology of Commerce* and had an epiphany.

'Unless we can make carpets sustainably then perhaps we don't have a place in a sustainable world,' he explains in the film *The Corporation*.[16] 'But neither does anyone else making products unsustainably. One day early in this journey, it dawned on me that the way I'd been running Interface is the way of the plunderer... and I said to myself: "My goodness the day must come when this is illegal, when plundering is not allowed... someday people like me will end up in jail."'

Ray embarked on a journey to make Interface sustainable – a journey that has led to the company promising to eliminate negative impacts by 2020. They are making good progress; using 25% renewable and recycled materials, reducing fossil fuel energy intensity by 60% and shutting a third of their smoke stacks and 71% of their effluent pipes. Their aim is for a zero footprint.

The initiative has been commercially successful too. The company website declares: 'Costs are down, not up ..., exposing the false choice between the economy and the environment. Products are the best they have ever been, because sustainable design has provided an unexpected wellspring of innovation. People are galvanized around a shared higher purpose, better people are applying, the best people are staying and working with a purpose. The goodwill in the marketplace generated by our focus on sustainability far exceeds that which any amount of advertising or marketing expenditure could have generated. This company believes it has found a better way to a bigger and more legitimate profit – a better business model.'[17] 🌿

7. Keep with your customer and keep up

'Discerning consumers now demand authenticity: they want stories about where their coffee beans come from. So the best coffees will increasingly be differentiated, like fine wines and spirits, and sold at previously unthinkable prices.'

Extract from 'Direct from the Source', *The Economist*, 19 April 2008

Consumer concern is one of the reasons why the organic and fair trade markets have exploded over recent years, with solid growth even through the downturn. Even Mars and Cadbury have committed to fair trade sourcing for some of their major brands. As a general rule, consumers embrace products that make them feel good about themselves, and this is one reason why greener products have been so successful.

Research by Havas of 10 markets in 2009 found 70% of active consumers believe the responsibility for tackling the sustainability challenge lies with business, with only 30% looking to governments to take the lead.[18] Havas found that, 'even in the economic downturn, consumers are not losing sight of the importance of sustainability.'

This was backed up by a Carbon Trust survey published in March 2009 that found that, despite the downturn, shoppers still care.[19] Two-thirds say environmental considerations inform their purchases as much as they did a year before, while more than a quarter said they were now even more conscious of the environmental impact of what they buy. Two out of three people think it is important to buy from an environmentally responsible company, with about one in seven saying they had decided to take their custom elsewhere if they felt a company's environmental reputation was not up to scratch.

Frustrated by the lack of action from government, consumers are using purchasing power to signal their support for a more sustainable way of life. Perry Abbenante, global grocery buyer at the ethical supermarket Whole Foods Market, has seen this effect at first hand: 'We have a small supplier in Africa that makes bodycare products containing shea butter. It's a high quality product from a small company in a small village, with a story behind it that talks to our customers. Our staff love it, our customers love it and, best of all, supplying Whole Foods Market has changed people's lives for the better.'

Bear in mind that while heart-warming stories, green attributes and ethical credentials can help sell products or allow you to charge a premium, it's dangerous to make this the sole plank of your business case. Consumers can be fickle and unpredictable.

Business customers tend to have a different set of drivers. These often focus on cost (especially concerning energy, with 40% of running costs associated with energy and power equipment), risk (to reduce the company carbon footprint and to prepare for regulations) and growth (organisations still want to grow, albeit without increasing their impacts). Therefore tailoring your operations or products to fit with these concerns can be beneficial.

◗ A real competitive advantage

How can you connect with thousands of potential customers, tap the public for innovative new ideas and support new sustainability initiatives all in one go? You set the public the challenge of solving one of your company's sustainability challenges.

This is what Green Mountain Coffee Roasters did when it announced an $800,000 grant competition to fund innovative work to combat climate change in four key focus areas: threats to coffee-growing communities, transportation-related emissions, building political will and empowering individual action. They were bowled over by the results.

'We launched the competition on sustainability social networking site Just-Means.org and we got over 1.1 million page hits in just over a month,' says Mike Dupee, vice president of corporate social responsibility (CSR). 'We had applications from all over the world and our network on JustMeans went from 30 people to 30,000 in just one month.

'At the same time we announced the contest – we created a Twitter account to help us create conversations about corporate social responsibility. In about six weeks, over 6000 people signed up.

'It was amazing! It introduced us to some terrific organizations we can collaborate with to fight climate change and generated an incredible buzz for the company. Now we're looking forward to seeing how the winning grantees come together as a group to do their work and help us reduce our footprint.'

8. Enhance your brand reputation

'Greener products inspire greater brand loyalty,' says Steve Yucknut, vice president for sustainability at Kraft Foods, 'and there's a connection between brand loyalty and brand equity.'[20] As social and environmental concerns move up the public agenda, investors and customers want businesses to use their enormous power to set the world on a better path. Major companies have discovered how being seen to have weaknesses can seriously damage their brand value.

'I think we're at the beginning of an age of environment and social enlightenment – a new industrial revolution which, unlike the first one 300 years ago, will need to recognise from the outset that success will be measured not just in terms of achieving commercial and market objectives but also societal ones', says David Vincent, from the Carbon Trust. 'Business has an important role to play. Some business leaders are beginning to recognise the significance of these wider, non-commercial aspects of the new world in which they will be doing business in the future. These early starts need to be recognised and applauded, and the lessons learnt promulgated across businesses and sectors.'

Dov Seidman sums it up well in his book *How: Why How We Do Anything Means Everything... In Business (and in Life)*, 'In our hyper-connected and transparent world, how you do things matters more than ever, because so many more people can now see how you do things, be affected by how you do things, and tell others how you do things.'[21]

As Joel Makower said on GreenBiz.com: '[This] seems to be the New Green Gospel: Judge thyself, lest ye be judged.'[22]

'The more sustainable we become, the more media we attract, and the more revenues we generate,' says Karen Lewis, owner of the award-winning Lapa Rios Eco Lodge, a resort in Costa Rica. 'However, this only works as long as the quality of the product and service are in line with expectations.'[23]

Bolstering the brand and ensuring efforts are genuinely authentic are two reasons why certification standards and partnering with nongovernmental organisations are so popular.

'Lots of people put "carbon neutral" on their letter head,' says David Vincent, from the UK's Carbon Trust. 'But it's hard to know exactly what this means and how they've achieved it. That is why we launched the Carbon Trust Standard. It's a badge you can earn as a public or private organisation when you demonstrate that you have achieved a good standard of energy efficiency and that you're prepared to continue on a reduction pathway. It's a way of rewarding corporate behaviour to reduce emissions and improve energy efficiency. It's also a way of differentiating those organisations who are genuinely taking action.'

Tensie Whelan, President of the Rainforest Alliance, agrees:

'Companies like working with us because we lend credibility to their brands as our work and standards are well respected. It's win-win. They get media coverage and it bolsters their reputation because brand reputation and reputational risk are very important, especially for well-known companies.

'The people we've worked with have told us it translates to sales. For example, Kenco put 100,000 acres of farmland under sustainable management and helped 200 000 farmers and their families. That increased the company's market share and helped secure a contract with McDonald's to sell Rainforest Alliance Certified coffees.

'Unilever's brand Lipton has increased sales in key markets where it's been advertising Rainforest Alliance certification by 5–10%. It also landed a contract with McDonald's European and Australian stores.

'For McDonald's, these investments have also paid off. When they brought in Rainforest Alliance coffee, sales went up 22% in UK outlets. So, investments in issues like worker rights and sustainable farming practises do lead to real increases in actual value.'

A good call

Doug Shaw, head of CSR and sustainability for BT Wholesale, has seen at first hand how sustainability initiatives can strengthen brand and bottom line:

'We implemented a mobile handset recycling scheme which delivered cost savings in excess of £3 million whilst generating cash for charity and making customers happy.

'A colleague and I had discovered we were sending old mobile phones to landfill. At the same time, a customer survey had revealed customers wanted us to recycle more and to keep doing our bit for charity. So, we developed a simple system for our employees and customers to return unwanted handsets while a third party took over the phone disposal, recycling and reuse process.

'The company gained by reducing hazardous waste and meeting stated customer needs. The customer gained by seeing us act responsibly. Our charity gained by receiving some of the profit from the sale of reusable handsets.'

9. All stakeholders count

The case for being a good corporate citizen – i.e. actively involved in the community – may seem harder to pin down. However, the benefits of presenting an improved image to your customers *can* be demonstrated and quantified (as described in **Keep with your customer and keep up** and **Enhance your brand reputation** above). An improved relationship with your local authority can also lead to more work as many prefer to award contracts to businesses with a record of community involvement.

There are many ways to get involved. Some businesses support a local charity or sponsor a local event. It makes sense to get involved in an activity related to your product. This lets you use your expertise as well as showing the human face of your business. For example, restaurants provide food to local homeless groups, while builders give free labour and materials to community projects. You can look for opportunities that directly benefit you – for example by generating publicity or improving the neighbourhood around your premises.

'Different stakeholders want different things,' says Mike Dupee from Vermont-based Green Mountain Coffee Roasters (GMCR). 'Your employees want to have a sense of meaning in their work; they value the idea that they are there for something more than just a paycheque and that they are part of something bigger than themselves. Consumers are indicating they want something more from their products beyond quality, convenience and price; they want to know what you are doing to make the world a better place. Your local community wants to know how you are helping make it a better place. Your government wants to know that you are ethical and operating in compliance with law. People who represent the environment want to understand how you account for your environmental impact.

'So there are a bunch of stakeholders out there that you need to pay attention to, not just current paying customers. These stakeholders care about this work – a lot. And when you are able to put resources into programs around social impact and environmental responsibility, execute on them and talk about what you are doing and how you are improving, you are going to create positive outcomes that accrue to the benefit of the business. For example, we had a tremendous experience opening a new facility in Knoxville, Tennessee, because we had developed a great relationship with the local community, based in no small part on our track record and commitments as a responsible corporate citizen. You will have an easier time keeping and attracting high quality employees. You'll also gain market-share and earn more of the money your customers spend on the products you make.

'With each stakeholder group – make the connection to what they care about, communicate with them about it effectively, and you will have an outcome that is beneficial to the business.'

10. Attract, retain and motivate skilled employees

'Sustainability is fundamentally a people issue,' says the Society of Human Resource Managers.[24] Strong sustainability strategies attract top quality talent, motivate staff, reduce turnover and absenteeism, increase productivity, reduce disputes and inspire innovation and creativity. This is the consensus from business leaders and employees in organisations across the globe, and you can use the following figures to prove it:

- 49% of MBA graduates rated a company's social responsibility and community involvement as 'extremely' or 'very' important when job hunting.[25]

- 92% of students and entry-level hires seek an environmentally friendly company.[26]
- 83% of employees in G7 countries say a company's positive CSR reputation increases their loyalty and motivation.[27]
- More than 80% of US workers believe it is important to work for a company or organisation that makes the environment a top priority.[28]

'You need to persuade people you really care,' says Jo Confino, head of sustainable development and executive editor at British newspaper and website *The Guardian*. 'People don't want to have to check their values at the door when they come into work. It makes you feel bad and takes away your motivation.'

Taking a strong stance will allow you to attract employees who want to work for a sustainable company. Their passion will in turn strengthen the culture. Natalia Oberti Noguera, director of New York Women Social Entrepreneurs agrees: 'If employees care about your business success because it matches their values, they will be engaged and motivated to achieve – even surpass – the company's business goals.'

'A strong CSR approach can change the whole culture and feel of a company,' says Katherine Allison, HR manager at the UK law firm CMS Cameron McKenna. 'It can make an organisation stand out.

'CSR makes people feel better about their life and their work. Lots of people feel a bit stuck in their jobs. They need to work to sustain a certain lifestyle but they'd also like to feel they are contributing to their community and the environment. Having a strong CSR policy taps into this and allows employees to live their values at work, which is much more fulfilling and leads to a more motivated workforce.'

An engaged and motivated workforce can also directly affect the bottom line. 'If our suppliers treat their employees better or manage the factories more efficiently,' says Bonnie Nixon, director of environmental sustainability at Hewlett Packard, 'we realise cost savings. In some of the emerging countries we have seen employee turnover on an annual basis go as high as 60 to 70%. There was no question that cost us money.

If employees are not working 16-hour days and they have a normal, healthy lifestyle, they will be less fatigued, likely to have fewer accidents, fewer health issues and injuries. They will have higher morale if you treat them well and train them. With proper training, motivation, incentives and positive labour relations, we have seen turnover rates decrease by more than 50%.'

'The number one thing that motivates people is not always money,' says Mike Dupee from GMCR. 'People are motivated by receiving respect, being challenged, or by being part of something bigger than themselves, contributing to doing something worthwhile in the world. The best instance of this at our company revolves around Fair Trade Certified™ coffees. In 2000, we began selling Fair Trade Certified™ coffee. Today, it is over 30% of our coffee sales. It means a great deal to our employees to understand what fair trade means and how it plays out once it reaches the coffee communities; they know that they are part of creating an opportunity for thousands, if not millions, of coffee farmers in our supply chain to create a better life for themselves selling coffee for us.

'The response from our workforce to our sustainability strategy has been tremendously positive. We have an overwhelmingly engaged workforce – people care about what they do and they want to see the company succeed not just because it's their financial future but because they believe we are doing something that is worth doing. The company's financial performance has been very strong over the past few years and we are very proud of that performance, especially in a difficult market environment.'

Sustainability is also a good way to strengthen your own career, so the more you understand now about sustainability, the more you will be ahead of your peers.

PRESENTING YOUR CASE
This chapter has given you the skills to work out which sustainability issues you should tackle, as well the skills to demonstrate that business case. Putting your ideas into the hard, clear language of business should give you ammunition to persuade even the toughest cynic that

your idea makes sense, while you gain kudos for presenting a strong, savvy case.

Once you've been given the okay to go ahead, you can use the tools in the next chapter, **Get your colleagues on side**, to roll out your programme in a way that engages your colleagues. Then your business case will become a full-blown success story.

Chapter 4
GET YOUR COLLEAGUES ON SIDE

❛Tell me, I'll forget. Show me, I may remember. Involve me, and I'll understand. ❜
Chinese proverb

How do you convince nearly 30,000 students and 7000 staff to recycle their waste on campus? Simple, says Dr Keith Pitcher at the University of Leeds who achieved just that. Get them engaged in your recycling initiative.

From persuading colleagues your company would get more contracts if you specialised in sustainable builds or getting colleagues to turn off their monitors at night, when you assess successful sustainability initiatives in the workplace, they usually have one thing in common – *engagement.*

Successful initiatives often succeed because the people behind them, from one person to a whole team, realise it is vital to get colleagues on side. The brains behind successful initiatives have instinctively realised the crucial role engagement plays in getting people to buy in.

However, what does engagement actually mean and how do you facilitate it? It's a popular buzzword, but while most people know what it means in a general sense, many feel clueless about how to translate the idea of engagement into practice in their own working environment.

This chapter will explain what engagement means and why it is crucial in implementing sustainability strategies. Then, it will describe the best ways to facilitate engagement with lots of practical examples and case studies to show clearly what facilitating engagement actually means in the everyday world of work. This will allow you to design strategies that will inspire, motivate and *engage* your colleagues to ensure your initiatives don't end up floundering because people have not bought in.

🌿 A new way of getting wasted

As the Environmental Manager at the University of Leeds, Dr Keith Pitcher was keen to reduce waste and increase recycling rates for the 30,000 students and 7000 staff who used the campus. With an ambitious environmental policy in place and landfill taxes increasing annually, the university could not afford to continue sending over 1300 tonnes of waste to landfill each year. The cleaning services team were also enthusiastic about improving performance in this area. Changing the behaviour of staff and students would be crucial for a successful initiative.

The process started by taking staff environmental coordinators to the university's waste site. Seeing and sorting through the mountains of recyclable waste being sent to landfill had a profound effect. The photos the team took of the piles of recyclable material they salvaged then became a vital tool in the wider campaign. 'Those photos and images did more than any words to grab student and staff attention,' explains Dr Pitcher. 'The material was used in conversations, presentations and poster campaigns and was very powerful. A pilot project had demonstrated that the most effective way to get people to recycle is to remove office waste bins. Simply providing new recycling facilities only had a marginal benefit, whereas recycling rates from individual offices increased to over 60% when bins were removed.'

Yet removing the bins without engaging the community in the initiative first can cause uproar and lead to the policy being revoked.

'So, before we implemented our "no bin" policy, we always took the time to talk one-on-one to department directors and then to staff and students. Engaging the university community in the initiative was crucial to its success. This meant we had an informed debate, answered a lot of questions and got the majority on side before we removed their individual desk bins. Of course, for some, change is difficult, so it was important to explain the overall benefits of the initiative and why the change was required. There is always a short settling-in period and bit of fine tuning, but we backed up the campaign with the infrastructure to make recycling easy and the norm.

'Interestingly, staff and student suggestions have widened the range of recycled materials and overall recycling jumped from 16% before the scheme to over 40%. A new waste management contract has extended the programme and now collects food waste for composting and sorts campus general waste. The recycling rate has now increased to over 80%. In addition, there was a big jump recorded in the level of satisfaction with recycling facilities provided.'

Engagement explained

Facilitating engagement means getting people participating in something in a way that makes them feel interested, involved and influential.

Engaging your colleagues is actually pretty easy. All it boils down to is finding a way to make your strategy interesting and relevant to your audience, and making sure that they feel their contribution and influence matters and makes a difference. This means they will automatically feel a connection with it, and understand its aim and purpose. Do this, and you'll have brought your colleagues on side and achieved that all-important buy-in, which can be used to motivate them to action.

The good news is that as concerns grow about climate change and the unsustainable use of our planet's resources, more and more people want to take action in the workplace. In the Climb the Green Ladder Sustainability in the Workplace Survey, 66% of respondents ticked the 'I try to be as sustainable as possible – at home and at work' option.[1] A further 14% chose the 'I do what I can when it's easy' option, bringing the total who are willing to act sustainably at work up to 80%.

A whopping 85% said they 'bring it up whenever it feels relevant' or that they were 'working with others to discuss issues and solutions for my company or organisation'. The message is clear – the vast majority of people want to feel they are working in a sustainable way. All you have to do is get them interested in your initiative by showing them its value and how their behaviour can make a difference. Then make it as easy and convenient as possible and they'll do the rest.

Our findings support research undertaken by others. Tandberg/Ipsos MORI undertook one of the largest surveys into global attitudes to climate change and how companies' efforts to become more environmentally responsible are perceived by employees and consumers.[2] They found that 24% of the 16,823 people surveyed believed 'that their individual action should be a key to driving environmental change – a sense of personal responsibility that is potentially borne out by their choice of consumer purchases and workplaces'. The survey also found that 45% had taken personal steps to reduce climate change. This indicates that strategies simply need to tap into this sense of personal responsibility in order for employees to engage.

Sounds easy, and it is. However, whether you're starting small and want to get your office to stock fair trade tea and coffee – or whether, like Keith Pitcher, you want to get a huge organisation recycling – the same simple principles will help you get your colleagues on side.

Six tricks to successful engagement
1. Stop, look and listen
2. Find allies
3. Harness the power of peers
4. Make it the norm
5. Give people the freedom to develop their own solutions
6. Set up green champions and teams.

Drinking it up

With 185,000 workers around the world and five different divisions, how does PepsiCo facilitate engagement across different cultures and processes? One way is by supporting employee efforts to be proactive.

One initiative that started as a grass roots effort but has now gained management support is the idea of 'Carbon Cafes'. A group in Chicago started meeting at lunchtime to discuss ways to measure and reduce carbon in both their personal and professional lives. It was such a success, senior managers supported the initiative and publicised it throughout the group. This encouraged more and more employees to start reducing carbon.

Other divisions have informal programmes where it is part of the culture to look for ways to help improve the company. Bottling plants have 'Tag and Flag' programmes where employees are encouraged to look for ways to improve operations or the production process, including environmental impacts such as conserving water or energy. Some plants offer incentive programmes to encourage their employees by using such programmes as 'employee of the month' recognition or gift cards.

Maria Figueroa Kupcu from Brunswick Group, who has worked with PepsiCo on some of their environmental initiatives, believes these types of programmes go to the heart of motivating employees and keeping them engaged. This is because they harness the energy and enthusiasm of employees to make a difference, and give them an outlet when they see things they'd like to change.

1. STOP, LOOK AND LISTEN

'You need to start the journey by looking around and asking questions of the company, your bosses and your co-workers', says Anthony Kleanthous, Senior Policy Advisor, WWF-UK. 'What do they believe about sustainability? Because, before you start anything, you first have to deal with reality on the ground. If that reality doesn't respect the agenda you're trying to push, you're going to bang your head against the door.'

It's tempting to dive straight in when you've had a great idea like recycling facilities for water bottles or insisting suppliers commit to reducing their carbon emissions. Enthusiasm is a valuable asset, but you'll get better results if, like Keith Pitcher, you take a moment to take stock of the existing situation and to assess the company or organisation's culture first.

'You need to ask: "What is the organisation's role, its motivation? What is its sense of identity?"' says Professor Tim Jackson of the University of Surrey. 'Because these things can be used to stimulate change. It's the same basic principles you'd use for social marketing. Your starting point is to understand where the people you are trying to persuade are coming from. What are their needs, aspirations, and norms, and what are the rules that constrain them? You need to know what the organisation is doing on an everyday level.'

This means one of the easiest ways to make things happen is to work within the existing corporate culture. It's like a lock and key – you have to fit, and the best way to do that is by looking and listening. This will help in two important ways.

Firstly, it will allow you to identify key issues that need to be addressed and to find the best overall solutions. Even if your goal is simply to get your small company to recycle plastic drink bottles, looking and listening is important. All it really means in practice is pausing to look at what's happening around you and asking and listening to your colleagues to find out what matters to them. This can be as simple as bringing up the subject with your colleagues when you're fixing a drink so you can gauge how other people feel about the issue, and start to drum up support. Then you can start the debate in a way that will make people listen. By talking to people, you might discover colleagues also hate bottles going to waste, and that switching to filtered water instead of installing plastic recycling facilities would actually save resources far more efficiently and make your co-workers feel happier.

Secondly, taking stock and talking to those people involved could lead to a much greater impact. They can help you devise a system that they understand and believe in – and which works within the company or organisation's existing structure and culture.

It also pays to take **Stop, look and listen** further by conducting a survey or by measuring behaviour. This is especially helpful when you're implementing business-wide change. Behaviour change experts like Global Action Plan advocate measuring existing norms first. In this way, you can build up a really accurate picture of the attitudes and behaviour of employees before designing any initiative.

Questionnaires and surveys allow you to measure the knowledge, attitudes, confidence and skills of your employees. You can then move on to conduct a 'business scoping' exercise, which does surveys and looks at facilities, buildings and actual behaviour among other criteria to get a good picture of the whole organisation. This two-tiered plan allows companies and organisations to identify hotspots for action and evaluate what will engage and motivate their employees. It will also provide benchmark measurements, which can be used to continue to evaluate and plan your company's sustainability initiatives.

Working in a systematic and analytical way will help you to understand the challenges, and to work out how to remove barriers to action. Such an exercise could reveal whether the organisation has a negative attitude towards sustainability. This would suggest that an information campaign or strategy that focuses on changing people's attitudes by showing them the benefits of sustainability would be more powerful.

The power of listening and effective communication will be discussed more fully in **Chapter 5: Have two-way conversations**. However, the important thing to remember is that taking stock and appraising the existing situation will help you plan a more effective approach and solution. It's also worth remembering that there is no need to feel under pressure if you don't know what the solutions are. Once you've identified trouble spots, you can work out what you need to know and set about finding the answers.

2. FIND ALLIES

If you've been getting frustrated that machines are left running overnight or wishing that your business did more for the community it operates in, it's likely that other people have been too. The trick is to find these people so you can band together to press for change.

'Talk to colleagues,' says Anthony Kleanthous, WWF-UK, 'and try to get some kind of consensus at a lower level. Talk through the issues so you can work out what the implications are for your business. Then use this detailed information when you begin to discuss your findings with management. Then you can say, "We're concerned about these issues and changing our behaviour could have these types of positive outcomes for the business." That way management will listen.'

You will be taken more seriously if you go to management or to your colleagues and you're able to say that others within the organisation share your views. It also means you'll have more people to bounce ideas off and more people to help share the tasks, thus lightening the load, making the task more enjoyable, helping you feel more motivated and stopping you from burning out.

It's easy to find others who share your views once you start bringing up the issues that matter to you at the coffee machine, over the printer or at lunch. Sending an email or putting up a notice are great ways to find supporters from different departments or parts of the organisation, and can often help you make new contacts in the business too.

Taking the time to bring the right people on side can make your task much easier. If your initiative depends on getting the support of the foreman of the factory, that's the person you need to make a beeline for.

Use the communication tricks from **Chapter 5: Have two-way conversations** to find out what motivates and worries them so you can angle your pitch. Show how your initiative can help them achieve their goals or make them feel good about their work, and you'll have a powerful ally.

♪ The multiplier effect

As a senior partner and planning director at global advertising agency Ogilvy & Mather in New York, Freya Williams wanted to set up a sustainability consulting arm that could speak to consumers and employees about the need to go green. By bringing up the issues and being prepared to take on the challenge, she quickly found allies who could help her make things happen:

'Lots of people supported what I wanted to do, but not everyone wanted to take on the challenge. But once I raised my hand, people came out of the woodwork. I started to find kindred spirits to work with. I found once people know what you are into, you can find out who to call. People say, "Oh you are into that – you should meet so and so." This allows you to build that support network so you don't feel like you have to do it on your own.

'When I started working with Seth Farbman, my business partner, it made a real difference. One person is an idea – two is company!' ♪

---

3. HARNESS THE POWER OF PEERS

The 'I will if you will' campaign launched by the UK's Sustainable Development Commission was successful at helping people to move towards more sustainable consumption. This is because it harnessed the power of social groups. Research has consistently shown that when people believe others are participating in pro-environmental behaviours, they are twice as likely to do the same. For example, residential energy users are twice as likely to install energy-efficient appliances and bulbs, and adjust their thermostats, if they believe other people are doing the same, even though the behaviour of others isn't consciously recognised as an important personal motivator.[3]

Trewin Restorick, the UK founder of Global Action Plan – a charity committed to engaging people in sustainable solutions – believes the key to facilitating behaviour change is recognising the importance of people acting in groups. People are more likely to change their behaviour if it is done in socially supported groups. A good example of this is giving up smoking – and numerous studies have shown that people are much more likely to give up if their friends and family do the same.[4] Change behaviour in a group and you'll soon reach a tipping point where sustainable behaviour is normal and it becomes adopted by everyone as a virtually unconditional norm.

Scott Davidson, a behaviour change specialist working with Trewin at Global Action Plan, has no doubt that peer-to-peer groups are one of the most effective ways to facilitate behaviour change:

'If you try to change behaviour individually, people won't do it for several reasons. One, they won't want to stand apart. We've all got social identities which often belong to groups, and we only move as part of that group. And there's loads of literature, such as Tajfel & Turner's work on social identity,[5] Deutsch & Gerard's work on social norms[6] and Asch's work on influence of group pressure,[7] which demonstrates this.

'By utilising people in their peer groups, they will relate to each other and listen to each other – which allows you to make change happen much more simply. Peer-to-peer is important because most people won't be spoken to or told what to do by government; by 'holier than thou' environmental groups; by senior management or by those they manage. They want to hear from people they relate to. So if it's postmen you're trying to talk to, they'll listen to other postmen. If it is senior management you're talking to, it is senior management they'll listen to.'

Messages about the need to save energy or to be socially responsible sound more genuine, relevant and credible coming from colleagues at a similar level, rather than from a faceless corporate HQ.

'If you use the same peer networking to move people as one group,' adds Scott, 'they will feel safe and they will support each other on the same level. This will give you the space to allow habits to be broken, and to make unconscious habits, such as throwing things in the bin, become conscious by talking it through.

Making habits conscious means they can be changed – so that instead of throwing things in the waste bin automatically, items are put in the correct recycling bin. And once habits have been changed, they'll sink back down into the sub-conscious, so recycling becomes the new unconscious habit. And all this happens much more easily if you get people to do it alongside their peers.'

Using peer groups is particularly helpful as people often approach sustainability with an armload of ready excuses and justifications. Peer groups are excellent at confronting these irrational justifications. For example, a colleague may say they don't recycle because it's too heavy, too far, too dirty or too inconvenient to carry their recycling to the bins. However, if a peer who they respect and who is in a similar position says they manage just fine, it transmits a serious social implication. It makes that person think: 'If they manage and they're just the same as me, and I don't want to be different but to be accepted in this group, I should be able to do it too.'

Peer power can also be harnessed when communicating with other stakeholders who are crucial to your organisation or company, such as customers, clients or local communities. When London's Islington Council wanted to get residents across the borough behaving more sustainably, it launched a peer-to-peer campaign. People from the community were trained to become champions, who then went out within their own housing estates and neighbourhoods to engage their neighbours.

The 'champions' talked to friends and neighbours about the types of activities individuals or families could do – from recycling rubbish and putting a hippo water saver in the toilet cistern to changing light bulbs or washing clothes on a lower temperature setting. The campaign was hugely successful: it saved 195 tonnes of CO_2 and 32 million litres of water. Uptake was much higher because residents were engaged by peers, rather than an outsider from the council or another agency. In addition, when figures came back showing how many people had participated, the power of that story became part of the engagement tool itself. People wanted to be part of the communal achievement and part of the new norm. This leads us to the next component of successful engagement: **Make it the norm.**

4. MAKE IT THE NORM

One of the most effective ways to change behaviour is to make it the norm. Imagine you have ten people. Six of them are doing a green behaviour but it's invisible; for example, they always print double-sided with two pages to a page. However, their four colleagues don't know this is the norm because they've never seen the other people's printouts. Get all ten people together in a meeting where they swap printouts and the other four will adopt the green printing behaviour almost immediately.

The power of social norms has been well documented. Although they can be incredibly powerful, people rarely recognise that their behaviour is influenced by others. If you can make people feel unsustainable behaviour is abnormal, you can facilitate behaviour change on a much larger scale.

The power of norms may actually be one of the reasons why some environmental messaging has failed to change behaviour. Research has demonstrated that when environmental messages try to change behaviour through shock tactics – for example by showing how much litter there is or that the majority leave lights and appliances on – it can actually lead to more of the negative behaviour, as subconsciously people feel vindicated to litter or waste energy because that is what the majority is doing.[8]

This is why it's important to give people the tools and infrastructure to change their behaviour, while also tracking the impact of any initiatives. Clearly, as Keith Pitcher's experience at Leeds University demonstrates, strong imagery of issues such as waste can help change behaviour, but the difference in the success of these initiatives is often one of responsibility, relevance and infrastructure.

Photo campaigns or building waste towers or sculptures in office buildings can be successful because they are a visual representation of an environmental problem directly attributed to that campus or office community. This allows people to feel their actions in that community could make a difference, rather than the messaging being directed at the general public or a wider group who did not share a sense of community or feel connected to the problem. This latter group are therefore unlikely to feel their behaviour can and will make a difference. People must also be given an easy and convenient way to act on the message, for example by ensuring there are lots of recycling bins available or setting up a simple system for double-sided printing. In this way, a powerful message can demonstrate a problem, while people are given the ability to address it.

🌱 A different lesson

As the environmental representative at Sherborne Girls, an all-girl boarding school, assistant housemistress Vicky Forster despaired at the amount of rubbish her boarding house sent to landfill. Recycling facilities existed, but they were tucked away so the girls didn't use them. So Vicky took action.

She removed individual bins from the girls' rooms and put recycling bins at the end of each corridor. This took the ease out of throwing things away while making it easier to recycle and made this the new norm. This simple initiative reduced the amount of waste sent to landfill by 87%.

Vicky engaged the girls in the initiative by holding a house meeting. She explained the changes that were going to take place before they were implemented so the girls were aware of what was going to happen and why. She put a laminated recycling guide by the bins so it was clear what should go where. She also utilised green champions to make displays and put up posters with waste facts and figures.

If Vicky had changed the system overnight and not explained why she had done so or what she planned to achieve, she would have had a revolt on her hands. Instead, the girls accepted the change with just an occasional grumble. As it was, raising the profile of rubbish also had an interesting knock-on effect.

'On top of the massive increase in recycling, a 30% drop in the total waste was also recorded,' explains Vicky. 'Not only were the girls recycling more, but they were also producing less waste generally.' Making the previously unconscious behaviour of throwing something away conscious again had made the girls more careful about what they bought and what they threw away.

On top of diverting 9.5 tonnes from landfill each year, Vicky estimates that the scheme could save the school £480 a year in reduced landfill taxes after accounting for setup costs. If the scheme was rolled out across the other six boarding houses at the school, these figures could be multiplied to produce savings of £3360 and 66.5 tonnes of waste.

Make the invisible, visible

Help people to realise that they are behaving differently to those around them by making invisible social norms visible is an effective way to change social behaviour. It's usually simple to do; it just takes creativity to make these behaviours explicit and obvious.

For example, if 80% of the office already turn off their computer monitor at night, all you have to do is make it explicit by leaving them a fair trade chocolate above their monitor as a thank you. The only caveat is that it must be something simple but visible that can be done again and again, perhaps weekly or monthly. Once this previously invisible behaviour, such as switching off the monitor, has been made visible, almost all of the minority 20% will do it straight away. The minority don't want to be left out or to be shown as massively different; plus they too want the thrill of finding a balloon or a chocolate on their desk in the morning.

'When we help our clients kick off campaigns,' explains Scott Davidson from Global Action Plan, 'we'll often suggest they start with a launch week with lots of visible activities, such as giving people balloons or chocolates for turning off their monitor. It's amazing because, throughout that week, you can really see the change. At the beginning of the week, 50% of people have balloons, and by the end it might be 90%. And the 10% who still aren't turning off their monitor are really feeling the squeeze.'

These strategies always work best when the focus is on the positive, rather than persecuting or embarrassing those not participating in sustainable behaviours. It is better to take the positive examples and make them explicit so it is about leading and making people follow. The workplace is a sensitive environment – people don't want to feel pressured into doing things – but if you are clever, using social and norms networks will change people's behaviour for you.

 Monitor magic

Stephanie Chesters, from London's Brent County Council, moonlights as a monitor fairy. Periodically, she and other members of her team will leave small chocolates on the desks of those people who have turned off their monitors at night. The next morning, there is always a buzz to see who got chocolate and who didn't, reminding those who didn't turn off their monitors to do so in future, and rewarding and reinforcing the behaviour of those who did.

A new kind of normal

Julie Chang, a chief economist for Ecology and Environment, an environmental consulting firm, demonstrates the power of sustainable workplace norms. 'I would actually say I am on the receiving end of being influenced at work. Our corporate headquarters is the oldest existing LEED[9] Platinum building in the country. We have a carpool/public transportation program that awards staff for reducing miles driven and our branch offices are encouraged to adopt specific policies such as recycling, composting and environmental building certifications. Our corporate norms are a subtle but persistent reminder to identify ways to be more environmentally efficient.'

There are always people who don't want to engage and get involved, but it isn't worth expending a lot of energy and frustration on the naysayers.

'Don't try and get people involved who don't want to be involved,' says Scott. 'They'll come later when you've built up a critical mass and reach a tipping point. You don't need to change the entire population of your office. You just need to change the first 40–60% and the rest will follow. So take those who are open to it, and don't fight with the rest. Find the ones who share similar interests. If you've got an office football team or people working on the same project, get them working together on a sustainability initiative.'

The key is to harness that shared interest or relationship. People don't have to be in the same department or share the same job title but, if you find the common link, that will provide the social glue to get them working as a team to find a solution together.

🌱 Stubborn for the sake of it

Bob Gordon has learned from experience that some people just won't budge and that railing against it leads to frustration:

'I was working for an ethical investment company. It was an organisation where sustainability was at the centre of what we did but, even in that environment, there were still challenges.

'Every desk had two bins next to it – one for recycling and one for waste. One of my colleagues refused to separate her waste into the separate bins. Despite the fact many of us would approach her and say, "It's no more difficult to separate your rubbish than to put it all in one bin – you've got two bins by your desk for a reason," she would reply, "I work for a charity, I'm not a charity," and stubbornly refuse to change her behaviour. I think she is an exception, but I think that there is an unwillingness ingrained in people's thinking that it is not their problem. Getting frustrated with her just didn't help. So while I think it is important to keep taking consistent and significant steps forward, sometimes you just have to accept that you aren't always going to win everybody over and that's okay.' 🌱

---

5. GIVE PEOPLE THE FREEDOM TO DEVELOP THEIR OWN SOLUTIONS

Give people power and ownership over business sustainability challenges and they'll usually rise to the challenge with relish. Most businesses know that direct instructions or communications from senior management or government insisting behaviour changes to fit in with a new corporate strategy or regulation tend to be met with resistance. It plugs into that very human trait: people hate being told what they should or should not do.

Change the balance of power and allow those affected to decide within that group what has to change, and they will come up with a solution that they will actually buy into and support. All you have to do is introduce the problem and let them discuss what they have to do. By utilising the teams you have in place around the business, you just have to be a facilitator. By getting them to vocalise the issues they're experiencing on the ground, you can help guide them towards finding solutions.

This makes sense after all. Even if an organisation or a company does have a dedicated CSR or sustainability department, that department or representative can't be an expert in implementing sustainability across all areas of the business. Nor should they want to be. Their role should be to guide others throughout the business to finding their own solutions. In a truly sustainable business or organisation, staff at every level should be incorporating sustainability principles into their everyday thinking.

Ensuring that responsibility for solving sustainability challenges rests with the people across the business allows them to come up with innovative ways of thinking, or even just implementing the obvious solutions in their particular area.

'The best solutions come out of empowering the process owners – they are the people who are best placed to come up with solutions,' explains Richard Ellis, head of corporate social responsibility at Alliance Boots. 'I wouldn't claim to be an expert in logistics, marketing or procurement, but I can work with the people who do understand these things – to get them thinking about these issues – and then innovative solutions tend to come out of that ongoing process.

'We haven't set specific targets for different departments. We have an overall carbon reduction target and it is the responsibility of everyone in the business to meet it. If we can use more recycled material and reduce our carbon – all of those things together are helping us to meet these targets. Because they own the processes, they can influence how they're being done. So from my point of view, I know we should be reducing our delivery transport miles, but I don't know which routes should be streamlined or which deliveries could be shared with other retailers. This is where the expertise of logistics comes into it.

'Another example is recycled plastic. I know it must be good for us to use bottles with greater recycled content in them but it's the manufacturing team who know exactly how much recycling content they can put in before the structure will lose its rigidity and crack. I don't need to tell them how to do it – they know the targets so they'll find the best way to meet them. Often, it's just a case of getting people to be aware of these things. All people are members of the human race and what they want is a good world, one that future generations will find worth inheriting. You need to get people thinking about the issues.'

Huge international companies, such as Diageo, also find that providing a framework and assigning responsibility also works well. 'The company's One Million Water of Life CSR programme provides clean drinking water to one million people each year in Africa until 2015,' explains Camilla Flatt, head of corporate citizenship practice for Africapractice, London. 'But, as the programme was too complex to implement from a single head office, the company provided a framework which enabled its operating companies across Africa to implement the programme and shape their own solutions.'

This included a step-by-step handbook. This outlined how to find a good water and sanitation project; how to select a good nongovernmental organisation (NGO) partner; what information they need to get the NGOs to report back; what systems needed to be in place; and an outline of how the project supports Diageo values. Each regional office was also provided with a press release kit and employee mobilisation kit. The latter has basic ideas on how to create interesting events, which can be used to spark ideas and remind people of how they can use successful events from the past, such as a fun run or sporting event, as part of the new initiative. In this way, Diageo was giving its regional offices the tools to carry out the challenge, while allowing them to build their own structure and solutions and to use their own contacts and ideas.

This premise works whether you're a huge multinational or a small ten-person charity. Human beings are enormously creative: we have evolved to be curious and to embrace challenges. By harnessing this natural instinct throughout the business, you'll spawn much more effective systems. You'll also often find that you motivate, energise and inspire people by empowering them to develop their own solutions.

🌢 Stimulate then leave to innovate

Dr Paul Toyne, head of sustainability at the international property developer Bovis Lend Lease UK, knew that the best way to solve sustainability challenges was to let people help develop the solutions.

'Once we had set our goals, we formed action groups with representatives from across the company,' Paul explains. 'They weren't necessarily people engaged in sustainability. We wanted a cross-section of business units so we had a high degree of representation. We wanted to hear from the right people. So we asked the directors of the business units to recommend who should be involved. This ensured we had top level buy-in and endorsement. It also meant new initiatives were more readily embraced because management wouldn't disagree with the outcome, as they'd be disagreeing with their own people who had put it forward in the first place!

'A lot of people were expecting me to tell them what to do and what the answer was. But if you harness the skills and experiences of the employees, quite often they know what to do. We asked: "Who needs to be involved? How can they be supported by the business?"

'We made sure that people were given the space to participate by getting their line managers on board. In this way, we have people who are in place delivering the tools and guidance to get sustainability strategies working, rather than a sustainability unit trying to solve these problems in isolation. We've got a team of advocates who are out there – day to day, week to week – incorporating sustainability into the workings of the business.

'One innovation that came out of this process was an online waste management process we developed with the operations guys and planners. We said, "Let's map out the journey of waste through our job and work out where the key interventions are required, and what we are expecting the supply chain to do, so we can cut waste as much as possible." At the concept stage, you input what materials you are looking to purchase, how much waste you are expecting, and the system then allows you to think about how you can design the waste out. And if you can't, it helps you work out how best to use the waste streams so they are either reused, or recycled: avoiding landfill wherever possible.

'Harnessing the intelligence and expertise of people throughout the business meant that we've developed systems that are really practical, that make sense and are fit for purpose.' 🌢

6. SET UP GREEN CHAMPIONS AND TEAMS

'How do you create change in a company?' asks Trewin Restorick of Global Action Plan UK. 'It's like a communal scene – say in a church – the organist starts playing and you get silence for a few seconds. Then a few people start singing, loudly and off key, and then lots more join in. That's how change happens. You need to find those singers who are brave enough to make that noise and, when you do, the critical mass join in. Wherever we work, that's how change happens. You need enough people to sing and those singers need the confidence, the time and ability to make some noise, knowing that they are supported by management.'

Helping people to voice their feelings and ideas about sustainability in the workplace gives them the power to make a difference. Often dubbed 'green champions' or 'teams', these people can be highly effective at galvanising others to action.

Just the simple act of nominating people or allowing them to put themselves forward – as green champions, environmental representatives or sustainability officers – raises the visibility of the issue within a company or organisation. The role can also be incredibly rewarding for the individual involved, increasing their motivation, dedication and enthusiasm for their job in the process.

'Champion workshops can be a great way to give people the tools to design effective strategies and to influence their colleagues,' explains Jeff Melnyk from UK sustainable communications agency Futerra. 'And they also fire people up to go back to the office and start spreading the message so that initiatives are implemented correctly. Well-developed champion schemes where champions are well-respected by their peers and the sustainability targets become part of their job, with measurements, tools and information, are usually the most effective.

'We did this for a campaign we ran with Tesco. An energy champion was assigned to each store who was responsible for energy monitoring to see that energy is being used most efficiently. We designed a workshop to show them the impact of their decisions and actions across the entire brand. This helped them to see how their actions, such as shutting oven doors, freezer doors, switching off lights, etc., add up to huge savings across the business. It also shows them how important they are and the role they play in helping to save energy across the UK.'

Having a champion in place within the business, from a small café to a large multinational, gives other employees a focus for their concerns or suggestions. They now have someone with whom they know they can discuss environmental or social issues without embarrassment and who they can approach with their own ideas and suggestions. It also creates a space for people to focus efforts together so that they aren't struggling on their own.

🌿 In-store people power

With over 1000 retail stores, JCPenney knew that rolling out green initiatives would be much more successful if each store had its own champion, an 'energy captain'. These captains could be the eyes and ears on the ground to look for ways to conserve energy and 'green' their workplace. One energy captain in Salt Lake City, Utah, found hidden light switches in a massive stockroom and began turning lights off at night, which instantly reduced energy bills by 25%. She also posted large signs to alert co-workers where the wall switches were located so they could also get in the habit of turning off lights at night.

At the company's larger distribution centres, the creation of green teams increased employee engagement more generally. Volunteers felt excited and rewarded when their efforts led to energy savings and other environmental benefits, as well as recognition from their supervisors. 🌿

🌿 Making things happen

Sustainability wasn't officially part of Will Rowberry's job as an assessment manager in the UK's public sector. However, as someone who cared about the environment, who reused and recycled bags as a matter of course, it drove him mad to see many of his colleagues throwing away a brand new lunch bag every day. He was sure putting a 'bag reuse bin' in the office kitchen would help people reduce their waste. Having a sustainability officer in the company meant Will knew who to go to with his idea.

'Knowing who to go to made it really easy,' says Will, 'and meant I could get my idea up and running almost overnight. I'm always going to him with ideas, such as suggesting we switch our fruit supplier to an organic company I use at home, and I'm still working on him to remove all the desk bins. But having a point of contact is fantastic as it gives me a focus for my green ideas.'

Creating a ripple effect

Having champions in the workplace can also ensure that sustainability initiatives maintain their momentum throughout the organisation. They take responsibility for ensuring an initiative is introduced to interested workers throughout the organisation, who can then champion the cause within their own sphere of influence.

Champions are therefore invaluable but, to really maximise their effectiveness, the best thing to do is to form teams. As almost all of the previous points have confirmed, getting people to work together in groups magnifies their impact. Teams also perform an important function because they provide allies. They help the people who are interested in promoting sustainability to maintain their motivation and enthusiasm as they feel supported in their endeavours.

Alliance Boots use a network of champions to learn from each other. Each champion outside the UK is assigned a 'buddy' – a responsible business expert from the UK where Boots' corporate social responsibility (CSR) strategy is well established. This buddy is then on hand to provide help and support.

'These champions are then the focal point of CSR activity,' says Richard Ellis, head of CSR. 'That doesn't mean they do everything but they pull the strings. It also means that I can go to any part of the company's operations to find out what progress it is making on corporate responsibility targets. The network also collects information for our annual corporate responsibility report.'

Green teams also open people's eyes to the rest of the organisation, which can provide benefits in several different ways. Firstly, they allow green efforts to be coordinated across departments so they are more effective and work together. Secondly, by getting individuals across the company talking to each other, their understanding of the business grows, leading to new innovations and better partnerships. Thirdly, networking throughout the business raises your profile as a dynamic, innovative thinker, which can help get you noticed and improve your career.

Once you have your team in place, focus on getting expert opinion and doing targeted research to ensure that any solutions, strategies or recommendations are safe and truly sustainable. In that way, changes will be genuinely green rather than greenwash. This is especially important as many environmental decisions are very complex and require a life cycle approach. For example, introducing compostable plastic packaging into your supply chain might not be environmentally beneficial if those bags end up releasing methane in landfill. However, if that packaging is composted, biodegradable plastic is preferable as methane release is not an issue when bags degrade in the right environment.

◗ Raising the profile

When Matthew Hawtin put himself forward to be sustainability officer at the employment agency he was working at, he discovered that the role raised the profile of sustainability issues as well as his *own* profile.

'People were really positive about my role – they said they felt the company needed it,' Matthew explains. 'Now, in head office where I work, people are more aware of their actions and it's made them think a bit more about the issues. So if someone's flying away for the weekend, they'll talk about how much CO_2 is associated with their trip. A lot of the time, that's all I'm really asking. I want to raise people's awareness because, if they're aware, they can make more educated decisions. I don't want to tell people to throw waste in the recycling bins but, if I educate them and make sure we have the infra-structure in place, they can make decisions for themselves. And I have noticed that just seeing me around also reminds people to recycle!

'It's also made it easier to have those conversations. There was always a bit of apprehension when I was talking about recycling and putting paper in the bins, and I do try to be aware of whether I am going on about it too much. But the way I see it is, if someone wasn't filling in their timesheet right, someone would be telling him or her the same thing. And so if it's part of my job role, then I go for it. It's also worked quite well – a lot of people did what I said because I was respected enough as a worker, so they took on board what I was saying and doing.'

Picking the right people

Choosing the right sustainability champions and green teams is also important. While getting people to nominate themselves could prove fruitful, often the best results occur when you have a 'persuader', a charismatic, well-liked person with powerful negotiation skills – ideally one of Malcolm Gladwell's 'salesmen'.

'When we go into corporations,' explains Scott Davidson from Global Action Plan, 'we identify ten key people. Then we get those ten people to go into their relevant departments or wherever they work and form their own groups to work with. The formation of the groups is the trickiest part and that's where having these strategically placed and chosen environmental champions comes in. Form that group and get them involved and then just provide them with basic information for discussion. Then they will be able to come up with an action list and they shouldn't need much support to help them move it on from there.'

'I'm the only person who works full time in corporate social responsibility,' explains Shelley Rowley from UK-law firm Speechly Bircham LLP, 'but having a CSR committee made up of about 25 people, from throughout a company of about 350, really magnifies the amount we are able to do. Having the green teams is a great way to get people engaged, and to harness people's energy and enthusiasm to work on sustainability projects. The CSR committee is really good – they might not know exactly what to do but they're happy to meet up and talk it through. We've started giving everyone responsibility for different things. For example, one of our trainees has taken on a community project. At first he had no idea how to start, so I really supported him. But now he's taken it forward and he's got all the trainees engaged and they're really excited.'

It's also important to have the support of senior and middle management to allow staff to allocate time to green initiatives without being pressured. It's often the case that senior management buy in, but middle management – the line managers – are resistant because it's their responsibility to see that targets are met. It has to be clearly communicated from senior management that employees should be allowed to dedicate time to sustainability initiatives without worrying about the consequences. Many organisations give employees time off for voluntary work, so including champion work in this category can help managers and co-workers to accept it as a priority more readily.

It's also important to be specific about expectations and goals. Champions need to know what it is they're signing up for – whether it's an hour a week, a day a month or a one-off event. The more they know, the more likely it is that you will find the right people to participate who will effect the most change.

♦ Choose the right champion

When Sarah Daly wanted to instil sustainability thinking into the agenda at UK-based Heath Avery Architects, she realised a champion was the way to do it. As managing director, she realised getting the 14-person architectural practice to specialise in sustainable buildings and environmental auditing would help them stay one step ahead of the market as client needs become more environmentally focused. However, she recognised that to change the culture, they needed a sustainability champion as well as a director on the board.

'We wanted our new strategy to be part of our culture as a team working together at all levels. But we needed the right personality for the champion. This wasn't necessarily the person with the most knowledge or who is most senior, but someone who could convey messages in a friendly, team-spirited way without nagging or preaching.

'So we chose a champion who was engaging and creative. He was able to inject a little bit of humour and colour into his emails about leaving lights

> or the photocopier on, which had a big impact. We noticed every time he came up with a fun message or graphic and sent it round, behaviour improved immediately.
>
> 'It's also important to reinforce and support the messages coming from the champion. So every time he sends an email, I always reply, copying everyone in, saying: "Brilliant idea, well done." Then everybody feels that they want to support the champion and help him come up with even more good ideas.'

Ann Finlayson from the UK's Sustainable Development Commission observes that leadership and champions can lead to people displacing responsibility for action on to others. This is why green champions or teams won't be effective if they are used in isolation.

Having champions or teams, or even a sustainability or corporate social responsibility department, is enormously helpful and can provide a focus and assign responsibility for action. The key is to avoid segregating sustainability into a separate department or making it solely the role of one person or group that can become cliquey. They are most effective when they operate as catalysts to inspire and promote others to think sustainably throughout the company or organisation. Once you have a team of champions leading the charge, you can work to engage a broader audience.

THE WAY TO ENGAGE

Getting people engaged and thinking about sustainability in the workplace can be incredibly simple – from dishing out chocolates for turning off monitors to showing pictures of the organisation's waste to make it feel real. It's just common sense – get people involved and they'll take ownership of the issues. They will start applying sustainability principles to their work life and they'll innovate to find the solutions to issues facing your business. Connecting to their work in this way will inspire, satisfy and motivate them, often leading them to think more innovatively and creatively about other areas of the business too, leading to bottom-line benefits such as innovative new products or money-saving initiatives.

Therefore, don't be put off if sustainability initiatives have failed in the past or feel worried that people will respond negatively to your suggestions. Just remember the six tricks for successful engagement:

1. Stop, look and listen
2. Find allies
3. Harness the power of peers
4. Make it the norm
5. Give people the freedom to develop their own solutions
6. Set up green champions and teams.

Then apply as many or as few as you feel apply to your situation. You'll find that once your colleagues are on side, you will unlock incredible energy and potential to achieve more than your wildest dreams – while also advancing your career.

The next chapter, **Have two-way conversations**, will build on this theme of engagement. It will discuss more specific ways to draw in your audience and communicate sustainability messages effectively – in a way that captivates, inspires and actually leads to behaviour change.

Chapter 5

HAVE TWO-WAY CONVERSATIONS

6 Seek first to understand, then to be understood. 9 Stephen Covey

How do you get the buyers at one of the biggest retailers in the world to care about organic cotton? You give them a packet of kitty litter.

That was the attention-grabbing solution Coral Rose and Andrew Fraser devised to persuade the buyers at Wal-Mart to use organic cotton (see box **Say it with kitty litter**). By attaching kitty litter to a meeting invitation, the packet acted as a visual aid which powerfully showed the equivalent weight of chemical fertilisers and pesticides used to grow cotton for a single T-shirt. This nifty idea made the issue of chemical use in cotton growing seem real, and ultimately led to the company adopting organic cotton clothing lines and a new sustainable value business model.

Finding engaging, interesting and eye-catching ways to communicate sustainability messages and promote initiatives is vital. Once you've decided what you want to do, the way you tell your colleagues about it can mean the difference between an initiative taking off or being ignored.

Fortunately, a vast amount of research has been done to reveal the best way to communicate messages around sustainability that actually lead to behaviour change. Choosing the strategies that will work the best for you will depend on your audience and your organisation. The first thing you need to do is to **listen** and **understand** your audience. After that, whatever strategy you choose to use, the underlying elements of successful communication are the same: make it **real**, **relevant**, **fun** and **feel good**.

In this chapter, we've pulled everything together so you can use the latest insights, inspiration and downright flashes of genius from some of the best eco-communicators out there to make your sustainability strategies fly. Meanwhile the high-profile success of your initiative that will result will also give your career wings.

Firstly, we'll reveal the secrets of human psychology that will help you **open the communication channels**. Then we'll explain the best ways of **getting it out there** to outline the most effective ways to convey your messages and launch initiatives so they grab your colleagues' attention and keep them engaged.

EIGHT WAYS TO DRAW IN YOUR AUDIENCE
Opening the communication channel
1. Remember, positive messages work
2. Understand where they are
3. Information isn't enough
4. Beware: people are not logical.

Getting it out there
5. Make it fun and catch their attention
6. Make it relevant and real
7. Use a variety of different messages
8. Keep up the momentum.

♦ Say it with kitty litter

Coral Rose knows how important it is to make messages personal and feel real to people. When she was trying to persuade the buyers at Wal-Mart to start using organic cotton, she and colleague Andrew Fraser unveiled a secret weapon: kitty litter.

'We had already started a grassroots movement in the company by talking to people, sending e-mails and posting flyers,' Coral explains, 'but it was the kitty litter that clinched it.

'Andrew and his children spent a weekend creating the invitations to our first meeting. These were a small note attached to a bag of clean kitty litter. We chose kitty litter as it was the material that most closely resembles actual chemicals used in agriculture. The note read: "The kitty litter in this bag weighs 1/3 pound – the amount of chemical fertilizers and pesticides used to conventionally grow enough cotton for a single T-shirt. Think of how many T-shirts we sell in one year!" It really grabbed people's attention.

'You have to educate people and keep them informed. Initially, a lot of people said to me: "We understand why people care if their food is organic, but we don't eat our clothes, why would people care?" So we appealed to their human side and showed them the reality of what cotton production means and how they could personally affect it with their daily decisions.

'I would explain that with cotton, the use of pesticide and chemical fertilisers affects the health of farmers, families and eco-systems; that cotton also enters the food chain as cotton seed oil (which can be found in cookies and other products) and feed for dairy cattle and chicken so it winds up on the table. This really made people click, because a lot of people understand why organic *food* is important but they hadn't understood why organic *cotton* is important. By getting involved, people felt that this could make a difference, while also being good for business.

'By communicating with everyone in this way, it meant people joined our team not because they had to, but because they wanted to. They realised how important this issue was so they got behind it, and felt really good about their contribution. This ultimately led to the success of the sustainable fibers team and Wal-Mart becoming the largest user of organic cotton in the world.'

OPENING THE COMMUNICATION CHANNEL

1. Remember: positive messages work

Make them feel good about themselves

You know that warm glow you get from doing a good deed? It was this feeling that Coral Rose inspired in her colleagues at Wal-Mart to get them to change their behaviour. She did this by showing them a problem, but also how they could help solve it. The warm glow that comes from doing good is proven to be a massive motivator,[1] which will drive your colleagues to spend time reading with schoolchildren in their lunch hour, recycling their rubbish or thinking up creative ways to make the packaging on a PC smaller, lighter and less environmentally damaging.

Use this basic human trait and tell everyone why taking part in your initiative is a sure-fire way to feel great. Plus, when you make people feel good about themselves, they'll love you for it, upping your stock in your colleagues' eyes too.

Appeal to their human side

In his book, *Creating a World without Poverty*, Muhammed Yunus writes: 'Human beings are not just workers, consumers or even entrepreneurs.

They are also parents, children, friends, neighbours and citizens. They worry about their families, care about the communities where they live, and think a lot about their reputations and relationships with others.'[2]

He makes a salient point which is often overlooked in business – people are human beings, not one-dimensional workers. If you approach someone as a human being first, not just as a business person or employee, then you'll create a connection that will enable you to find joint solutions and help you to persuade that person to change his or her behaviour.

The key is to open the conversation in a way that finds your common humanity rather than diving straight in with a focus on the profit angle or the business case. If you start by coming to someone as a business person, that's how they'll respond – in terms of the budget and the bottom line. Money and the business case *are* important as they give your arguments credibility, but you also need to talk to someone as one human to another, with respect for who they are and how they feel about things. In this way, people will open up and be prepared to change because the action is based on moral issues not profits.

'The trick is to talk their language *and* be radical,' says Jo Confino, head of sustainable development and executive editor at British newspaper and website *The Guardian*.

'People get sucked into the idea that business is business and you have to put your human side away. But that is what has got us into this mess in the first place. Like any good journalist, to win someone's trust, you need to come alongside them. You don't look up or down at them, or have any judgements or criticisms, you have a conversation, you have a shared humanity – then you can talk to them and start to change the direction of that conversation.

'It doesn't matter if you are the Queen of England or a bricklayer, or how commercial or business minded you are. People are human beings first, and the vast majority would like to do good – they often get divorced from the ability to do that. They need to see that they are supporting the company but also that they are supporting a greater good. So much of business is designed to cut off those feelings – you're either at home or at work, they're two different worlds, but it doesn't have to be that way. You don't want to pigeonhole people. If you relate to a businessman as a businessman – you're less likely to get any humanity out of them. It's much more effective to let people be people first.'

Be positive

Smiles are infectious (test it out today by smiling at every colleague and you'll get a near 100% return rate) and so is positivity. Positive messages are one of the best ways to get people interested and engaged in your initiative. Fear, panic, impending catastrophe and doom are a massive turnoff, and as has been learned to the planet's cost, people don't respond well to negative messages.

'The trick to communicating eco messages is to be positive,' says Chantal Cooke, founder of Passion for the Planet radio station. 'In general, environmental messages are negative and overwhelming. When you confront someone with a really big problem, they freeze, so it's better to give them inspirational positive messages about the things they can do, along with examples of how things can be done better. If you focus on telling people how fantastic the solutions are, they will want to support them rather than slumping into despair.'

Therefore, make green behaviour something to aspire to. Use your messages to paint a picture in people's minds of what sustainable behaviour would look like – such as seeing 20% of your company's energy bill savings going to a local charity, which is the message the Royal Mail used when they wanted to get workers to reduce energy use (see box **Saving energy, changing lives**). Painting a vision of the future where good things are possible and which allows people to measure their contribution towards this goal is much more motivating than being told about some awful, apocalyptic future.

'Giving people concrete positive stories is the way forward,' agrees Roger East, consulting editor at *Green Futures* magazine. 'A lively story is much more arresting. That doesn't mean only focus on the positive but you need to communicate a clear positive potential outcome: some way of addressing a problem.'

Being positive personally can also have a big impact. 'Having a positive attitude is the secret to getting people to change their behaviour,' says Shelley Rowley, CSR coordinator at the UK law firm Speechly Bircham. 'Being positive engages the people around me and makes it more likely that they'll pass on the message.'

Inspire them

People also respond well to being inspired. 'People engage well with a role model,' says Chantal Cooke. 'Inspirational stories can inspire people to change and help people find their own power. Hearing the story of a teacher who experienced a messy divorce, then quit her job to open an orphanage in Ghana gets people thinking, "Wow! If she was just an ordinary person who did that, maybe I could do something too!" In every company, there is at least one person who wants to make the company more sustainable but they don't feel they have the power. Positive stories show us that while we might feel like a nobody, we can step up and do something too. Then, when one person leads the way, others will follow.'

2. Understand where they are
Find out what makes them tick

Different groups and people have entirely different motivations. If you understand what motivates someone personally (do they care about the environment, social justice, worker rights, are they more motivated by saving money, kudos, convenience?) you can find the angle that appeals to them and use this.

Edward Chambers, co-author of *Roots for Radicals*,[3] advocates that building a relationship first is the most important task, rather than launching straight in with the business case. Ian Christie, a sustainability researcher and consultant in the UK (see box **Playing politics**), admires Chambers' approach. He says you should start with what Chambers calls 'relational meetings', getting to know the person and asking questions like:

- Why do they work for the company?
- What are they proud of?
- What worries them about their job?
- What's keeping them awake at night?

You can then reveal the same information about yourself. This process allows you to understand their point of view and shows you are interested in them as a person. Then, at the end of the conversation, when relations are established and you have shown that you understand your colleague's concerns, you can begin to outline your suggested solutions and ask: 'Would this be useful to you?' This will help you gain acceptance for your sustainability goals, while simultaneously presenting you as a valuable problem solver to your colleagues and to your company or organisation.

Talk to people

'It's so worthwhile to sit down with everyone in the office, it doesn't have to be for long,' says Dr Victoria Hands, environmental and sustainability manager at the London School of Economics and Political Science (LSE). 'When I want to get people on board, I get everyone around and say, "I just wanted to tell you that I'll be coming round to speak to each one of you for five minutes, or feel free to approach me." I mean, what's five minutes in your lunch break or even a full lunch hour, spending it with a colleague, getting to know them and asking: "How do you feel about this? What turns you off about this? What lights you up about this? What would you prefer to see?" If you start engaging with people on that level then you will have allies, a team that can support each other and that is really important.'

By asking colleagues what their concerns are, and what they see as the barriers, you can work out a way around the problem to find a solution that is sympathetic to their professional needs but that also reaches your goal. You will also have the information to make it real to them as an individual, both *personally* (for example by demonstrating how much waste they are personally responsible for) and *professionally* (by showing how your suggestion will impact on their targets), as Professor Ian Christie did with the British government (see box **Playing politics**).

Say you wanted to introduce recycling facilities, but you were encountering resistance from the facilities team. By sitting down and talking with your colleagues, you might learn that their concern is that there isn't enough space on site to store recycling. This gives you the opportunity to find a different solution – perhaps you can ask suppliers to remove the packaging on delivery (as HP now does for many of its business customers) or you can ask suppliers to reduce the packaging that comes with their products in the first place (as LSE have done successfully to reduce on-site waste).

🖋 Playing politics

How do you get a busy politician to pay attention to climate change? You show him or her how it affects the policies he or she cares about. That's the top tip from Ian Christie, a sustainability researcher and consultant who has advised influential players from the British government to the WWF for many years.

'I've been in situations where I was surrounded by people whose agenda and priorities meant that, in effect, they wanted to stop me achieving things. In these cases, the only way to have an impact is by finding out what makes people tick. I go round having "get to know you" meetings. I ask, "What makes you want to do this? What do you hope to achieve? What frustrates you?" Then I can say, "Now we have this shared understanding, here are some ways in which I could help you achieve some of your goals – and some of mine too, since we have important shared objectives and values."

'I learned some of this when I was taught basic marketing – you've got to sell the FAB to the MAN. The FAB: the Features, Advantages and Benefits; the MAN: the person with the Money, Authority and Need. And it can work everywhere you go. It works because you first find out what matters to the person in question. The worst thing you can do is launch straight into what interests you – show them your samples, as it were, and tell them what they mean to you. People are sceptical and they can easily be put off by such enthusiasm and focus on *your* own agenda.

'An approach which tries to understand their goals and needs allows you to present yourself as what you are and aim to be – someone who can help solve their problems – is more effective,' says Ian. 'It makes all the difference if you can understand what's important to them first so you can show how your solutions can help. This happened once when I was trying to persuade a senior politician to make far more of a priority of action on climate change. I'd been telling him how important climate change was to me, and about how it was a huge global issue his team wasn't taking on board. But I hadn't got through to him.

'So I started asking his advisors, "What motivates him? What does he care about? What defines him as a politician?" And I realised, I'd been going about it the wrong way – his passion is for social justice and helping the poor. I realized I'd been arguing the wrong case. So I changed my angle to show

> him how many of the things he was fighting for to help the poor would be impacted by climate change, such as the UN's Millennium Development Goals. And the result was the politician embraced it – and he changed tack to give climate issues a much higher profile in his speeches and policy development.'

Really listen

Once you've asked people what matters to them, the next step is to *listen* to the answer. It's amazing how often we don't actually do this. Don't believe us? Think back to the last time you asked for directions – we'll bet you had to turn to a companion afterwards and ask: 'So, where do we go?' because you switched off halfway through.

It's also easy to switch off if you don't like what you're hearing but if you shut out what you don't want to know, you'll be shutting your ears to finding a workable solution to the problem.

'To get into other people's worlds you have to be a good listener,' says Dr Victoria Hands from LSE. 'You need to develop listening skills, which is not the same as just keeping quiet.

'And you can't make changes until you really acknowledge what's going on. Students throw away tonnes of useful items, like pots, bedding and furniture, at the end of each term. I wanted to find a way to store these unwanted items over the holidays so we could offer them to new students the next term. But I realised it didn't matter if I don't like the fact that halls of residence don't have storage I can use, that's just the reality: there just wasn't the space. Once I acknowledged that and started to work within those restrictions, the problem became more flexible, there was more cooperation and I could find opportunities.

'This doesn't happen if you start by telling someone "you have to do that differently". That just alienates them and puts them on the defensive. By sitting down with people to understand what the issues are, I've discovered lots of students buy cheap storage units as there isn't enough storage in the rooms. That's allowed me to ask: "What would happen if we made the wardrobes bigger so students don't need to buy new ones every year?" So in this way, I can stop one whole pile of waste from being created in the first place, in this case, old storage units. So, because I've listened and can now ask the right question, the guys at the dorms are helping me make that solution happen. So I'm reducing waste, even though I'm doing it in a different way than I had originally envisaged.'

Roger East at Green Futures agrees. 'Being good at listening encourages a climate in which people will come forward with ideas. If you listen carefully to people, you can understand where there may be resistance or concerns. It will also help you see where there may be doors that are ready to swing open.'

By listening first, you can try to devise a strategy that meets other people's goals as well as your own. This means your colleagues are more likely to be supportive and you'll also be more successful as you won't be battling to get people on side, but working together to find solutions cooperatively, because, as **Chapter 6: Work together** shows, the attainment of one person's goals increases the chances of reaching the goals of the other group members.[4] This will raise your stock internally in your organisation too as people will think about you positively as a person who helps them meet their targets.

Reverse mentoring where people in operations can actually give feedback and explain the issues to management can also work well. For example, by getting someone who maintains water meters to mentor the leadership team to show them the practical barriers to a suggested solution, a workable one can be found. Reverse mentoring can help break down the barriers within a business to stop people feeling cynical about solutions.

◗ Saving energy, changing lives

How do you make employees excited about saving energy? You tie it to something they care about, advises Dr Martin Blake from the UK's Royal Mail:

'We wanted to reduce energy use by 10%. But when I told the operators and union representative we wanted them to turn off lights and save energy, they said: "No way! All you care about is saving money so you can have fat cat bonuses, we're not interested." It's a typical response in the union environment. But postal workers care about community so one of the postmen suggested we donate some of the money saved to a charitable project, and that hooked them in straight away.'

Royal Mail trialed a scheme in Edinburgh where 20% of on-site energy savings were given to a mental health charity called Enable and it's been a huge success:

'Staff love it, and the money has allowed Enable to train 24 people with learning disabilities to become postmen,' enthuses Martin. 'They're star employees – diligent and loyal. And having a job and a role to play in society has done wonders for their self esteem and self worth, and gives them an enormous sense of satisfaction. The programme also helped staff understand learning disabilities – and some even realised they've been struggling with them undiagnosed their whole life. The whole programme created an enhanced degree of tolerance and understanding which was unexpected, but amazing.

'It's saving money, reducing emissions, reinforcing the sense of community and satisfaction for staff and the socially excluded, while taking people off government benefits. These are the sort of multiple wins you can achieve if you construct your programme right.

'We're rolling the programme out nationally and looking at ways to apply it to other parts of the business, such as telling drivers that for every litre of fuel they save by driving more slowly or sensibly, we'll donate to charity. It just shows what you can achieve when you listen to people to find out what they care about.'

Lead from behind

'There are two things people need to remember if they want to be truly successful,' says Dave Stangis, vice president for CSR and sustainability at the Campbell Soup Company, New Jersey. 'One: they need to check their ego at the door (or leave their ego at home). Two: they can't let their passion interfere with the existing corporate culture. Every company has their own way to get things done. You have to listen and you have to give credit to others – to all the people who help you execute your strategy: such as the environmental engineers at a plant, human resources, the community relations team. They are the ones you want to shine the light on.'

People are naturally more interested in their own ideas than those of other people. 'One of the most influential things you can do,' says Ian Christie, 'is make people think your idea is theirs. It's one of the quickest ways to make ideas stick – don't take credit. There is an old saying that there is no limit on what you can achieve if you let someone else take the credit. It's true. You've got to give away opportunities for people to shine. Listen first, give away ideas and then let people run with them.'

Neat phrases to help do this include: 'Have you thought about this?' or 'I noted down some ideas that came up in our conversations – is this what you meant?'

When things take off, you also need to be prepared to hand over and relinquish control of your pet project. 'When you do succeed, you have let go and allow other people to make the project their own,' says Dr Victoria Hands from LSE. 'It can be difficult to deal with your feelings of loss, and it can be hard to let other people take over when it's your baby, but it's a true sign of success when your initiative becomes bigger than you and your individual input. By allowing other people to get involved, you can really start to maximise your impact.'

Leave the preaching behind

In many organisations, people don't see sustainability as a priority or part of their job role. It's important to respect that instead of evangelising. The good news is that simply talking about sustainability gets people thinking about the issues. Presenting the information in a neutral, nonjudgemental way can win people over as they don't feel they're being preached at.

'People pick up when there is judgement in your voice and are easily turned off by a preaching attitude,' says Sofia Busamante from Turn Up the Courage, a UK-based leadership and coaching organisation. 'If there is respect for their thinking or their life, they will be more open to hearing what you have to say.'

'Our strategy is to give people information,' says Chantal Cooke from Passion for the Planet. 'We treat our listeners as intelligent people. Rather than trying to persuade or wagging a finger, we just explain the impacts and ways you could change. If you give people the option to start somewhere, they might take it, but if you tell them it's all or nothing, they'll do nothing.'

This also means learning when to let go. 'I have to stop myself sometimes,' explains Kristen Thomas from the US marketing agency The Phelps Group. 'I have to tell myself, it is okay if someone leaves the water on too long to wash that plate. At least we now have proper plates instead of Styrofoam!'

♦ Walking the line

'Initially, I would feel apprehensive when reminding people to put paper in the recycling bins,' explains Matthew Hawtin, project and sustainability officer for the UK's Careers Development Service. 'There is a balance. You don't want to be an eco-evangelist. In my company, people are not at work to learn about sustainability. My company's purpose is to get people back into work. I think sustainability *will* become part of the business mandate as it is becoming more important to demonstrate our commitment when we tender for new contracts. But you have to work with where colleagues are now.' ♦

Don't overload people

One of the barriers to engaging people is that many don't understand the concept of sustainability or corporate social responsibility (CSR). However, if you break it down into bite-size chunks, people understand and identify with the components.

'People might not get the wording or terminology,' says Shelley Rowley at Speechly Bircham, 'but when they see events coming up, like a personal safety talk, healthy living week, volunteering, recycling – that's real to them. But if I just say "CSR" they wonder: "How does that affect me?" So when people ask me what CSR is, I say: "You know volunteering? Well that's a community project and that's what our community is." And they think: "Aha, I'd like to do that, I could read to kids in my lunch hour." If you say to someone, "Do you know what your carbon footprint is?", people may be unsure, but if you ask: "How do you get to work? Do you walk, do you cycle? Well that's a part of our corporate footprint – it is about you and how you get to work." You just have to explain it in a way that relates to someone and his or her daily life without being patronising.'

According to Kristen Thomas at The Phelps Group, 'It is also much better to start with small things and build. If you try to do too much too fast, people will push back. The programme I started at Phelps took 18 months and we started with easy things like switching from disposables to china plates and mugs. The solar panel installation took time but we got there because we started off small with a simple question like, "Hey, can you rinse off a plate?" People think to themselves: "Am I really going to say I cannot rinse off a plate?" When you approach it one step at a time, and you show people why you are doing what you are doing, and you get back to them with results, most people are smart people – they want to do the right thing.'

Be honest and above politics

Honesty and integrity are also important for getting people to respond well to your message. 'This just means doing what you said you would, when you said you would,' says Dr Victoria Hands at LSE, 'and communicating if you can't as soon as you know. This also means not gossiping about people. If you keep the level of conversation very high, productive and focused on your commitment to people and the planet, you can keep the discussion above office politics. Make sure people realise that it's about a higher vision so they don't get bogged down in petty issues.'

'I think it is more attractive for people to hear about the truth of who you are,' agrees Trewin Restorick from Global Action Plan. 'If you appear as a perfect person who is there to show them how they also can be perfect, your approach will meet with limited success. If you are there primarily to understand their world first, and then only suggest an aspect of sustainability that could make a difference in their life, then you will have far more impact. You will have the context for that action and they will trust they are not a project of yours but a human being.'

People respond when they perceive you as being genuine and authentic. If you lead by example, not only will your colleagues respect you and respond but you may also find your initiatives will win you new clients while existing clients will value your efforts and may even be inspired to change their own behaviour.

This is what happened for Kristen Thomas at The Phelps Group. Living her values rubbed off on her colleagues and when clients saw what the company was doing, they asked to see their sustainable business plan. This inspired them to take action and strengthened the business relationship.

Take negative reactions in your stride

Sustainability strategies are usually well received but you can't please all of the people all of the time. Fortunately, climate change detractors are now a minority. In fact, a study by Ipsos reveals that 70% of people from 23 countries from around the world (including the US, UK, China, India, Italy, Russia) agree that climate change will affect their generation.[5] This means that while it's important to take the views of those who disagree with you on board, it's best not to become bogged down trying to win hardliners over. As was explained in **Harness the power of peers** in **Chapter 4**, if you focus on the majority, the detractors will follow in the end.

'You do have to be prepared for some headaches,' says Debbie Ledbetter, director of environmental sustainability at global IT giant HP. 'For example, some of the simple tips I sent round on email riled a few people, which took me by surprise. There are people out there who don't believe in climate change or who are not ready to make changes or admit that they are needed. So it's important to manage your expectations – you cannot get to everyone. We were able to engage more and more over time – but we couldn't engage everyone.'

When someone is being critical, bear in mind you don't have to answer their challenge on the spot. If you don't have the evidence you need at that moment, be polite, then find the facts and get back to them.

3. Information isn't enough
Give them the facts and the power to change them

Information is not enough to change behaviour on its own, especially when it comes to persuading people to engage in socially and environmentally responsible behaviour, such as switching off their monitors at night or turning off the engine instead of idling.

The US government discovered this to their cost when they assessed the impact of the education programme launched during the energy crisis of the 1970s.[6] Pamphlets, videos and other information services resulted in paltry energy savings of between 0 and 2%. In *Motivating Sustainable Consumption*, Professor Tim Jackson from the University of Surrey outlines why information must always be presented alongside solutions:

'One of the many paradoxes that haunt the debates on behavioural change is that more information is not always better ... People like to feel in control of their lives and resist feelings of helplessness. My attempts to impose more information on your already crowded life may simply reinforce your sense of helplessness about the situation.

'Kaplan and Kaplan (1989) identified three evolutionary insights into the information processing and problem-solving properties of human beings. They concluded that people are motivated:

- to know and understand what is going on: they hate being disorientated or confused;
- to learn, discover and explore: they prefer acquiring information at their own pace and answering their own questions;
- to participate and play a role in what is going on around them: they hate feeling incompetent or helpless.'[7]

This reinforces the point discussed in **Give people the freedom to develop their own solutions** in **Chapter 4**. It is important to create a situation where people feel able to do what they believe in. This is because the most effective way to turn people off environmental issues is by making them feel they don't have the power to change things.

This is backed up by Michelle Shipworth's research on the best way to facilitate behaviour change in home energy use. She concluded that:

'A person is more likely to take environmental actions if they believe that they can bring about change through their own actions. Psychologists call this concept "locus of control" ... Energy action programs need to underline the positive impact that each person's actions have.'[8]

Help people change their behaviour, not their attitude

You must back up any information or messages with infrastructure that gives people an easy way to align their behaviour with their attitude. If you're going to build a waste tower to demonstrate how much paper the company sends to landfill, make sure you install plenty of convenient recycling bins at the same time.

Otherwise you're making people care about something but giving them little scope to address the problem, leaving them frustrated. This can make them feel anxious, and the unconscious desire to get rid of these feelings of anxiety and frustration can lead to apathy, or a change in attitude so the issue won't make them feel bad any more.[9]

Making (radio) waves

'How do you persuade a meat-loving public to eat veggie?' This was the question facing Chantal Cooke at Passion for the Planet radio. She knew intensive meat production accounts for 18% of global emissions, but that making listeners feel bad about eating meat wouldn't turn them vegetarian. Instead, Chantal knew if she gave them the facts about meat's impact on the planet, and then an easy and painless way to do something about it, she'd be more likely to win them over.

'We never take the line: "It's bad, terrible, who can we blame?" We acknowledge problems and issues but we end on a positive way that people can make a difference,' explains Chantal. 'So the campaign explained that rearing livestock for meat accounts for 18% of global human greenhouse gas emissions and 8% of water use; that it is responsible for 70% of Amazonian deforestation; that 7 kg of grain is fed to a cow to produce just 1 kg of beef.

'To complement the facts, we worked out the difference it would make if someone had one meat-free day a week to show people that this easy, achievable action could make a difference.

'We calculated that by having one meat-free day a week for a year, you could reduce your greenhouse gas emissions by 600 kg; save 84,000 gallons of water and 7700 square feet of rainforest; while saving a wallet-boosting average of £320 and improving your health because vegetarians have a lower risk of developing heart disease, diabetes and cancer than meat eaters.

'In this way, we showed that swapping to meat-free dishes one day a week could save money, improve your health and save the planet *and* make you feel good. This approach makes people think "I could do that!" '

Make things clear and simple

Often people don't do something as simple as recycling because they aren't quite sure exactly how to do it. 'People don't need to know *how* things get recycled,' says Jeff Melnyk of British sustainable communications agency Futerra. 'They just need to know what *they* need to do in a clear way. Visual, illustrated examples which are very specific – like telling people which bin to put coffee cups in – solve this problem simply, and get people recycling.'

4. Beware: people are not logical

'Any communications strategy which assumes that well-formed, rational arguments will result in attitude or behaviour change is likely to be unsuccessful.'

The Rules of the Game: Principles of Climate Change Communication, Futerra[10]

It is often assumed that when faced with a choice, we make a rational decision to do the thing that benefits us the most. However, as the current economic and ecological crisis has shown, as well as a huge volume of research, man rarely makes the rational choice.[11] Instead, people rationalise their own actions. As psychologist Richard Gross says: 'The human being is not a rational creature but a rationalising one, attempting to *appear* rational both to others and to oneself.'[12]

Research has also shown that people emphasise the positive and ignore information that they don't like or which doesn't fit in with their ideas. This is known as *dissonance following a decision*: we actively avoid information describing the desirable qualities of an item we have rejected. People pay *selective attention* and *selectively interpret* to perceive ambiguous information as being consistent with our opinions.[13] These are probably some of the main reasons why climate change and the problems associated with the unsustainable use of resources have been ignored for so long: people didn't want to hear bad news or information that might mean they had to change their behaviour. It's also why it was a flash of genius to call Al Gore's film *An Inconvenient Truth*.

The knowledge that humans don't make the logical, self-interested choice is important because it means you can't rely on appealing to logic. Again, that's not to say logical arguments aren't useful, but the reality is that people respond best to personal stories, or the promise of feeling good (see **Make them feel good about themselves** above).

Don't expect attitudes to influence behaviour

Another strange but true facet of human psychology is that attitudes don't necessarily predict behaviour. Attitudes 'represent predispositions to behave, but how we actually act in a particular situation will depend on the immediate consequences of our behaviour, how we think others will evaluate our actions and habitual ways of behaving in those kinds of situations'.[14] In other words, just because we care about something doesn't mean we will act on it.

Don't fall into the trap of thinking that just because your colleagues say they believe using public transport is the right thing to do, that they will. If it is awkward, or they think it will embarrass them in front of their co-workers, they might not act on it. Therefore, while you can appeal to people's attitudes in the poster campaigns, emails and other communications you may use to tell people about your initiative, you must have the infrastructure in place that makes it easy for people to act on their attitudes as well. This understanding of psychology is also why, as explained in **Make it the norm** and **Harness the power of peers** in **Chapter 4**, it is so important to use social norms and peer groups to ensure that sustainable behaviours are the norm.

GETTING IT OUT THERE

Now you've opened the communication channels to work out what matters to your colleagues and how you can get them to care about your initiative, it's time to start telling people about it. This section will outline the best ways to get your message out there in a way that engages your colleagues, leads to long-lasting changes in behaviour and leaves you feeling satisfied, empowered and looking like a leader.

5. Make it fun and catch their attention

Successful sustainability initiatives often work because the people behind them have made them fun and engaging. MTV gave out green lollipops to reward green behaviour, which got the whole company showing off their green tongues. The BBC had people cycling to power a light bulb. IBM held a web-based 'World Jam' to get employees across the world talking (see box **Web around the world**).

'Make communications as exciting, innovative and relevant as possible,' says Trewin Restorick, Founder of Global Action Plan UK. 'Try to communicate imaginatively. Getting on a bike to power different appliances lets people feel the energy needed to charge a mobile phone, or the difference between a low energy bulb and a traditional incandescent one. This helps them to physically make a connection between energy use and energy generation and to feel responsible for the energy they use. But even if you just put green footprints on the stairs, the secret is to make things fun.'

Generate a buzz

Giving out chocolates to people who turn their monitors off at night, without explaining why, generates a buzz that a simple, straightforward reward couldn't achieve on its own. People will try to work out why some people are given chocolates but not others.

'It's also worthwhile to get them to realise the scale or urgency of the problem in an interesting, eye-catching way,' says Trewin. 'Waste sculptures are a great way to grab attention while being fun too. We worked with someone at a London bank who built a waste tower several storeys high out of paper boxes which stunned employees into changing their behaviour to use less paper.'

Making your initiative visual and high profile also helps, for example by putting a display in the reception area or lobby to get people talking.

'We've seen time and again how providing engaging information can influence behaviour,' explains Neil Turner from renewable energy company RES. 'When we put in a renewable energy installation like solar or wind power for a client, we always put a big display in reception explaining what we're doing. We make it fun and attractive with lots of visuals, info and interesting facts. It's really powerful because showing people how renewable energy is being generated makes them connect to the issue of energy use. Electricity becomes tangible to them, it becomes something important that shouldn't be wasted, so energy use tends to drop too. One client told us this had led to a drop in energy use of 30%. This means that installing renewable energy means that not only do our clients get a larger proportion of their energy from low carbon sources, but they're using significantly less too!'

Companies like Global Action Plan and the Energy Saving Trust use engaging tools like an eco driving simulator game, which tests (and teaches) players to see how far they can drive with a certain amount of fuel. Tools like these generate an enormous amount of interest, which can be raised further with a competition for the best score.

Competitions, games and online simulations are a fun way to get people engaged. From guessing how many old batteries are in a jar to zapping carbon, Space Invaders style, there are lots of engaging games. Search online for inspiration or speak to the plethora of NGOs and government agencies who are skilled at promoting sustainability in fun ways (see **Appendix 1: Who can help**).

Make a day of it

'Sustainability fairs or themed days can be a really effective way to kick off or round off a campaign,' says Sophie Hanim of the UK's Energy Saving Trust. 'Fairs draw people away from their desks with games, activities and giveaways, which means people get involved.

'We have Earth Day events every year,' says Debbie Ledbetter from HP, 'and employees love it! People email me afterwards to tell me how inspired they were. We have a vendor fair where we bring in socially responsible products, nonprofit groups, solar companies, organic farms, recycling facilities and so on. People are passionate about climate change and they want to know and do more.'

 Words that work

Choosing the right words can make the difference between an initiative seeming cool or corny. The trick is to use words that confer kudos or glamour, rather than seeming worthy or deeply green. Here is a list of eco-words that work:[15]

Smart, e.g. '**smart** appliances'

Savvy, e.g. '**savvy** driving'

Green, e.g. '**green** lifestyle'

One planet living

Carbon footprint

Zero waste

Less is more

6. Make it relevant and real

To make your initiative have maximum impact, all the evidence points to the need for messages and mediums to be tailored to different audiences.[16]

Talk in their language

Many innovative channels used to convey climate messages don't work because people don't realise they should be paying attention. For example, factory workers might notice eye-catching posters announcing that the company is looking for green champions, but they don't respond because they assume the message is targeted at office staff. Make it explicit – in this example, by making it clear you're looking for champions from all sections of the business.

It's also important to talk in a language that people understand. This may mean, once you've made a human-to-human connection (see **Appeal to their human side**, above), using the business language of legal, compliance, risk, bottom line and budgets to draw links between your initiative and the issues that matter to a colleague's everyday work life. Choosing the angle that matters to people can lead to major breakthroughs.

'There are multiple benefits to going green,' says Yalmaz Siddiqui, global director of environmental strategy at Office Depot, 'but, to be effective, you need to understand which benefits will appeal to which function. The sales team is excited by the unique selling point of a green product or solution; a supply chain executive is persuaded by the argument that smaller, lighter packaging reduces costs for materials, inventory and transport; for facilities managers we show how going green can reduce energy costs. Each function has its own priorities and those should be highlighted when trying to influence in a greener direction.'

Using the right message for the right audience is important, because if you don't, you'll turn people off. For example, asking employees to bring in their own mug while highlighting how much money this could save can turn employees off if they think the company is dressing up a cost-saving scheme as a green initiative. However, tie in these savings to something they care about, such as a staff party or a charity, then the reaction will be different (see box **Saving energy, changing lives**).

Making it real

The other problem is that some people don't see how climate change affects them. Therefore, show people the links that affect them and make your sustainability initiative and messages relate to their jobs, and make it as easy as possible. Linking sustainability to people's targets and everyday work activities is also a great way of dealing with the 'I'm too busy' or 'It's not my responsibility' line because it makes the issue seem relevant while giving people a clear course of action.

Thus, a construction worker working for Bovis Lend Lease on site in Britain may not care, understand or feel able to make a difference to the impact carbon emissions will have on climate change or people in the developing world. However, he or she can identify with wasting fuel by leaving his or her car running, and that can be used to draw very simple comparisons with wasting energy by leaving lights, printers and air conditioning on in the workplace, as was done in a Bovis Lend Lease poster campaign (see Figure 5.1). In this way, a fuzzy and intangible issue, such

Figure 5.1. Bovis Lend Lease campaign poster. Reproduced by permission of Bovis Lend Lease

as emissions, becomes rooted to an employee's everyday reality in a way that feels real and relevant. Making sustainability real to your audience will maximise your impact.

 In the driving seat

If your business racks up lots of road miles, give employees a driving lesson.

'Smarter driving lessons are a great way to teach employees about the way they can reduce emissions and save fuel costs,' says Sophie Hanim of the Energy Saving Trust. 'People enjoy it, as it's a hands on experience which takes them away from their desk and helps them to do something to help the environment.

'The stats show that after one hour-long lesson, fuel use was reduced by 20%. We did some lessons for Heinz. One of their employees used to fill up twice a week but, after the lesson, he told us he now fills up just once a week, saving him enough money for a lovely meal for two every week. A lesson seems to cause a mindset shift which leads to real, tangible results.'

Put things in context

Have you ever felt frustrated to be told you can save the planet by changing to low-energy light bulbs when it feels an utterly futile gesture? We were familiar with this feeling until we discovered that one-fifth of the world's electricity is used to power lighting.[17] Suddenly, the obsession with light bulbs made sense – because if every American changed just one bulb, it would save more than $600 million in annual energy costs, while preventing the greenhouse gas equivalent of the emissions from more than 800,000 cars.[18]

This is an excellent example of why context matters. If you simply tell people to switch their workplace lights to low-energy bulbs, you'll get a small effect. However, if you tell them that switching to low energy would save a certain number of tonnes of CO_2, and the company a big chunk of money (therefore swelling employees profit share or bonus – if relevant), your colleagues will be more likely to switch.

 Three-tree challenge

Shelley Rowley from Speechly Bircham hit upon a way to reduce her law firm's paper use: by making people realise exactly how much they used each year. 'We calculated, in trees, how much paper every single person in the building used. It worked out to three trees per person – so we devised a campaign using a tree-o-meter to encourage people to reduce their paper usage by a tree each. We're going to have a meter on each floor to see who is doing the best to reduce their usage, to get everyone vying with each other.'

7. Use a variety of different messages
Different days, different ways

As different people will respond to different messages, you need to use a variety to reach as many people as possible. 'You're never going to get everyone,' says Shelley Rowley, 'but the more events I do, the more people I engage as different people are attracted to different things. For example, someone who takes part in a health check, fair trade fortnight or has his or her carbon footprint assessed might not do a community project. Someone else might decide to donate a present in our Christmas appeal. The broader you can be in your initiatives, the more people you can capture. Plus, I try all forms of communication to promote initiatives; such as email, internet, posters, and asking the CSR committee to tell people in their departments.'

Debbie Ledbetter from HP agrees: 'You cannot have one campaign that will be done in six months. It's an ongoing process and you have to find ways to engage those who are less interested. We were able to engage more and more over time – but we couldn't engage everyone. You have to be mindful of the cultural differences of employees from across the world. The same programme can't necessarily be rolled to India, China and the US – but we do what we can to be as effective as possible in each market. Direct tips on email are really effective. Email gets their attention and colleagues would look forward to getting tips every two weeks on how to reduce their impact at home and at work.'

Segment your audience

'Blanket messaging usually fails,' says Jeff Melnyk of Futerra. 'When we're designing a communications strategy, the first questions we ask are: "What are the values of the audience?" and "How do we segment the audience to target the right people with the right messaging?"

'So, when one of our clients wanted to commit to more sustainable carbon reduction behaviours, we didn't blanket message everyone. We looked for the people who will manage the issue of carbon. This could be anyone from senior management to the personal assistants (PAs). People like PAs are often forgotten in the equation, but they are decision makers and it's they who have a huge impact on day-to-day operations.

'So rather than watering down a generic message in an all-company email – such as "Cut our carbon", which doesn't assign any responsibility – we said to the PAs: "We need to cut carbon and you manage travel so when you book UK travel, only use the train." Targeting your messaging means people know what to do in a way that is relevant to their job.

'In segmenting the audience, you might think you've left out quite a bit of the company. But when a company has 20 000 employees, you can't hit everybody with every initiative.'

Give your messages credibility

If the source of your message is seen as expert or knowledgeable, people are more likely to be persuaded. Partnering with organisations such as the WWF, Rainforest Alliance, the Carbon Trust or Global Action Plan can bring enormous credibility to your campaign. Expert partners can provide you with salient facts and figures, and may be able to help you plan your campaign, although the benefits of collaboration will be discussed more fully in **Chapter 6: Work together**.

Another way to communicate messages powerfully is via sessions with internal and external speakers – from getting a member of the green team to explain the latest initiative or a WWF representative talking about the effect toxic chemicals have on wildlife to a spokesperson from a waste management plant explaining what happens to waste, experts engage and motivate.

'Bringing in experts is fantastic,' says Debbie Ledbetter from HP, 'as people like the face-to-face interaction and being able to ask climate change questions (either in person or via a webcast) directly to a credible expert. It's a very effective way to communicate with employees and everyone leaves feeling inspired.'

Look for the leaders

People are also heavily influenced by their peers (see **Harness the power of peers** in **Chapter 4**). Some peers and employees are more influential than others. If you can identify who these people are within your organisation and persuade them to lead the charge, your initiatives will be more likely to gain traction as research studies have shown that these 'transmitters' (or sneezers, trendsetters, opinion formers, influentials) are key to creating the momentum for change.[19,20]

Explain to these leaders why sustainability issues such as carbon or fair labour practices are an issue for the company and that they need to display leadership behaviour in thinking through the technical issues or infrastructure changes that need to be addressed. This empowers them by giving them license to tackle the challenge while being identified as a leader elevates their status, which is incredibly motivating. Raising your profile with these influential individuals while you make them feel good about themselves is also very beneficial to your own career.

Identifying leaders is one of the reasons why creating champions works so well, as was discussed more fully in **Set up green champions and teams** in **Chapter 4**. It allows those employees to feel they are personally involved in finding solutions, which motivates them to inspire their colleagues.

Credible sources such as experts and leaders are also valuable because an information overload means people feel confused about environmental issues and the unsustainable use of the planet's resources. By using people your colleagues already trust, and partnering with experts, you can find information and transmit it in a way that cuts through the mire to give people the facts to help them act.

Make it personal

Another neat trick to get people engaged is to make it personal and individual, and to make them take ownership.[21] If you want to get someone to start recycling, give them name stickers to put on their bin, or give out fun pin badges that people can wear. These methods make people identify with the initiative and make it more likely they will take part because if you label yourself as a recycler, you become one. Using these simple methods to turn residents into recyclers helped Waltham Forest Council in London achieve a 35% increase in recycling in the first month of the programme.

Use peripheral messages

Seeing the characters of your favourite soap putting items in the recycling as they leave the house is peripheral messaging – a message that's transmitted in such a way that people don't really notice it. Getting the CEO to launch a sustainability initiative via a video conference, as Bovis Lend Lease UK did when they had a Q&A coffee morning promoting greener travel, or having in-house communications printed on recycled paper will transmit subtle, almost imperceptible, messages that can help to change behaviour.

Get on the web

Technology and social media can be an excellent way to share knowledge, connect with and influence others, and it is well worth looking at the ways you can use mediums like intranets, web chats, email newsgroups, Facebook, YouTube, Twitter and blogs to get people engaged.

These channels are so effective as they allow you to connect with key audiences in a more transparent and authentic way. They also open communication channels so employees across an organisation can feed back and connect with each other even if they've never met, such as when IBM managed to get 320,000 employees sharing ideas and solutions via a web platform called 'World Jam' (see box **Web around the world**).

♨ Web around the world

When IBM wanted to engage 320,000 employees across the globe, they knew the web was the way to do it. The company created 'World Jam': a web-based platform that allows employees to share ideas and help each other. The initiative has grown into a five-day event during which employees around the world log on to share ideas, ask for help and look for practical solutions to global challenges.

Tying this technology into a specific event allowed IBM to engage more than 320,000 employees in 20 regions worldwide at one time. Across industries, disciplines and national borders, staff shared ideas and learned from each other. ♨

Use your existing systems

Most companies and organisations have already worked out efficient systems of communicating with and training their staff, so use these. Often, sustainability initiatives and training can be slotted into your existing communication and training channels, in the same way you would treat new regulation on compliance or the launch of a new product.

'We recognised we need to up-skill and train our people around sustainability,' says Dr Paul Toyne from Bovis Lend Lease UK. 'We created training programmes to give people the right information for their role so they could be part of the team delivering sustainable solutions on site. We have entry level training and foundation courses leading up to assessor courses on green building schemes. This means the people who have done training become green enablers. It helps them to understand the implications of what they're doing.'

8. Keep up the momentum
Feedback, remind and reward

You also have to keep reminding people what you're doing and why they should act. This is one of the reasons why feedback and reinforcement is crucial.

'There is a lot of research which shows that, while programmes can get people engaged, they may revert afterwards if the message isn't reinforced,' says Scott Davidson at Global Action Plan. 'However, if you measure what they did and feed this back to them, it makes people think, "Wow, I can actually make a difference, so I'll continue that behaviour." Often this will lead to bigger behaviour change in other areas such as flying or driving less. People want to make changes, so showing them that they are making a difference by using measurement feedback is absolutely critical. It does have to be a robust measurement though; you do actually have to look at water usage and electricity meters, do spot checks on bins, monitor the tonnage of recycling and get all those measurements as best and robust as you can. It's usually quite simple to do but it makes a huge difference.'

'There are always success stories along the way which show the initiative is working,' says Jeff Melnyk from Futerra. 'Grab those stories and use them to keep the momentum going to keep the change. It's not as simple as: implement strategy; engage employees; measure in a year. You need a holistic approach which keeps going back and making sure the communications strategy is working. This is why taking measurements as you go along is so worthwhile.'

Measure and show progress in a way your audience can understand

People love visuals and graphs, charts and eye-catching image that measure and present findings so they can see problems and progress. Steve Lanou, deputy director of the sustainability programme at the Massachusetts Institute of Technology, argues that using graphs and targets is invaluable. They can inspire and motivate people to get behind an initiative whether the subject is something as dry as the efficiency of dormitory radiators in university accommodation or as fun as funds raised for charity. 'If you do an inventory of something like emissions, and show it to people in a visual way like in a graph, it shows them the story,' explains Steve. 'They can see where the organisation or company has come from and where you are going.'

This is where good measurement systems come into their own. American department store JCPenney has used real-time energy monitoring in some stores to help measure and reduce energy use through a web-based energy centre. This allows store managers to log on and get energy consumption data at that site from the previous day, with comparative information from the same day the previous year. Energy consumption data can be shown from the previous day in 15 minute increments, which helps stores to find spikes in energy use and to find a way to reduce that usage.

Hard physical measurements are also useful. This type of data is often necessary to help you get support and funding for your initiative, for example by being able to demonstrate how much waste your initiative is diverting from landfill and therefore how much money you're saving the company.

Praise and reward

Creating a reward system to incentivise volunteers can be powerful, but the most successful incentives aren't always cash or gifts. Often, recognition at a high level of the organisation is enough. This has been Andrei Aroneanu's experience at PepsiCo. 'We used to give out a T-shirt or something small as a thank you. What we quickly learned is that publicly thanking those who make a difference at company meetings was the best recognition they could possibly ask for.'[22]

It's striking how powerful and important praise can be to help employees move the sustainability agenda forward at their firms. From our research with sustainable innovators from Campbell Soup Company to Office Depot, Ecology and Environment to Global Action Plan, the message came through loud and clear; praise is a powerful tool.

Pointing out and recognising the efforts of those who have taken part in initiatives motivates them to continue their efforts. Meanwhile, the public recognition inspires others who have not previously engaged to take part.

Professor Ian Christie agrees: 'Once, I was trying to persuade a procurement department to care about sustainability. I knew they felt unrecognised and taken for granted. I realised that I could motivate them by showing them how they could win recognition by winning awards in sustainability because there might be a category they could shine in. It worked, and they started working with us on a sustainable procurement strategy.'

Money is not a big motivator

Another surprising thing is that people aren't particularly motivated by money. This can be especially true in a business environment when people don't feel it is their own money they are spending or saving, but instead the fat cats' at the top of the company. Financial incentives and small rewards do help to change behaviour, but they will only have a limited effect if used on their own.

Material rewards can reduce people's motivation as they switch from being motivated by the enjoyment or good feeling they get from participating in an activity to being driven solely by the promise of reward.[23] Rewards can work but if you are going to use incentives, such as tying bonuses to sustainability targets or giving gift card rewards for walking, biking or using public transport to get to work (see **A new kind of commute** in **Chapter 6**), do it sparingly so colleagues still do it for the love of it rather than the incentive. Public recognition and anything that improves their status is usually the most successful.

Check your communications are reaching their targets

It's also worth checking for gaps in the communication channel. For example, there's no point sending everyone an email or putting information on the intranet if half the company doesn't work on computers or if nobody is visiting the site. You also need to check that your messages are grabbing people's attention and getting them to engage.

Think about the most visible place to site events or communication materials so they get the most visibility. In many companies, this can be the canteen or the reception, as this is often the place where most people are likely to see and spot campaigns and events.

The reality is that there are many different ways to skin a cat and there are lots of different ways to communicate. The trick is to keep checking to see what is working and what isn't so you can tweak your strategy as you go along. You've got to see what staff respond to and you may have to improvise halfway through.

Communication as a two-way street

The way you communicate, and listen in return, is a key component of success. However, as we've shown in this chapter, opening the communication channel and getting your message out there is actually very simple if you just keep the maxims we've outlined in mind:

- Remember, positive messages work
- Understand where they are
- Realise information isn't enough
- Beware: people are not logical
- Make it fun and catch their attention
- Make it relevant and real
- Use a variety of different messages
- Keep up the momentum.

Once you've learnt to **listen** and **understand** your audience, you just need to communicate your initiative in a way that makes it feel **real**, **relevant** and **fun** and makes people **feel good**.

Do this, and you'll be rewarded with the satisfaction of knowing that your initiative is making a big difference. You'll know it is helping to make the planet a better place, motivating your colleagues and enriching their lives and improving your company or organisation's bottom line and image. And all this will happen while showing your colleagues and your company or organisation that you are a person who makes good things happen, which is a sure-fire way to make good things happen for your own career.

Chapter 6
WORK TOGETHER

❛Climate change is not a problem that can be solved by a single entity – be it government, business, civil society, or individuals ... Long-term solutions will come from the combined efforts of all of the above. ❜ JustMeans and Green Mountain Coffee[1]

Have you ever wished the individual commuters sitting in their cars causing congestion would get together and share rides to cut traffic, pollution and emissions?

It was this thought that inspired Erika Vandenbrande from the City of Redmond, USA, to join forces with environmental experts and local employers to set up a ride-sharing programme called R-TRIP. By collaborating and working together with Ecology and Environment and key employers in the city, such as Microsoft, R-TRIP has had a huge impact. It has helped employees from across the city save over 22 million vehicle miles, conserve almost a million gallons of gasoline and reduce emissions by over 20 million pounds in just over one year.

To do this, the City of Redmond called upon Ecology and Environment's 30 years of experience in running green transport programmes. Ecology and Environment knew how to persuade employees to exchange the comfort and convenience of driving solo for greener transport modes such as biking, walking, public transport and carpooling. The City of Redmond also knew they needed the area's big employers – such as Microsoft and its 40,000 staff – on board to ensure workers in the area had easy access to the scheme.

By tackling the problem together, each organisation was able to have a much greater impact than either could have dreamed of achieving on their own. Meanwhile, the teams behind the schemes were recognised both within their companies and externally for being the brains behind the much-feted initiative.

This is an excellent example of how joining forces to **work in partnership** can help you and your business make real progress towards achieving your goals. Partnership-driven initiatives can strengthen brand and value while marking you out as a dynamic achiever who thinks outside the box to bring ideas and skills together. This chapter will show how working with others will maximise your impact and elevate your career.

THE POWER OF PARTNERSHIPS

Many businesses and individuals within them are making incredible progress because smart employees have engaged with the unexpected. These individuals have started conversations with those who come from 'across the aisle'. They have engaged in conversations with colleagues across disciplines and departments, joined forces with their competitors or co-created solutions with their customers. Many have sat down with groups who are concerned about social and environmental issues – such as nongovernmental organisations (NGOs), nonprofits, social entrepreneurs or shareholder advocacy groups – to share information and use each other's expertise to find solutions.

There is no one route to sustainability and, as the old adage says, two heads (or three, four or five) are better than one. Plus, if you work with others in networks and find allies, you'll have support and encouragement that will help keep you inspired and motivated. Building a like-minded team will also impress internal and external stakeholders, such as your co-workers, customers and community. Team efforts, such as R-TRIP, demonstrate that collaboration can give you the power to transform not just your workplace but also your town, borough or city – and, perhaps, even your country.

You might want to form a casual, one-off partnership to organise a screening of an eco-film like *Age of Stupid*. You might like some advice from a conservation charity on creating a wildlife area. You might want to collaborate on developing products for a low-carbon economy like GE and Google (see the example coming later). Whatever your aim, linking with others to enlist their expertise can help you maximise your impact.

◗ A new kind of commute

Erika Vandenbrande, senior planner from the City of Redmond, Washington, knew that to reduce traffic, increase transport efficiencies and manage growth, she was going to need help. Erika enlisted Tony Gale and the GreenRide team from Ecology and Environment, along with people from state and local agencies and companies, such as Microsoft, AT&T Wireless and Nintendo, to grow a city-wide green ride programme called R-TRIP.

'Working together with Ecology and Environment,' explains Erika, 'and with others within the City of Redmond, meant we were able to take our original program to a whole new level.'

The R-TRIP web system lets users search for other people in the city or at the same company with the same commute so they can find a ride share. Its route planner shows public transport options so people can search for alternatives to getting in the car. It also allows users to log and track their savings – and those of the company and the programme – while earning credits towards a gift card reward.

'Ridesharing has been part of Ecology and Environment's employee program since the 1970s,' explains Tony Gale, 'and we have learned how to ensure the right levers are used, like financial incentives, personal recognition and easy-to-use, web-based technology. In fact, since we implemented our internal program for our employees, we have saved 32 million miles from being travelled in single occupant vehicles and thousands of tons of greenhouse gases from entering the atmosphere. We understand how to encourage employees to give up driving solo as a daily commuting routine in exchange for transportation modes that are better for the environment like biking, walking, using public transportation and car-pooling. This knowledge helped feed into the development of the R-TRIP program.'

Ecology and Environment's expert knowledge in designing a useful, engaging programme helped ensure that the initiative was adopted by companies like Microsoft, who employ 40 000 people in the area. 'Employees at Microsoft can log onto their R-TRIP page,' explains Lynn Frosch, transportation services manager from Microsoft, 'and easily see what they are doing to help reduce road congestion, gasoline usage and CO_2 emissions. They can also follow the overall successes of their company and the entire City of Redmond.' The companies taking part have found that employees find this immensely satisfying, and getting to know others through the ride-sharing scheme has boosted morale and strengthened relationships between workers within companies and also the Seattle community.

For Erika, the success of the programme has also translated into job satisfaction. 'One the biggest positive benefits of working on the program has been that it has given the things I am really passionate about credibility in the business community. It shows to the world – including upper management, elected officials and our business community – that these things have value, and that they can be mainstream and empowering.'

A new era of cooperation

Successful collaborators have realised they can have a much greater impact by sharing ideas and enlisting the help of others, both to find solutions and to spread the word. 'There's definitely been a realization that a small group of people can't achieve a huge amount on their own,' explains Trewin Restorick of behaviour change NGO Global Action Plan in the UK. 'The only way to really effect change is by building constructive partnerships with the people who share your views for a more sustainable world.'

From multinational corporations to tiny companies, smart people within smart businesses are realising that by working together they can achieve more. One famous example is McDonald's. The fast food chain started working with Environmental Defense Fund, an NGO specialising in environmental issues, in the 1990s to help them eliminate the nonbio-degradable Styrofoam 'clamshell' in which McDonald's had sold over a billion hamburgers. Another multinational, technology giant Hewlett-Packard, is working with the WWF on using information and communication technology to reduce greenhouse gas emissions. Meanwhile, technology multinational General Electric and internet giant Google have joined forces to lobby for renewable technologies and to create new smart-grid and energy-saving products (see **Practise co-opetition with your competitors**).

Across the spectrum are the Massachusetts Institute of Technology (MIT) in America and the University of Surrey in Britain. They are just two examples of universities who, independently of each other, collaborated within their own communities to use students to tackle sustainability issues on campus. They have done this by setting students the task of finding solutions as part of their academic coursework (see box **The future by degrees**).

Smaller organisations are collaborating too, such as the UK-based Riverford Organic Vegetables. They have been working with their customers to develop products and services that fit with customer values and needs. Meanwhile, they have also been working with the University of Exeter to research the environmental impacts of different types of packaging. In countless offices around the world, savvy individuals are phoning up organisations like the Carbon Trust or plugging into networks such as

CSR Chicks for advice on things like low-energy light bulbs or purchasing green office supplies (see **Appendix 1: Who can help**).

Enlisting help from all departments, skill sets and outlooks – from factory workers and logistics staff to customers, suppliers and stakeholders – can help you understand the issues and design effective solutions. The whole is definitely worth more than the sum of its parts!

To help you find your own collaborative solutions, here are some of the types of people you can partner with and some of the unique and creative ways in which people are reasoning together. Next, there is a checklist of useful guidelines on the best ways to make working together a success:

1. Work with your colleagues
2. Co-create with your customers or clients
3. Practise co-opetition with your competitors
4. Work with your supply chain
5. Engage with NGOs and social partners.

I. WORK WITH YOUR COLLEAGUES

It's crucial to bring people together across departments and across the business. In this way, your organisation works as a team and sustainability initiatives across the company complement and support each other. It seems obvious but often initiatives don't succeed because this basic maxim has been ignored.

Savvy employees recognise the importance of working together. When asked to rate 'how important you think each element is in making sustainability strategies successful' in the Climb the Green Ladder Sustainability in the Workplace Survey, 87% of respondents said it is important that their employer coordinates efforts across the business.[2]

Every element of business from product development to procurement has a financial, social and environmental component. Sustainability principles should underpin every person working in every part of the business. Yet how many times have you seen your company or organisation working with little communication between departments or co-workers, leading to a duplication of efforts? Often, buildings, facilities, legal, compliance, transport and procurement set up their own individual systems for dealing with an issue such as energy efficiency or waste, rather than pooling efforts to create a simpler and more cost-effective solution.

As discussed in **Give people the freedom to develop their own solutions** in **Chapter 4**, collaboration is vital because other areas of the business have knowledge and expertise that can be brought to the discussion to ensure that realistic, workable systems or targets are designed. The case of Yacob Mulugetta and John Davis at the University of Surrey (see box **The future by degrees**) is a great example. The pair are trying to get their organisation working together as a whole by applying the university's expertise in solving sustainability challenges to all of its operations.

Dr Paul Toyne, head of sustainability at Bovis Lend Lease UK, gave us another great example that demonstrates the power of one person to bring people together to find solutions. John Morrison, a building services manager at the international property management and construction company, thought it was crazy that the company was wasting energy and money by keeping lighting on in temporary project offices and on sites. This, and the fact Bovis Lend Lease was participating in a high profile 'London Lights Out' radio campaign, made him think, 'Let's turn out *all* the lights.'

John knew the company couldn't just introduce a 'lights off' policy overnight, so he, and a team from legal, insurance, risk management and the building services community, worked to develop a 'lights out' policy that will reduce the company's carbon footprint by 3% and save approximately £250,000 per annum. 'This is an example of someone taking responsibility; driving change through and making a difference,' says Paul. 'Simple things can equal big changes!'

Collaboration is one of the reasons why initiatives like sustainability champion networks (see **Set up green teams and champions** in **Chapter 4**) work so well. As more and more employees around the world at all levels understand the need to tackle climate change, conserve materials, water and energy, they want to participate and feel empowered. Collaboration brings people together across a business so people can find solutions together, rather than efforts being the sole concern of the CSR or sustainability department.

✿ The future by degrees

By giving students research projects to solve real-world challenges, Yacob Mulugetta has been working across the University of Surrey to turn undergraduates into a sustainability army. Yacob, the deputy director at the Centre for Environmental Strategy, was keen to help the university escape the confines of academia and put knowledge into practice. He was also fed up with directing undergraduate effort into tired multiple choice questions and essays when that energy could be used to reduce environmental impacts in the real world.

However, Yacob couldn't turn the assessment system on its head on his own. He joined forces with the sustainability and energy manager, John Davis. Together, they have worked with others to set up over 40 projects that focus on solving real-life sustainability issues on campus and at two local schools.

These include researching the demand for, and benefits of, introducing a new school bus and helping the university cut carbon, manage waste, improve transport and map its eco-footprint. These projects have the potential to make a genuine, lasting difference. They also provide students with valuable skills and experience, which will give them an edge when looking for careers after university.

'It's been incredibly hard work,' explains Yacob. 'But it's amazing seeing the projects coming together, and to see students, local schools and the university all working together to solve sustainability challenges. Most of the students are really enjoying getting their hands dirty by working on practical projects. They're also realising the importance of collaboration as they learn to work with their own team and with other teams, as well as with staff from the university and the participating schools.'

2. CO-CREATE WITH YOUR CUSTOMERS OR CLIENTS

Keeping your clients happy is essential to business success, and, as every marketing man knows, working with your customers to create and road test products or systems is one of the best ways to ensure success. Tying products and services to client values is also another well-established winner. As social and environmental concerns move up the agenda, more and more customers are demanding that the organisations that serve them – from governments and schools to retailers and internet service providers – be part of the solution, not the problem. A new breed of 'ethical' consumers is trying to use its purchasing power to support companies who are making progress in solving our toughest social and environmental challenges.

'There is a growing interest and concern about how companies use resources and engage in transformational practices,' says Wood Turner, executive director of ClimateCounts.org, a US-based organisation that rates companies on their ability to tackle environmental issues. 'This clamour for action is coming from all ages and segments of society – not just the affluent or the younger generation who are known for being passionate about these issues.'

It is more important than ever to fully understand your customers' and clients' values and needs. This will help you create brands and products that reflect and meet them, ensuring repeat custom and long-term success.

'I know if something feels right to me, then it will feel right to my customers,' explains Guy Watson, founder of Riverford Organic Vegetables (see box **Delivering *value* for money**). 'If I am genuinely doing something worthwhile, genuinely adding value, genuinely giving people what they want, I've always been able to turn that into a commercially viable venture. Doing something worthwhile has always been the starting point. Then you work out how to make it pay!

'Being close to our customers has always been part of that. I know our customers tend to be just like me – people with children who question the way the world works. Things that have seemed right to me have seemed right to our customers. When I've strayed from that into areas I'm uncomfortable with, it's ended in difficulties. That intuitive guidance is quite a big factor. I will bend to being rational with commercial facts when I come to make a decision, but it always starts from what feels right.

'Listening to your customers is a good thing, but just wanting to please people is not enough: you need to stand for something (and be prepared to be occasionally unpopular) to earn trust.'

🌱 Delivering *value* for money

Riverford Organics keeps in close touch with its customers to make sure they're providing the service and products that suit their customers' needs. One of the largest organic vegetable delivery services in the UK, Riverford grows and purchases organic products that it delivers direct to its customers' doors in a weekly seasonal vegetable or fruit box. The boxes arrive at 40,000 homes with a newsletter from the farm, often written by founder Guy Watson, which talks to the customers directly.

This newsletter is backed up by surveys to reveal what customers feel about that week's delivery, as well as canvassing opinions on extra products and services, and how customers want Riverford to operate. These results are fed back into the system and the findings are shared with the customer via the newsletter.

Riverford also attends suppers at customers' houses to find out how they used their weekly packages and what they found frustrating. Riverford shares what it learns with its customers through the newsletter, even when the tips are uncommercial, such as 'Buy less until you've used up your veg backlog'. The openness of this dialogue has allowed Riverford to explain and win customers round to unpopular decisions.

'Our customers are pathologically opposed to plastic but I had an inkling that despite all the money we were spending on it, biodegradable plastic wasn't actually better for the environment,' explains Guy. 'But we can't do anything unless our customers support it. Sometimes we can persuade them but sometimes we have to do what they want us to do. This is why we partnered with Exeter University to do a lifecycle assessment on biodegradable versus conventional oil-based polythene plastic. It's all about knowledge and credibility. I was frustrated by wanting to do the right thing but not knowing what the right thing was. Sometimes the right thing isn't what everyone else is doing – it is often counter-intuitive. If you are going to challenge people's norms, you need to be extremely well informed. Partnering with Exeter gave us credibility and gave us the real facts.'

Riverford's life cycle analysis on the plastic in their supply chain revealed that biodegradable plastic had greater environmental impacts. This is largely because much of it ends up in landfill where it releases methane – a potent greenhouse gas – something that isn't an issue if the plastic is composted. 'Having this evidence allowed me to go out and argue for the change. Having a close relationship with our customers meant we could explain why we were switching to conventional oil-based polythene plastic fully in the newsletter and online, and explain that our customers could return the plastic bags to us to be recycled, so most of our customers accepted the switch.'

Customers also have an open invitation to visit the farms. Events such as Easter egg hunts are staged to tempt visitors to come and see their vegetables growing in the field and to interact with the farmers. This entire process encourages the customer to feel that they are co-creating the product with the company, and that Riverford lives and understands their values. This ensures that the company has happy and loyal customers and farmers.

3. PRACTISE CO-OPETITION WITH YOUR COMPETITORS

There's a new buzzword in town, and it's **co-opetition**. The term describes a new movement towards cooperating and collaborating, as well as competing,[3] to create the maximum benefits for all parties. This could be something as simple as sharing deliveries such as in the Alliance Boots example (see box **Mileage in a good idea**) or joining forces to ensure that industry standards reward sustainable behaviour and your organisation's efforts towards best practice. More and more businesses have realised that it is possible to reduce energy and material use, and negative environmental and social impacts, while protecting profits and corporate secrets.

Mileage in a good idea

'Why are retailers driving their trucks around half empty when we could just team up with other retailers to share deliveries in Scotland?' This was the question troubling Ian Barnes, delivery drivers and the logistics team at the British pharmacy and retailer Alliance Boots. The company realised that if they could collaborate with other retailers, it would help them meet carbon reduction targets, while reducing costs, pollution and traffic and increasing transport efficiency.

Boots UK tapped into an initiative called Far Flung Places which helps businesses with similar delivery routes to partner-up. Multiple retailer deliveries, to out-of-the-way places, could be mapped together by individual routes. Ian Barnes says:

'The scheme helped us work out that we were sending full vehicles from Glasgow to Inverness for delivery direct into stores, while another company, JBT, were bringing vehicles down from Inverness into the Glasgow area for delivery. In between, JBT were running back empty and we were running back moderately empty, apart from recyclables. By getting together, we used the space on the JBT vehicle on its outbound journey from Glasgow up to their distribution platform in Inverness. They then deliver the stock to stores using their delivery fleet while bringing our recyclables back.

'We started by running a trial to see if we could get it to work – because, obviously, there are complexities. Technically, there are vehicles available, but do they match the delivery times and the slots that both parties need? You need to compromise: it might be worth the vehicle waiting an extra hour, or getting the stock ready an hour earlier.'

The manager in Scotland had to engage the distribution centre, as well as the stores around Inverness.

'They needed to be on board,' says Ian, 'and aware that non-Boots branded drivers would be turning up at their store to deliver and take stock away which was a fundamental change. It may have been the same driver delivering to the same store for years, so it's important to get the stores to understand why you're changing the system.

'The initiative is about being open with other people – so we can say we've done this and it's worked, so we're prepared to share our learning. It means we save 6000 delivery miles a week and 150,000 litres of fuel per annum and we've reduced our carbon footprint. These benefits are good for Boots UK as it is helping to meet the company's carbon reduction targets and saving money, while also saving emissions in Scotland.'

By working with others in your industry, you can also unite to help governments ensure that legislation is fit for purpose and that sustainability initiatives are *actually* sustainable. This is because if you tackle an issue before legislation comes in to address it, you will have more time to work out a really robust solution using the expert, insider knowledge that governments tend to lack. Developing your own solutions will also give you more time to adapt your systems sympathetically, so you don't have to implement new systems in an expensive rush (for more on this, see **Minimise compliance risks** in **Chapter 3**).

A good example of co-opetition at work is GE and Google – two companies who share investments in renewable energy. This may come as a surprise to those who know Google as a search engine, but the energy-hungry data centres that power web searches have led the internet giant to make it part of their business to find low-carbon energy solutions. Therefore GE and Google have joined forces to lobby the American government for renewable energy power and to develop clean technologies. The companies will push for government programmes to modernise the electrical grid to enable wider use of renewable energy, such as the wind power generated by GE and Google's wind businesses.

These businesses could be said to compete but, by teaming up and bringing their combined power towards lobbying government, they are more likely to succeed and both should reap the benefits. They will also work together on technical collaborations to develop a range of cutting-edge products such as hybrid cars, geothermal energy and 'smart grid' technology. This ranges from software that makes the grid more efficient to 'smart' meters and in-home displays, which let consumers understand and control home energy use to reduce energy bills. By working together in these areas, rather than competing, GE and Google are hoping to create groundbreaking new products that generate income streams and help tackle climate change as the world shifts towards a low-carbon economy.

You might expect big players in the electronics industry to be fiercely competitive, and often they are. However, that hasn't stopped HP, Braun, Electrolux and Sony working together on sustainable initiatives. The electronics giants established a pan-European take-back and compliance system for used electronic products years before the Waste Electrical and

Electronic Equipment Directive (WEEE) made it compulsory for them to do so.[4] The companies aimed to prevent old electronics such as computers being disposed of in landfill where they can leach toxic chemicals into the environment. In addition to protecting health and the environment, the collaboration also strengthened the brands of the companies involved and reduced compliance costs when the WEEE directive came into force.

Dr Martin Blake, head of sustainability at the UK's Royal Mail, champions the idea of co-opetition. His attitude is one of openness and sharing – one where the Royal Mail's sustainability initiatives are freely available for anyone else to use and learn from, such as the eco-driving tips or vehicle tracking systems the company has used to reduce fuel use in one of the largest fleets in Europe.

'We're all in the same game,' Martin explains. 'There is only competition in how well we meet those shared goals. Let's give other people the opportunity to share what they're doing so we can all learn from each other.'

◢ A healthy partnership

In Mali where one child in five does not reach the age of five because of preventable diseases like diarrhoea or malnutrition, Anne Roos-Weil was desperate to get her life-saving Pesinet service up and running but she was stumped. A micro-financed health insurance service, Pesinet provides regular checkups with a roving trained field agent who sends symptoms and vital statistics to a doctor via mobile phone. The doctor can assess whether the patient needs to come in for treatment, allowing curable diseases to be treated before it's too late.

To convince families to pay for the service, there is a need to offer a very affordable subscription fee and to raise awareness of the value of prevention. When Anne heard about an initiative called Telemigrants, she realised that a collaboration could help achieve these objectives while ensuring more resources would be available for both projects to develop. Telemigrants provides a pre-payment internet platform that allows Malian immigrants in France to pay for services for family members in their country of origin. Through the financing mechanism of Telemigrants, Pesinet could reach more people to help them get treatment, while increasing awareness of the value of prevention as expatriate family members become the advocates of the project within their community back home.

'It's amazing how it works for both of us,' explains Anne. 'More subscribers equals more income for Telemigrants, allowing them to offer their services more widely. This also has the effect of creating more jobs in France for people to run the service. Together, we are able to help more people than our projects could have done independently. Our programme is more robust and solid than when we were alone, allowing the partnership to apply for more funding, rather than us competing for the same funding pot. This ultimately means we are all able to help more people.'

A coalition of winners

'Many companies worry about competitive issues,' says Anthony Kleanthous, senior policy advisor at WWF-UK. 'They worry that talking things through with their competitors might give away their competitive advantage. They also worry about legality, since sharing price-sensitive information can open them up to accusations of acting as a cartel. However, sustainability is a systemic challenge. There is no such thing as sustainable business, only a sustainable system, so you have to get used to talking to a broader constituency of people with whom you can face these challenges.

'If you get people together, you can have a roundtable learning exercise. You can admit you don't have the answers, but you can say, "Let's work on the issue and be prepared for the answers to emerge as we go." At the end of the day, as long as you focus on what's important and what your real impacts are, and you avoid token gestures, you will come up with a much better, more sustainable solution than if you try and do it on your own.'

Other people, such as Guy Watson at Riverford Organic Vegetables, are finding that a cooperative model can lead to business success. The cooperative model can be effective as it allows companies to grow while still retaining their personal feel as they remain as lots of smaller businesses working together, rather than one sprawling, faceless corporation. This makes it easier to keep values – not just pure profits – at the heart of the business, which helps to keep that all-important connection with your customers alive.

Other collaborations worth considering include industry associations and councils. If you work in the food industry, you might consider joining the Marine Stewardship Council to help and show your support for sustainable fishing practices. If you work in the paper or timber industry, the Forestry Stewardship Council can help you support sustainable forestry (for more details on these organisations, see **Appendix 1: Who can help**). Organisations such as these have done a huge amount to see what being sustainable means for a particular commodity or particular part of the system. By uniting, you can benefit from their expertise and they can benefit from yours.

Industrial symbiosis or industrial ecology is another growing field which looks at ways companies can help each other by swapping products and services that would otherwise be considered waste. For example, a factory could pipe its waste CO_2 into greenhouses to make crops like tomatoes grow faster or a manufacturing plant that has waste heat could use it to warm a nearby swimming pool.

It's also worth considering clubbing together with organisations around you, such as the other tenants in your office block, neighbouring retailers on the high street or the other schools in the district. Having the backing of other stakeholders gives you enormous clout when it comes to lobbying landlords, suppliers or local governments to make change happen, such as installing recycling facilities (see box **One voice, many partners**), water-saving measures or energy-efficient lighting.

The key is to look for support all around you. If *you* care, the people who share your business environment probably will too. You should be able to find a way to work together that is beneficial to your businesses – and by coming together, you will amplify your ability to make change happen.

One voice, many partners

'We're in a big building with lots of little companies in it,' explains Chantal Cooke, the co-founder of the digital and internet radio station, Passion for the Planet. 'There are a number of things we've done in the building by getting the support of the other tenants behind us. For example, we spoke individually to all the different business owners and asked them if they would recycle if we organised a system. They said yes, so we did some research on the best way to install the recycling facilitates – so they weren't in the way, and so on. Then we went to the building owner and told him, "Everyone wants recycling, this is how much it would cost, so can we have it?" Because we had the weight of all the other tenants behind us, he didn't really have a choice but to say yes!'

4. WORK WITH YOUR SUPPLY CHAIN

One of the most effective ways to achieve far-reaching results is to focus on greening your supply chain. Whether it's a hospital canteen, a multi-national retailer or a small office, organisations and companies wield enormous power over their supply chain because suppliers can't afford to lose business, whether it's supplying food, fabric or filing equipment (see box **Ask and you shall receive**). Even a small business can make a significant impact by setting sustainability standards. The bigger your supply chain, the greater your power.

Ask and you shall receive

'How can I get greener office supplies and electricity without increasing my budget?' This was the challenge facing Matthew Hawtin, project and sustainability officer at Careers Development Services. The answer was, 'Ask them.'

'We use one major stationery supplier quite a lot. So I went to them and said we wanted to change our catalogue with them – to cut costs and switch to more environmentally friendly products. We wanted to limit the options and make those choices eco-friendly. We go through a lot of paper and the 100% recycled paper was double the price of normal paper. Because we buy a lot, they agreed to reduce it to the same price as their normal paper. We also switched to markers, pads and envelopes with recycled content. The suppliers were helpful, and they met us in the middle as much as they could, so we made good savings from the switch.

'I also looked into energy suppliers which started off being really time consuming and complex because we have 25 centres. Then I realised they would do it for me. So I just went to EON and British Gas and gave them all our meter numbers, and they worked out which contracts were up for renewal and so on. This made it easy for them to give me comparative quotes for regular and green electricity.

'It was actually incredibly easy to start a conversation with your supplier, and because they're keen to keep you as a client, they always try to help you as much as they can.'

Wal-Mart is one high-profile example of a company that caused global ripples when it launched a far-reaching sustainability strategy in 2005. The massive American and international retailer announced that it wanted to work with suppliers to achieve three core sustainability goals: 'Being supplied 100% by renewable energy; creating zero waste; and selling products that sustain resources and the environment.'[5]

'We recognized early on that we had to look at the entire value chain,' said Tyler Elm, who was Wal-Mart's senior director of corporate strategy and business sustainability at the time the initiative was launched. 'If we had focused on just our own operations, we would have limited ourselves to 10% of our effect on the environment and eliminated 90% of the opportunity that's out there.'[6]

He was right. The decision made factories cut waste, reduce energy use and look for more sustainable materials right around the world. The manufacturers knew that finding solutions would make it more likely that they would continue to win business from the retail giant in the future.

Today, you ignore your supply chain at your peril – weaknesses in this area can cause significant brand and profit damage. Nike experienced this type of backlash when, in 1992, they were held responsible for human rights violations in their supply chain. Tariq, a 12-year-old boy from Pakistan, was featured in *Life* magazine making soccer balls for only 60 cents an hour, while Nike was using its substantial marketing dollars to advertise the soccer balls to children from wealthier backgrounds. Today, Nike factors in social and environmental impacts across their supply chain. 'We see corporate responsibility as a catalyst for growth and innovation,' says CEO Mark Parker.[7]

Unsustainable business practices far up the supply chain – such as converting rainforest to farmland, intensive farming and the production of toxic chemicals in fossil fuel refineries – have exacerbated problems such as climate change, habitat loss, biodiversity loss, water scarcity and environmental pollution. Today, there is a growing awareness among many stakeholders, including customers and, increasingly, governments, that businesses should be responsible for their entire supply chain.

'The days when a company's responsibility for a product began and ended at its own door are over,' says Michael Passoff, from American shareholder action group As You Sow. 'Companies are no longer able to claim they are only responsible for the T-shirt they sell, but not the slave labour used to pick the cotton or the pesticides used to grow it. We tell them that since they are the one who is responsible for selling the products, they are responsible for all elements along the entire supply chain.'

Having weaknesses in your supply chain can be extremely costly. In their book *Green to Gold*, Daniel Esty and Andrew Winston tell a sobering story about the Sony Corporation from Christmas 2001. When a small but legally unacceptable amount of the toxic element cadmium was found in the cables of the PlayStation game controls, the corporation's entire European shipment of PlayStations was blocked by the Dutch government. The presence of the pesky chemical cost the company an eyewatering $130 million, led to an 18-month search of over 6000 factories to find the problem and forced Sony to introduce a new, more robust, supplier management system.[8]

We have heard many stories of suppliers doing their best to help businesses be greener. Examples included reducing and recycling packaging on food orders for university campuses, streamlining deliveries so that only full orders are despatched, switching to lower emission transport options by investing in hybrid vehicles or using lighter materials like plastic pallets instead of heavy wooden ones. The suppliers all made these types of changes because their clients – that's you – asked them to (see box **Ask and you shall receive**).

Even the greenest consumers understand that many businesses cannot green their entire supply chain overnight. However, smart individuals within canny companies have realised that the quickest and most effective way to green their supply chain and ensure products don't have inherent environmental risks is to work *with* their suppliers. Companies who are taking steps towards more sustainable operations, like Marks & Spencer (see box **Give and take**), have discovered that telling people your goals and exactly what you want – and giving them a time frame and plenty of support – is the best way to encourage them to convert to greener practices.

♣ Give and take

How do you start the process of making the products of a multinational food, clothing and homeware company more sustainable? You ask your suppliers to help you.

Marks & Spencer, a world-famous international food and clothing retailer, has used collaboration across its business to make its 'Plan A' sustainability strategy really gain traction. Launched under the tag line 'Plan A – Because there is no Plan B', Plan A made 100 commitments across the business to address the main sustainability issues of carbon emissions, waste, sustainable sourcing, ethical trading and healthy lifestyles. With over 840 stores in more than 30 countries, this was a daunting challenge, but Marks & Spencer knew that by collaborating with others, for example by working together with their suppliers and by learning together and sharing information, they could reach their goals.

To do this, Marks & Spencer developed goals for different industries and gave their suppliers access so they could work together to find joint solutions:

'We've done bits of work specific to certain industries,' explains Richard Gillies, Director of Plan A. 'So we produced a sustainable construction manual which lays out what it is we're looking for and what the targets are. The innovative suppliers realise: "If I can meet these requirements, then I will be in a competitive position." We are looking for suppliers to innovate and to come back to us with both a route to achieving the targets in Plan A while also achieving the commercial objectives of the business.

'Take a recycled paper papier-mâché mannequin. If I ask the five biggest mannequin manufacturers in and say, "I want a recyclable mannequin," the one who innovates is likely to get the work. If you bring your suppliers in and say: "Here are the things our customers are demanding and they want help getting access to them," then they understand and want to help you. We tell them: "It's not about charging a premium for a green product, it's about making what our customers want more sustainable at a good price." This approach allows the suppliers to get involved, and those that innovate and play that game will gain themselves a competitive advantage.'

To support their suppliers through the process, the company has created a supplier exchange website; run training classes on subjects such as ethical trading practices, energy conservation and refrigeration gases; and invited suppliers to see green factories in operation so they could put plans together for their own operations.

'There are certain commitments for suppliers,' explains Richard, 'but this is not about creating significant increases in costs for them. It is no good creating an eco factory that is not commercially viable – one-off costs we will help with but what we're looking to do is to create a commercial eco factory, so we're asking for suppliers to find ways to do it. We're also creating various forums to share information, such as taking a guy from a chicken factory to a furniture factory to look at their eco-plant. This is the kind of cross fertilisation we're promoting. We'll gradually raise the bar and increase the level of compliance monitoring that we already do – but first we have increased the numbers of people we have in overseas offices to do the inspections. So it's a step by step process. But we've already made so much progress and we've had an awful lot of market recognition for that, which has been fantastic.'

◗ Paper talk

As a major supplier of company catalogues, Yalmaz Siddiqui from US-based Office Depot was keen to reduce the environmental impact of the paper used to produce them. Yalmaz knew that demanding only Forest Stewardship Council (FSC) or recycled paper would be hard for his supply chain to deliver. He knew a gentler, more inclusive approach would yield better results.

'We're aware the dark green community wants us to only stock and sell paper with high-recycled content or that is FSC certified,' says Yalmaz. 'While sometimes these papers are available competitively, other times it is not realistic to make a switch to greener options because of cost or a lack of availability from the mills.

'So, working with the paper buyers internally, we added a nuance to our policy which had previously accepted all forest certification schemes equally. This said to our catalogue paper suppliers: "We're not asking you all to shift immediately to FSC sources, but if all other things are equal, we will opt for FSC-certified paper." This presented a carrot of additional business to paper mills who stepped up supply and didn't step up the cost.'

The results were significant. In 2008, over 50% of paper used for Office Depot catalogues and inserts was on FSC-certified stock. This was a substantial shift for Office Depot and represented huge volumes of FSC-certified paper in the wider office supply and catalogue-retailer communities.

'To work at all, the change had to be collaborative and not drastic,' says Yalmaz. 'By saying we can help give FSC paper suppliers access to our purchasing power, we thought we could grow the market for FSC paper. And, by being honest about it (i.e. not saying we would switch completely or irrespective of costs or availability) we implemented a green-ward shift in spending without over-promising to the dark green community, or imposing changes in direction that internal stakeholders may have been uncomfortable with.' ◗

5. ENGAGE WITH NGOS AND SOCIAL PARTNERS

Can one initiative get customers spending in-store, raise money for charity and divert used clothing from landfill? If you are Marks & Spencer and Oxfam, the answer is yes. The key to creating an initiative that achieves all these things at once is bringing business together with socially and environmentally aware organisations such as charities, social advocacy groups or government-sponsored advisory services.

The famous British retail giant and the international charity realised that, by working together, it was possible for them both to achieve their goals. For Marks & Spencer, that meant increasing sales and supporting social causes, and for Oxfam, it meant increasing good quality donations into their store to help them alleviate poverty. By working together to introduce a scheme where customers received a £5 Marks & Spencer voucher for donating old Marks & Spencer clothes to Oxfam stores, each organisation was able to achieve more than either could accomplish on their own.

'It used to be that when companies saw us coming, they ignored our calls,' explains one executive from a well-respected American NGO. 'Then we started to notice that they began listening to us. In the beginning, they were only greenwashing the issues to get us to leave them alone, but it was a step up from the past where we were totally ignored. Today, we see a big change – they are inviting us in, even convening senior level management teams for us. It is clear they are listening to what we have to say. It's such a change from even just five years ago. A few companies are even ahead of us when it comes to addressing issues related to PVC and toxins.'

This shift towards working together with business is a new paradigm for both parties, with businesses more used to fielding attacks for their negative corporate behaviour rather than being extended the hand of partnership. Many NGOs and nonprofit organisations have decided to give up their adversarial stance to adopt a new outlook, which reasons and works together with business to help them move towards more sustainable practices. They have realised this will actually achieve much greater results, even though they know some of their supporters will feel working with business is like getting into bed with the enemy.

Social advocacy groups like WWF, Friends of the Earth, Greenpeace, the Carbon Trust, Rainforest Alliance, Human Rights Watch and Oxfam can use their expertise in solving social and environmental problems to help you identify the issues for your business or industry. Their under-standing of issues such as human rights, pollution and toxic chemicals offers you the opportunity to view your company or organisation and its practices from a new angle, allowing you to identify risks and problems and work towards solutions (for more details on these organisations and others, see **Appendix 1: Who can help**).

Many of these organisations can give you the broad parameters to get started, from helping you work out how you can make energy savings to working out where to start with a product life cycle assessment. They can also help business establish accurate datasets, inform sectoral best practice and help identify common areas for intervention. The internet also means you don't even need to be in the same country to be able to receive substantial practical help and advice from some national organisations.

For example, UK-based organisations such as the Carbon Trust – a UK government funded company which helps businesses and the public sector cut carbon emissions and develop commercially viable low-carbon technologies – have an enormous amount of information, as well as guides and resources, on their website. This literature can take you through the steps you need to take to assess issues such as energy efficiency and employee travel in your workplace.

They also bring kudos. Developing solutions in conjunction with these groups will mean your organisation's efforts are more readily accepted, and your company or organisation will be more likely to be praised by your customers, peers, investors, networks and the press.

'Businesses want to partner with us because we bring credibility and expertise,' explains Anthony Kleanthous, Senior Policy Advisor at WWF-UK. 'They know we have huge expertise in conservation, especially in areas of ecological and water footprinting. We bring an outside perspec-tive. We are influential. We influence the media, and have the ear of decision makers in government and the civil service. Our brand is widely known and trusted, and we have a reputation for basing our work on science. The general public tends to trust scientists and NGOs more than any source of information other than their peers, and certainly more than companies or journalists.'

It is this expertise that companies such as the UK pharmaceutical giant Alliance Boots have tried to harness by working with a variety of organisations across the business. 'Different groups have different viewpoints and a different understanding of subjects and issues,' explains Richard Ellis, head of CSR at Alliance Boots, 'and each group has a particular area of specialisation. For example, WWF is highly knowledgeable on chemicals and the use of chemicals in products, the Carbon Trust can help us trial carbon labelling on some of our products, while the Ethical Trading Initiative is highly knowledgeable about labour standards in the supply chain. In our desire to collaborate with these important organisations, we have come to learn which of these "critical friends" we can turn to for particular needs. We're aware that some NGOs don't wish to be seen as being friendly with big business for fear of upsetting their supporters. So we don't force our critical friends to come out and say they support our company. Our goal is to continue to work with these knowledge power-houses to learn and to be challenged to do better. It's all about getting a different viewpoint, stance and understanding to help drive our progress forward.'

Nonprofits and social advocacy groups also need to adapt to find the most effective ways to work with business. David Vincent, from the UK's Carbon Trust, explains: 'When we started out, we were doing thousands of site surveys a year to companies and public sector organisations to give them advice to improve their energy efficiency. We quickly learned only a third or so of our recommendations were being adopted. We realised we had to invest in developing much deeper relationships with organisations to support them and bring energy efficiency and carbon emission reductions higher up their agendas. We had to start encouraging them to take action in a systematic way. These included showing them what their peers have done and suggesting they look at those opportunities; introducing an interest-free energy efficiency loan scheme for carbon-cutting action; and launching a Carbon Trust Standard to reward and recognise good behaviour within their peer group.'

♦ Give and receive

Partnering with NGOs doesn't just salve your conscience; it can also help to strengthen business.

'We want to help place socially disadvantaged people in work,' explains Dr Paul Toyne at Bovis Lend Lease, 'and build a workforce with the right skills. So we've set up a not-for-profit organisation called Beonsite. This helps train disadvantaged people to work on construction sites and helps to meet the needs of our supply chain by providing the right skills and training.

'These interventions have put about 360 people in full time employment and 2000 have been helped with skills and training as well. So we are on track to meet our target of helping 3000 people by 2010. And although we have had to invest a lot of time and effort and funding into the scheme, we hope it will be cash neutral in the future because we were able to gain funding from local authorities as it helps them meet their targets around employment and skills as well.

'We've also been working with Waste and Resources Action Programme (WRAP) to share the findings of an online waste reporting tool we've been developing. By opening up our books and being transparent about our results so far, WRAP can plug our information into a research project it is running to benchmark the data it is getting from other contractors. This will show whether WRAP's system and our waste reporting tool are really working. This helps us too as it's in our interest to have the correct figures for what we're sending to landfill, rather than having to use generic industry figures to calculate landfill taxes. This means we can be rewarded for our work on reducing waste. In addition, on the back of their assessment of our work as a "leading edge", we have been able to access free consultancy support through their work programme to help us fine tune our approach and improve our performance further. It really is win-win!' ♦

Some NGOs, nonprofits and social advocacy groups feel the knowledge transfer they can offer is invaluable. Michael Passoff from As You Sow, a shareholder advocacy group, says: 'A lot of times, our role is to educate the companies we work with. I have been amazed at how little they know about the issues we raise. This is the frustration from the grassroots communities – often companies are so big, they don't have a clue what is going on outside their immediate business operations. The companies get their information from their trade organisations who are concerned with protecting the old guard – or they hide behind regulatory agencies which are completely ineffective or corrupt.

'We try and show companies that it doesn't matter if the government approves or not – if there is a product recall – it's the company that will be affected. We tell them: "You don't want bad press or public resistance or rejection – this has nothing to do with regulation – this is about consumer preference." It's been too easy for companies to hide behind the fact that there is no real regulation in many areas, for example, using nano-technology in lipsticks and sunscreen. The question for the company and shareholders should be: "Can nano-particles get absorbed through skin cells and be carried to parts of the body, such as the lungs, and does that pose a health risk? And if they can and do, would that make your company liable?" '

Other organisations, such as the American environmental and public interest coalition Ceres, work hard with companies to create an accountability loop. Veena Ramani, manager of the corporate accountability programme at Ceres, explains: 'We push the companies that we work with to report back to stakeholders about how they have used the recommendations and feedback provided through the stakeholder engagement process. Robust stakeholder engagement can create a culture of candour within a company, which is useful in identifying and grappling with challenges and risks.

'We organized such a process for American Electric Power (AEP) – a large coal based utility in the US. We brought a diverse group of representatives from the investor, NGO and public interest community to the table with key senior executives from the company and organized a candid discussion on tough issues, e.g. the impacts of climate change legislation on the company's business, use of coal, water, etc. As a part of this process, AEP reported back to the stakeholders about what recommendations they would be able to follow through on, what they would not be able to use, and the business imperatives for the decisions being taken.

While all parties agree that there is still considerable progress to be made on key issues, the dialogue has led to greater understanding on both sides on the issues and stakes involved. This will help in developing solutions that marry financial sustainability with environmental and social priorities, which is what sustainability is about.'

'Having a partner helps people to visualise solutions,' says Jo Confino, head of sustainable development and executive editor at *The Guardian* newspaper and website. 'Bringing in Forum for the Future made a real difference. As an NGO dedicated to helping businesses become more sustainable, they helped us to see how embracing sustainability can lead to the long-term success of *The Guardian*. That was the first time we got the board together and got them thinking through what sustainability means for the company and getting it.

'People know sustainability is important – that cog is turning – but they don't know what it is and how to achieve it. Forum are very good at setting a very ambitious vision to make things happen.'

Innovative and surprising solutions that steer businesses towards more sustainable solutions are also coming from interactions and partnerships with a whole new sector of business called social entrepreneurship. Social entrepreneurs operate their companies in a way that puts social or environmental impacts at the core of their business, and they can help traditional businesses to do the same.

A good example of this is Deloitte and College Summit. J. B. Schramm from College Summit teamed up with Evan Hochberg at Deloitte to roll out a mentoring and support service that helps underprivileged high school students obtain college degrees and improve their career prospects. Running the programme together allowed the programme to ratchet up its impact in a way that neither organisation could have achieved on their own (see box **Beneficial back scratching** in **Chapter 7** for more on this).

Don't go it alone

It doesn't matter how grand or humble your sustainability plans are – there will be an NGO, nonprofit or other similar organisations that can help. Just try and think laterally. If you'd like to create a wildlife area, can a bird conservation charity help? Or if you'd like some tips on reducing waste, most countries have charities dedicated to reducing waste; if not, can the WRAP website help? Perhaps your ambition is to carbon footprint your supply chain, to investigate options for on-site energy generation, or you just want to know what options there are for low-energy lighting; the Carbon Trust website is a great first port of call, wherever you are in the world.

Working together

Appendix 1: Who can help can give you some ideas of possible partners. There *will* be someone out there who can give you help and advice to make your dreams, and your ideas, a fulfilling reality. Don't give up until you find them.

GUIDELINES TO EFFECTIVE COLLABORATIONS

The following guidelines to effective collaborations will help ensure your partnership is a success.

Be open

One crucial element to making collaborative relationships a success is openness. Be honest about your goals and how far you're prepared to go – and if that means you won't consider any initiatives that aren't cost neutral, say so. If you lay your cards on the table, and are willing to talk, you will find that most often other people will respond by opening up in return.

◗ In you we trust

'It's all about trust.' This is the opinion of Rich Liroff from the US shareholder advocacy group the Investor Environmental Health Network. Rich has helped companies such as Wal-Mart and McDonald's to connect up to the right shareholders to tackle issues such as toxic chemicals and pesticide reduction.

'It's my job to share information. It could be information on what NGOs care about because I am networked into the NGO community, or I can help identify other stakeholders who can help businesses solve

---

sustainability challenges. My work cuts through lots of sectors so I can share best practices. Basically, I am a free research service. I build trust because I am willing to share information but I won't share it with the media. I just use it to help them improve their performance, but for people to be that open with you, you have to build trust.'

Identify your goals

Work out what you want to achieve. One of the keys to successful collaboration is working out what your goals are and then finding people with similar aims. If you know *clearly* what it is that you want to achieve, you can find the right partner as it will be easy to convey your goals. This lets potential partners see if their goals match and if they can help you.

Identify potential collaborators

It sounds obvious, but often the secret to identifying people who can help is pretty basic – just look around you and talk to the people who are key to your business. Whether you are a small shop, a school or a large multinational, this means engaging with stakeholders such as your suppliers, customers, local council, community, NGOs, green business forums, competitors and others within the industry.

'Try to find businesses around you who have done the same thing so you can share knowledge and learn from each other,' suggests Martin Horwood, the Shadow Environment Minister for the UK's Liberal Democrats. 'There are a lot of local organisations who support this kind of networking. For example, Vision 21 in Cheltenham brings local businesses together in one forum to share examples of greener businesses. Local resources and networking are also invaluable for sharing knowledge and expertise, especially for small and medium enterprises which tend to receive less support. Talk to your local politician, campaigning or non-profit organisation (such as your local Friends of the Earth) as they might have useful contacts they can put you in touch with.'

Anthony Kleanthous, Senior Policy Adviser from WWF-UK, has represented WWF-UK in stakeholder consultations and helped to convene multistakeholder partnerships, both at WWF and as a freelance sustainability consultant. 'It's fairly straightforward: all you need to do is pick up the phone and talk to people. A lot of companies have stakeholder engagement activities that involve identifying and polling the opinions of NGOs, such as WWF or Greenpeace, and suppliers who are engaging in sustainability, such as Unilever, to see how they can help. You might also want to get a big investor – maybe a big pension fund – to find out what issues matter to them. The key is to think about who it is who influences your clients, your investors, your staff and your community – and get them into a room. If you assure everyone that the conversation is confidential and/or nonattributable – for example, by imposing Chatham House rules – it's surprising how candid people will be. You can ask them what they think of you, and you can present your ideas, and gauge their reaction. You can then ask them to help you come up with fresh solutions.'

Expand your networking

Networks are a great way to find others who can help you, from industry associations and green drinks to online forums and email newsgroups. Traditional networks are a great way to find partners, but there are also now countless sustainability-related networks. Email newsgroups and communities can also be incredibly helpful – in fact, we met through the email newsgroup CSR Chicks. We even wrote this entire book without even having met (Shari is based in New York and Amy in London).

Just add your email address to the listing, and then you can see what other people are talking about on the network, such as posting details of interesting events or articles. You can also post questions if you have a topic you need advice on, such as how to write a sustainability strategy or where to find a green office supplier. The incredible thing about these networks is that people from all over the world are linking up and helping each other, even though many have never met.

Check you 'fit'

The rewards for collaborating can be enormous, but forming longer-term partnerships can be challenging and time consuming too. A seasoned collaborator, Trewin Restorick from Global Action Plan believes one of the best ways to ensure a successful partnership, especially when the partnership is with someone from outside the company, is to 'spend more time than is healthy' checking you have the same joint aims and understand each other's cultures. This is because partnerships that are not genuinely matched will be shallow and are often short-lived. Much more can be achieved when objectives are truly shared.

'Check your aims are consistent,' says Guy Watson, founder of Riverford Organic Vegetables, who has partner farms across much of Southern England. 'That often involves getting to know someone quite well and liking and trusting them. It's a good guide to do business with people that you like.'

It's also important to ensure that your partners have the right experience, knowledge and a willingness to collaborate, as the attitudes, values and behaviours of the people involved will directly influence the success of the partnership.

Work out your strategy

It's vital that you sit down and agree clearly what you hope to achieve and how you think you are going to achieve it. This should include establishing indicators of success. What needs to happen for both partners to feel goals have been met and what kind of rewards, in terms of value created, do they want to see coming out of the partnership?

It's also worthwhile to create a project plan so you know *how* you are going to get to where you're going. Doing this at the start can save time later. In reality, project plans are often developed as the process moves along, but even just a one or two page document can help get you started.

Assign tasks and responsibilities and be clear about ownership

In any business relationship, it's crucial to make it clear who is responsible for what so that everybody understands their role. It's also important to make sure you know who *owns* what.

'Governance and leadership arrangements, as well as intellectual property rights (where relevant), should reflect ownership, and need to be made explicit at the outset,' says Mike Jones from Open Minds Consulting. 'Be explicit as to where power and control lies and the attitude to risk – where is the freedom to experiment, and where not?'

Retain your independence

Partnerships can be wonderful, but it's important to retain your independence, and to be aware that the people you partner with may also have their own agendas. 'The key is to have partnerships but not be bound by them,' explains Trewin Restorick, 'and to remain independent from pressure groups as they may have their own agenda. Many pressure groups feel their survival depends on them being in the news all the time or on them having a narrow dogmatic focus. Our approach is to look at the evidence and make the best decision based on that. Some pressure groups tend to cherry pick an issue and narrow the debate, so it's important to be aware of that.'

◢ A chilling waste

'How can a man die from the cold a few feet from campus when students throw out perfectly good bedding at the end of every term?' This question haunted Dr Victoria Hands, a former student and now a member of the university staff at the London School of Economics and Political Science. Victoria had always hated waste, but it was returning to campus at the end of the winter holidays and realising that a homeless man had died from the cold just outside the campus that spurred her into action. She couldn't continue watching mountains of perfectly usable kit such as duvets, food, clothes and cooking equipment go to landfill at the end of each term as the students moved out of university accommodation.

What started with a few friends salvaging reusable items from a skip at the end of term has turned into a huge campaign that has prompted 212 halls of residence and 40,000 students to start recycling, and many universities nationally to run end-of-term reuse schemes. Eight universities monitored in 2008 diverted 85 tonnes from landfill and this is set to increase. This personal initiative also helped to propel Victoria to the role of environmental and sustainability manager.

'It's been by working with others that I've really been able to have a massive impact,' explains Victoria. 'After those first few skip dives, I enlisted the help of a particularly helpful and open-minded residence manager and a local charity, CRISP. We started having organised collections of unwanted items and working with a variety of local charities to place different items. Duvets and food went to a homeless charity; women's clothes to a women's shelter and so on. We also started a swap shop where people could swap unwanted items or just take and make a small charity donation. We brought it to more halls and started monitoring the items and tonnage so we could demonstrate to the council and the university the amount being diverted from landfill.

'Then we expanded the scheme. I took it to the Greater London Authority, and asked them if they would help us. They were really interested in recycling because this initiative could help the London Boroughs meet their targets. We won best partnership project at the national recycling awards in 2006. And best waste minimisation project in 2008 for diverting 85 tonnes in eight universities, led by the London School of Economics and Political Science and funded by HEFCE.

'We set up recycling facilities with local authorities in all 212 halls of residence across London, which means that 40,000 students now have the facilities to recycle. We're getting there! We've got great networks linking up local authorities, universities, halls of residence managers, re-use charities, recycling organisations. And we've also tested measurement systems so we can show evidence for how much can be reused and recycled, and what worked and what didn't.

'It's incredibly satisfying, and it does make me take a step back when people comment on those tonnes of waste diverted from landfill. I have a real sense of achievement from knowing that I'm helping to make a difference, but there is so much more that can be done to avoid this waste in the first place!'

THE WAY FORWARD!

As the examples in this chapter have shown, to achieve significant results, it makes sense to collaborate and work together, as the City of Redmond, Ecology and Environment and Microsoft did to reduce car use.

You can make huge progress by enlisting the help of those who have the knowledge to find solutions. Look around at your **colleagues, your**

customers, your competitors, your suppliers and **NGO partners**. Start thinking of ways you can join forces to find solutions, such as shared deliveries, greener products, safer supply chains and happier customers.

These partnerships and the creative solutions they will help you design will also propel your career on to another trajectory. They will give you the power to meet targets and exceed expectations while you work together to co-create a more sustainable world.

The next chapter, **Make it part of the culture**, will show you how to take sustainability one step further, so that it goes from being a successful initiative to part of your company's DNA.

Chapter 7

MAKE IT PART OF THE CULTURE

❝Sustainability is not a one time organisational initiative. It is a way of thinking, acting and operating, and it must permeate the fabric of an organisation.❞
Society of Human Resource Managers[1]

How do you make sustainability a part of your culture? 'You approach it on all levels,' says Sarah Daly from the UK-based Heath Daly Architects. She transformed her company's day-to-day operations and the services it offers clients by embedding sustainability across the spectrum.

In-house, there were quick fixes, like looking at paper and power use, and developing new products, such as sustainability audits, plus training staff to think green in their workplace. This won new business, kept the company ahead of the market, energised employees and cut costs. It's also been a process that Sarah found personally and professionally rewarding (see box **Sustainable by design**).

These are the benefits of embedding sustainability into your company's DNA. From your journey to work, to the way you design, source and use products, and your treatment of suppliers and producers, sustainable practices can become the new norm. Once they are the norm, your company's impact will grow as initiatives and innovations feed on, and into, each other. Two-thirds of employees say initiatives are most effective when sustainability is part of the organisation's culture and an everyday part of the business process.[2]

By integrating with company operations, rather than just bolting on a few quick green wins or using fair trade products, sustainability can become something that doesn't cost money but generates it, something that strengthens your business and brand.

How do you take sustainability into the heart of your company or organisation? This chapter will give you the skills and framework to help you ensure that a sustainable approach becomes second-nature to your colleagues. These actions will also demonstrate that you are a strategic, realistic, business-minded thinker who can help your organisation succeed well into the future.

The 12 steps to embedding sustainability into the culture are:

1. Win over management (again and again!)
2. Think strategically
3. Make an action plan
4. Work together and engage the entire company
5. Make it personal and part of everyone's job

6. Give people the skills
7. Innovate and use your imagination
8. Tell people the plan
9. Create a culture of openness
10. Look to the future
11. Check it's working
12. Accept it will be a journey.

◢ Sustainable by design

Sarah Daly has seen first-hand how making sustainability a part of the culture can make a business thrive. Her campaign to instil sustainability into the everyday business of the UK-based Heath Avery Architects has led to new products, new contracts and an empowered and energised workforce.

From saving paper and power, to developing new products and training staff how to think green, the company has transformed. It has taken time, and there is still more to do. However, by keeping everyone involved in the process and thinking creatively about how the company can evolve to help customers address sustainability, Sarah's experience is proof that it *can* be done.

'Sustainability is about survival,' says managing director Sarah. 'It's often pitched as an ethical and responsible "addition" to business but it is far more urgent. It's integral to the survival of all organisations.

'When I started, there were sceptics who trotted out arguments like "What's the point in saving energy when the Chinese are building new power stations every few days? We want to drive the cars we like, not use public transportation," and so on.

'So, to change the culture, I appointed a director of sustainability and a sustainability champion who was one of our graduates. This was important because action shouldn't just come from the board but be part of our culture at all levels. We hit the subject from the inside out by changing the way we do business and by changing our clients and supply chains in the process.'

Time and effort was devoted to making sure everyone understood what was happening and why. The topic was included in weekly project meetings so people could put forward ideas. It became an agenda item at board meetings so implementation could be monitored. Heath Avery Architects also engaged with local networking and support groups which advise companies how to introduce sustainable practices. 'The result,' says Sarah, 'is a very motivated and positive team which completely believes in what we are doing.'

There was another benefit to her hard work: a new service the company can offer for sale (always handy in a beleaguered world market). 'We innovated with the development of sustainability audits, which have given us a popular new product. This means we can advise clients on sustainability in key areas like health and education. We need more positive role models who can show the breadth of positive outputs from making sustainability part of the culture. I don't just mean the cost reductions. There are so many other benefits – like the improved feelings of health, well-being, positivity and the sense of achievement which people experience by working together to make a difference.'

I. WIN OVER MANAGEMENT (AGAIN AND AGAIN!)

Getting the buy-in of management is one of the quickest ways to embed sustainability into the culture. By making the business case (see **Chapter 3**), engaging your colleagues (**Chapter 4**) and understanding the issues that are important to them and how you can help (**Chapter 5**), you should be able to win management over. This will set the stage for you to effect a greater transformation.

'One employee can be the catalyst to advance the company,' says Frank Dixon, founder of US-based sustainability consultant Global Systems Change. 'The best thing they can do to make this happen is to make management aware of the issues. It's like ploughing the field before you start to sow because your specific ideas will take hold better and meet with more success if you have management supporting you.'

Sara Parkin, founder of UK-based sustainable development organisation Forum for the Future, agrees: 'One of the first steps you should take is to get the backing of the leadership. That's the learning from the research we've done at Forum for the Future. This gives permission for everybody else to embrace the idea and to give it their resources and support. If leadership haven't given their support, this is much more difficult.'

Top-level influence is also vital because management have control over the way spending programmes are structured. Their buy-in is necessary to authorise investment and to give line managers the green light to let staff dedicate time and resources to sustainability. They are also often the only people in the business who can appreciate how an initiative can have an overall cost benefit to the company. Individual managers are often reluctant if an initiative impacts on their budget while another department reaps the benefit.

'Often initiatives can create a cost saving in one place by investing in another,' observes Professor Tim Jackson from the University of Surrey, 'but this is not necessarily visible in accounting procedure. So you need someone with authority who has this structural oversight to give their support.'

Ideally, the best approach is to set up a body at board level with the power to install sustainability experts at management level *and* operational levels. This prioritises sustainability while providing support and a coherent strategy to the rest of the organisation. Having a sustainability expert at management level means that programmes are more effective, which in turn leads to greater cost saving.

'It's a compelling and persuasive case to appoint a sustainability expert at management level because the position will pay for itself,' says Steve Lanou, deputy director of the sustainability programme at the Massachusetts Institute of Technology. 'Having someone at top level can ensure that strategies are co-ordinated and supported by management which means that you'll get much greater savings, especially in areas such as energy, waste and water. And these savings can cover the additional salary of the sustainability manager several times over.'

Be an influencer

Depending on your position within the company, approaching management may seem daunting, but it needn't be. If you start with your area of influence, such as your peers and the people who are directly above you, you can start to drum up support: perhaps through chats over lunch, screening relevant films at staff events, showing people how simple changes can save money and changing your own behaviour to become more sustainable. Then, as discussed in **Chapter 4: Get your colleagues on side**, you can go to management with your colleagues behind you, which will make them more likely to sit up and listen.

'Start building relationships with people who have influence in different areas,' says Holly Fowler from Sodexo, US. 'Complex issues like climate change call for an all-hands-on-deck effort.'

By building relationships with people who have the power to ratchet things up, you add their authority to your influence. This will help you achieve deep-rooted change throughout the organisation.

2. THINK STRATEGICALLY

The ability to think strategically is crucial to the success of any business, and sustainability must be part of this long-term thinking. It's logical, after all, when all sustainability means is behaving in a way that can be continued indefinitely.

The *only* way to ensure your company or organisation can continue indefinitely is by knowing and understanding your social, environmental and economic impacts. If you deplete or mismanage just one of these components – your resources, your workforce, your suppliers, your relationship with your local community or your finances – you jeopardise your ability to continue operating.

Dave Stangis is vice president of corporate social responsibility at Campbell Soup Company – and, in a previous role, kick-started and integrated Intel's market-leading sustainability programme. He says strategies should:

- be **differentiating** for the company;
- be **identifiable** to employees, customers, suppliers and consumers;

- be **integral** to the culture;
- **leverage** company strengths or address weaknesses;
- provide strategic policy and operational **focus**.

In practice, thinking strategically means asking questions such as:

- What long-term environmental or social pressures could disrupt your business?
- What happens if you have to factor the cost of carbon into the balance sheet?
- What can you tell your shareholders, staff and customers when they ask what you are doing to address your social and environmental impacts?

These were the types of questions that Chiquita, the world's largest banana producer, asked when they realised that unsustainable farming practices were threatening the ability of their growers to continue supplying produce. Chiquita thought strategically to combat this. The company invested in the environment by upgrading all 110 of its company-owned farms, reducing agrochemical, water and energy use.

They invested in their social impacts by improving working conditions for their producers. This had a positive financial impact as the resulting efficiency helped the company cut costs by 12% and boost productivity by 27%. It also allowed all of the company-owned farms, and many of its independent ones, to become Rainforest Alliance Certified™ – which benefited the company's reputation.

Chiquita is a nifty example of how a strategic approach can help you use sustainability to build and strengthen your business.

♦ Flat pack for the future?

'We believe in low price but not at any price,' says Charlie Browne, IKEA UK corporate environment manager. 'Our aim is to do good business whilst being a good business. We also want to be the leading home furnishing company – that is our ambition. IKEA has made sustainability a part of business strategy and culture. Our culture is to make the best possible use of limited resources. The first time we sawed the legs off a table, we were doing this because you can then get 10 times as many products on a truck, which allowed us to reduce prices. It also had the environmental effect of reducing transport emissions dramatically.'

When you consider that logistics usually counts for the lion's share of a product's environmental footprint, flat-pack furniture suddenly takes on a greener hue. While it can seem counterintuitive, it turns out IKEA's strategy of selling flat-pack furniture at low prices actually encourages sustainable business thinking. This is because low cost margins encourage the maximum use of resources, minimal waste and high transport efficiencies. It turns out that IKEA's corporate thinking is rooted in the Swedish cultural mindset, which promotes protecting the natural environment and using resources wisely. Therefore, behind the scenes, IKEA has always taken its environmental and social responsibilities seriously.

'Our old business statement used to be: "IKEA will always try to minimise its impact on people and environment,"' explains Charlie, 'but we felt that was too passive. So now our statement is: "IKEA's business shall have an overall positive impact". So, if we take something away we'll add something of equal value back.'

For example, IKEA developed IWAY – a step-by-step staircase model to place increasingly higher demands on suppliers of IKEA products. Making this an explicit but gradual process that requires auditing, education and support, gives the suppliers the time and support they need to convert to more sustainable practices. This enables IKEA to use its influence to create ripple effects throughout the industry.

From constantly reassessing its production, logistical and packaging process, to giving all the staff folding bicycles as a Christmas present, the company is constantly finding innovative ways to save energy, materials and money. A commitment to 90% recycling of all waste and an increase in the use of energy-efficient construction and equipment in their stores (ranging from extra insulation to solar panels, biomass boilers and rainwater harvesting for toilet flushing) is helping to put IKEA's values into action.

'It's about making a choice, it's about making a difference, it is about leadership,' explains Charlie, 'that's our rallying cry. We still have challenges, but we'll continue to strive to be a good example of effective environmental management and initiatives. Because it makes sense as a business and as a responsible citizen to always make the best possible use of limited resources.'

3. MAKE AN ACTION PLAN

'The leaders who are pulling ahead,' explains Maria Figueroa Kupcu of US corporate communications firm Brunswick Group, 'are doing so because they took the leap and they see the returns. Employees love it and are buying in, they're getting good press, and it's helping to build up customer loyalty. But if you haven't articulated what you're trying to do, you don't know what you are hoping to gain. Which makes it harder to figure out where you need to prioritize and even where your successes are. The clearer you are about *why* you are doing it, and *what* you are doing, the easier it is to assign personnel, prioritize and set clear goals.'

This is why, to really effect change, it's vital to implement a sustainability *strategy* rather than relying on a *policy*.

This is because, although the terms are often used interchangeably, they are distinct. Policies can easily be stuck in a drawer and ignored, but strategies set targets and goals, give people responsibility and make them accountable so that words become action. Top tips for implementing a strategy are:

Step 1: Write it down! Work out what you want to achieve and clearly articulate it.

Step 2: Get the people who will be responsible for implementation to help you design it. They will have the knowledge to create workable solutions.

Step 3: Measure and set a baseline of where you are now. Then set targets of where you are going – and work out a way to measure if you get there.

Step 4: Work backwards from your targets to figure out how you will get there. This will help you to identify your options and risks.

Step 5: Assign responsibility, budget and targets to people and departments throughout the business. Tie these targets to job functions and make them mandatory.

Step 6: Measure and assess progress. This will allow you to check that your strategy is working, and to make tweaks where necessary.

Step 7: Feed back! Give updates on progress – this will help motivate staff and help you evaluate success.

Step 8: Revisit your strategy and assess how it should evolve.

Making your strategy explicit enables the people who support your business, such as your suppliers, to meet your goals. Companies such as Marks & Spencer, Bovis Lend Lease, IKEA and Hewlett Packard have reaped rewards by telling suppliers what they want, giving them an action plan and a timetable, and supporting their investment in the process.

◗ The three P's of success

'Lots of people think in terms of the three Ps of People, Profit and Planet,' says Dave Stangis of Campbell Soup Company. However, my three Ps for sustained business success are **Performance**, **People** and **Perception**. They are the lenses through which the leading companies of tomorrow will be viewing their success. Every single strategy or idea for business should use the concepts to ask: "What measurable performance improvement will result?"

'For the **performance** criteria, you need to ensure that every priority has a metric, a system to measure it, and a target. You need to ask: "Do the business units have the tools they need to assess and improve, and do executives have the direction they need?"

'For the **people** criteria, you need to ask: "What is the people dynamic of the idea – do employees have a role across the company? Can they affect the outcome? How will they learn what they need to do? And how can we measure that they are doing it?"

'For the **perception** criteria, there needs to be reliable and consistent communication across all outlets. You need to check that initiatives elicit an "I get it" reaction from customers, employees and others.' ◗

⚜ Building sustainability into the process

What would it mean for a construction company to be sustainable? This was the question Dr Paul Toyne and his colleagues asked at Bovis Lend Lease UK.

'We decided,' explains Paul, 'that it meant designing and constructing low or zero net carbon waste and water developments which also deliver sustainable social outcomes. The latter means thinking about the impacts of the built environment we've created on health and wellbeing. Making sure we've created a positive space that encourages a sense of community and sustainable lifestyles – and the health and wellbeing of its occupants and our workforce.

'When you think of it like that, you ask: "What are the key challenges we face in Britain today?" But if you try to address all of them, you will confuse yourself and lose traction. So we took a strategic decision to focus on a few things and asked how they impacted on the business.

'We also asked: "Do we only want to take on issues we have direct control over or do we want to present leadership that will challenge clients, government and competitors?" We decided we wanted to do both, so our activities range from trying to reduce waste on site to improving best practices across the industry.'

The company identified five priority areas (waste, carbon, design, sustainable materials and employment) and set clear baselines and targets to be achieved by the end of 2010. One aim was to reduce construction waste to landfill by 70% from the 2007 baseline. Another was to support 3000 people with skills, training and employment through their BeOnsite programme. 'Setting out what we aim to achieve in such a clear way has helped us work out how we will get there,' says Paul, 'so our goals can become a reality.' ⚜

4. WORK TOGETHER AND ENGAGE THE ENTIRE COMPANY

Tensie Whelan from the Rainforest Alliance has helped global brands such as Kraft, Chiquita and McDonald's to transform their operations. She says: 'The way to get a company to think sustainably is to engage people at every level from admin staff to the buyers, the marketing department to the sales team. It's especially important to target the people responsible for your major impacts – which will be different depending on your industry.'

Bringing people and efforts together across the business means you are more likely to get integrated efforts and thinking. This leads to solutions that work and prevents the duplication of efforts (see **Chapter 6: Work together** for more on this).

'Creating alignment within the company is vital,' says Maria Figueroa Kupcu from PR agency Brunswick Group. 'This means creating strong links between your business divisions so each piece of the puzzle works with one another.

'We often see clients who don't have the internal processes to get together and talk about things across divisions. The marketing department is doing one thing and they don't tell the communications people or the operations team who are doing something different. Everyone is stuck in their own silo doing their own thing. You need a big initiative that will force people together.

'Companies who are doing CSR well have figured out how to have this exchange of information on an ongoing basis. Sometimes this comes out of a crisis, because the company has realised that not looking at sustainability in a cohesive way across the company leaves them vulnerable.

'Nike is a great example of this. From their early problems with human rights issues in the supply chain in the 1990s, they changed the way they worked and now approach sustainability in an integrated manner. Their approach is now robust in terms of human rights and the supply chain, but they also look at product lines from a life cycle approach – they look at products from creation to disposal. The shift was born out of difficulty but now it's just part of how they do business.'

See the whole
To be truly successful, you need to be able to see the bigger picture, not only how your organisation works as a whole, as well as with customers, shareholders and suppliers, but also your part in the local, national and

global community, and how your actions impact on people and the planet.

Every effort counts. Projects that move your workplace towards sustainability – such as stocking fair trade beverages in the kitchen, or recycling and installing solar panels on the roof – are valuable and worthwhile. However, the biggest impacts come when you align the goals of the business with the goals of society.

Many firms are already doing this. For example, oil companies are investing in renewable technologies, while IT companies are spending millions on research and development to assess how their products can help the shift to a low carbon economy.

'Sustainable development is a social challenge; it is not limited to an organisational boundary,' says Sara Parkin at Forum for the Future. 'Sustainability doesn't *have* a boundary. So the question is: "What is the contribution of the organisation to meeting this challenge, not just in the way it operates but in terms of its purpose and the products or services it provides? How can the organisation use its relationships with others, such as the industry or government, or suppliers, to contribute to sustainable development?"'

'You need to have a recognition of values across the business,' says Jo Confino, head of sustainable development and executive editor at *The Guardian*. 'Because values have value everywhere! For us, at *The Guardian*, this meant recognising that sustainability was not just about trying to reduce the impacts of our printing, distribution and office processes, but also looking at how our ability to be a world leader in environmental coverage could be used to influence others towards more sustainable behaviour.'

♨ Climbing the Green Mountain

Green Mountain Coffee Roasters (GMCR) has always been a coffee company with a heart. The Vermont-based company grew out of one well-loved café. As it grew, it translated its values into a powerful sustainability strategy. This has had far-reaching benefits, which range

---

from helping coffee farmers improve their quality of life and reducing greenhouse gas emissions and solid waste to strengthening the brand, winning business and inspiring and motivating staff.

'A whole systems approach is the most effective business model,' says Mike Dupee, vice president of corporate social responsibility. 'Many companies have used phrases like "doing well by doing good", but those phrases don't necessarily mean much. Those phrases don't tell you a lot about the organisation's focus – is it poverty or clean water or malaria or something else? It's very important for an organisation to know what kind of change it wants to see in the world and to align its corporate social responsibility strategy with that end in mind.'

GMCR's journey began by identifying poverty, hunger, energy use and solid waste as areas key to their social and environmental programmes and critical to the business. 'For a corporate social responsibility strategy effort to be successful in the long term, it must triangulate around three areas,' says Mike. 'It must be meaningful in the world, connect with employees' passions and resonate with the brand promise. Without brand resonance, your stakeholders may have a hard time figuring out why you are doing it. So, for example, supporting arts education wouldn't make sense for us as a coffee company, but it might make sense for a record company.'

With these focus areas settled, GMCR has built on early successes and moved into more aspirational, bigger picture projects, which increase the company's ability to create positive change and extend its networks into the wider community. These newer projects include investments in solar power and creating an $800,000 grant competition to find and fund innovative programmes that fight climate change.

'We're often asked: "What do you do when you have a conflict between economics and principles?"' explains Mike. 'But, when you build sustainability and social consciousness into your business model, it's much rarer to have to choose between profitability and principles. If you're in a situation where you're forced to choose between one or other, you are probably not asking the right questions.'

5. MAKE IT PERSONAL AND PART OF EVERYONE'S JOB

For sustainability to be embraced across the organisation, it has to feel personal to people and it has to be part of everyone's job. This means showing people how it relates to their role and how they should automatically consider sustainability as an everyday part of the process. They must also understand how their behaviour can and *will* make a difference.

'We create a connection between an aspirational statement of sustainability and very specific things that a department or function can understand and do. This makes it become very real to people, and a part of their role,' says Richard Ellis, head of corporate social responsibility at Alliance Boots.

'One of the key things about Boots is that, with the exception of myself, there isn't anybody who does corporate social responsibility (CSR) as a job. It's the responsibility of everybody who works for the company to pick up this agenda. Lots of companies have CSR/sustainability departments and those departments have people and money and resources. Two things come out of this. One – the rest of the company can abdicate responsibility and say that this is the responsibility of the CSR department, which makes them less engaged and more critical. Two – the people who design the strategies aren't the ones who work with them so they won't be so effective. They don't have the day-to-day knowledge of how that part of the company works, and the people who work with these strategies won't be as committed, as they won't have ownership.

'By embedding activity in the routine of the business, sustainable systems are created by the people who own the process, which makes them a valuable part of their role.'

Organisations can make big changes quickly if they are undertaken in a thoughtful way that brings people along with them. To do this, however, you need to ensure that:

- People understand the need for sustainable systems.
- People have the knowledge and skills to behave differently.
- The right behaviour is recognised and rewarded appropriately. (Recognition is usually enough.)

Truly embedding sustainability into the culture also means tying sustainability targets and behaviours to employee goals. This can be through appraisals or even bonuses. You also have to help people see how the decisions they make in their sphere of responsibility can be part of the overall framework, so they feel involved.

It is also important to give people the power (as discussed in **Chapter 4: Get your colleagues on side**). Management often make decisions that are imposed on staff without them being involved in designing the programme.

'It's easy for companies to take a "Decide Announce Defend" or DAD approach,' explains Thomas Jelley, corporate citizen manager at Sodexo UK & Ireland. 'When they should be taking an "Engage Deliberate Decide" (EDD) approach. DAD struggles because the solutions are imposed on people. Some may think it works because a decision is made quickly but, in reality, it takes a long time to get people to accept the change or "buy-in".

'The EDD approach takes longer to deliberate and formulate a strategy up front, but the implementation phase happens more quickly with better engagement. For example, we often use focus groups that comprise different layers of the company and ask them what they feel needs doing. Some focus groups have really taken off – they have taken responsibility and are driving the agenda. It's absolutely fantastic.'

Once you open the floodgates, you'll probably get boundless enthusiasm. 'It's like *American Idol*,' says Dave Stangis of Campbell Soup Company. 'We have over 12,000 participants who want to provide us with their ideas but we may only be able to afford to implement 12. We need to find ways to get to the 12 best decisions in ways that don't alienate or take away the passion of our employees. One way to do this is asking them to help design and implement the programme, so they can see the challenges, and also help find the solutions.'

6. GIVE PEOPLE THE SKILLS

Whatever the size of your company or sector, changing thinking and behaviour requires education and training. Two-thirds of people feel they need more resources or training to address sustainability.[3] The skills and technology exist – the key is to get the knowledge to those around you.

A *lack* of knowledge and understanding can lead to counterproductive behaviour. For example, the UK's waste strategy is more focused on increasing recycling than on reducing the waste that goes into the system. Obviously, recycling is a good idea, but it is much better to prevent material from entering the waste stream in the first place.

In a field as new and constantly evolving as sustainability, some trial and error is inevitable. There are often tradeoffs, and no solution is ever 100% perfect – so setbacks should not be stigmatised, but built upon. However, a basic incomprehension about what sustainability means – including an understanding of the physical and biological constraints of the planet and what that means for the people, plants and animals who depend on these resources – has led to perverse policies and practices that can exacerbate problems instead of solving them.

This is why in order truly to embed sustainability in your company or organisation's culture, you need to get staff literate in sustainability. The best solutions are those that assess benefits across a whole system, to check that ideas that seem sustainable in one place don't have a negative effect elsewhere.

'One of the key factors that gives HP an advantage is that we have expertise *and* we take a systems view,' says Randy Boeller, from Hewlett Packard US. 'So, when we look at the environmental impact of our packaging, we look at the raw materials but we *also* look at the impact of transporting the item from where it's packed to the customer. In terms of carbon footprint, the logistics of moving from factory to customer can be four times as much as the processing of the raw materials and manufacturing them into a packaging component.

'Packaging and logistics are inseparable. If you make a change in packaging material that would increase the embedded CO_2 of the package but *decrease* the CO_2 of logistics because the packaging material is now lighter, you could still have a significant net gain. So you *have* to look at systems holistically before you can make the most intelligent overall decision.'

These skills can be built upon through workshops, training and communication campaigns. It can be very valuable to enlist the help of organisations such as Global Action Plan, Futerra, Rainforest Alliance, Ceres, Environmental Defense and our training and consultancy company, Climb the Green Ladder (see **Appendix 1: Who can help**). They can help you create relevant education programmes that ensure staff have the knowledge, skills and motivation to take action.

7. INNOVATE AND USE YOUR IMAGINATION

To power street lights, Ealing council in London is trialling green speed bumps that generate electricity as cars drive over them. To eliminate packaging, Hewlett Packard designed a laptop that didn't come in a box, but in a reusable laptop bag made from recycled material. Wherever you look, people are developing innovative solutions that solve sustainability challenges in highly creative ways.

The question is: 'How can *you* revolutionise your industry or change your processes to factor damaging impacts out of the equation?' From championing video conferencing instead of corporate travel to offering staff memberships to car clubs instead of company cars (which reduces impacts as people drive less, use public transport more and fewer cars means fewer impacts as fewer cars need to be manufactured overall), there are so many ways to innovate.

The key is to take a fresh look at what you're trying to achieve, rather than the means you are using to do it. In this way you can start to work out if there is another way to get the same result without so many negative impacts. It is this kind of thinking that needs to be encouraged at a company level, because, to paraphrase Einstein, we won't solve the problems we face by using the same kind of thinking that created them in the first place.

'There are massive opportunities,' says Sara Parkin of Forum for the Future, 'but the way everyone is approaching it is to keep the systems exactly as they are so we can keep living the way we do. We need at least an 80% reduction in CO_2 in the UK, and that has vast implications.

'Most of the focus on tackling CO_2 emissions is on end of pipe solutions. Literally: "I want energy so how do I stop things coming out of this pipe by capturing the CO_2?" We should be changing our focus so we don't think "I want to consume energy", but "How can we get the services that energy provides without the emissions?" We need to go right to the front end of the pipe and do things completely differently. The companies who do this are the ones that will be part of the future.'

Social entrepreneurs are skilled at thinking of innovative solutions and one way to transform your business culture is by enlisting their help. They recognise a social problem and use entrepreneurial principles to address it. Partnerships between corporations and organisations run by social entrepreneurs – such as the Skoll Fellows, Net Impact, StartingBloc and JustMeans.org – are becoming increasingly common as businesses align their goals with the principles of sustainable development (see box **Beneficial back scratching**).

♦ Beneficial back scratching

Barry Salzberg, CEO of Deloitte LLP, a leading professional services organisation, and Evan Hochberg, who oversees its community involvement, believe that an educated, diverse workforce is fundamental to business competitiveness. J. B. Schramm, a social entrepreneur, wanted to help disadvantaged American high-school students to graduate from high school, go to college and get good jobs through his College Summit programme. The men realised that, by working together, they could make progress towards their goals.

'In US high schools, close to 50% of African American and Latino students drop out between 9th and 12th grade,' explains J. B. 'As a leader in the professional services field, Deloitte is focused not only on recruiting high-quality graduates but also on increasing diversity as their teams work in every corner of the US and around the world. The organization was also broadly looking for ways to increase the volume and diversity of talent flowing into the workforce. The College Summit programme matched their goals.'

Therefore, after a series of meetings laying out their organisations' respective values and priorities, a relationship was formed, which included pro bono work, volunteerism, leadership and cash contributions. Notably, Deloitte has contributed pro bono technology support that has helped College Summit increase its productivity by 87% in some cases. The organisation also supplies more volunteer writing coaches to College Summit than any other company, which helps low-income students complete their college application essays and apply to college.

'Both organisations are helping to advance each other's objectives,' says Evan. 'As a result of working together, College Summit is reaching a much larger number of disadvantaged students and helping them to get to college, and Deloitte is having a measurable, positive impact on society.'

8. TELL PEOPLE THE PLAN

Once you've decided on a strategy, it's important to make sure people know about it: 86% of the people we surveyed ranked their employer taking the time to explain the issues and solutions as important to the success of sustainability initiatives.[4] Like any campaign, especially one that signals a seismic and permanent shift for the business, it will have the most impact if you market it with a strong identity and messaging.

'We chose "Plan A because there is no Plan B" for Marks & Spencer,' explains Plan A director Richard Gillies, 'because we wanted to have a strong and catchy brand name. A clearly articulated plan was heavily communicated internally and externally. As you walk through the office or the store, you can see the Plan A labels, so the branding brings together lots of activity that we're involved in.

'We used our normal cascade route to tell people throughout the company about it, with team briefings and director briefings. We launched it with key NGOs who work with us and the stakeholder community. We also have a network of Plan A champions. One volunteer from each store leads the implementation in stores and looks for opportunities, so we had a big launch event for the 450 champions.

'When there is any change of policy in the company, there is training which goes along with it. Sustainability is no different – we have training on everything from waste and energy to changes in our policy on hangers and bags.'

Educating your workforce in this way helps employees understand and sell products, while also getting them thinking about sustainability.

'The thing which had the single biggest impact was engaging staff with the sustainable auditing process we offered to clients,' explains Sarah Daly at Heath Avery Architects. 'These strategic reviews of clients' existing buildings give indications of how they can reduce costs, improve their green credentials and prioritise expenditure to future-proof their organisation.

'By getting everybody to understand the audit, they started to look at themselves in a comprehensive way, to assess issues like transport, waste, energy, water and their own behaviour. Learning about the product turned them all into ambassadors for sustainability – at work and at home.'

9. CREATE A CULTURE OF OPENNESS

As with any new strategy or target, there will be successes *and* failures. However, if you create an environment that is geared towards working together to find solutions, and which doesn't stigmatise failure, you will come up with more creative solutions. By being honest about what has worked and what hasn't, you'll earn respect, and people will be more forgiving, from the media to staff and customers. It will also help insulate you from the charge of greenwashing.

'You've got to allow people to fail,' says Sara Parkin. 'Most people are intrinsically innovative and entrepreneurial – you don't need to set up systems to facilitate it. So you need to think: "What is *preventing* staff from being innovative and entrepreneurial?"'

'In a company,' says Gwyn Jones of the UK-based Association of Sustainability Practitioners, 'how many people feel they can admit "I am failing"? How many managers can survive the next quarter if they say that? But I've heard stories where people opened up and, by telling others they were having problems, they found a way forward. Being able to admit your failings allows you to experiment and ask for help so a solution can be found.'

Don't succumb to spin

'A sustainability report is a bit like money,' says Jo Confino of *The Guardian*. 'As a concept, sustainability reporting is neutral. It's what you do with it that matters. We often get feedback on how honest and approachable our report is, and that's rare because most organisations fear admitting to failure.

'It's basic psychology. No-one likes to fail and companies don't want to write a report which exposes problems. But for me, integrity comes from being honest and you tend to win a lot more respect for doing it. The fact is we live in an extraordinarily complex world – there are always tradeoffs to be made and mistakes to learn from. Let's be honest about that. C. P. Scott, a former *Guardian* editor, wrote that the public can sense the difference between honesty and manipulation. Honesty brings trust. The PR-ification of the business world destroys trust because we know deep down it's just not true.'

Veena Ramani, manager of corporate programmes at Ceres agrees:

'It's important to create an accountability loop. When stakeholders raise issues, we push companies in our network to talk about these issues in their reporting – even if it doesn't necessarily show the company in a good light. So, for instance, if the company has faced an issue with public safety, we'd push the company to talk about it.

'This is the information world. Stakeholders tend to be informed about the company's record and they are often aware of the issues as well as some of the problems that the company has been facing. So where a company chooses to be candid and acknowledge where there are challenges and risks and to talk about in a forward thinking way by saying, for instance: "We see that public safety is an issue – here is what we are doing to address the issue" this gives them credibility and improves their reputation in the eyes of their stakeholders.'

Being open and sharing your evidence is a great way to win over critics and to drive change across the industry.

'My thinking is that, if we have problems,' says Dr Paul Toyne from Bovis Lend Lease, 'everyone else in the industry is going to have them and we've got to play a leading part in changing the way we do business. To help, I've created a sustainability advisory group comprised of external experts, consulted with staff and taken an evidence based approach to setting and delivering our targets.

'It has generated a lot of interest and publicity. People doubted us. They went in and looked at the evidence, ready to criticise us. But they came back saying, "Fair play: you are doing what you said you're doing, you are measuring your performance in an accurate way and we can't fault you."

'We have a long way to go, and much more to do, but we are going in the right direction. And we can learn and share with others. If we struggle, we'll tackle the issue another way and keep trying until we succeed. And the company as a whole is very supportive of that approach.'

🌿 Building on success

Has Plan A been scaled back in the downturn? That was the question for many Marks & Spencer customers, but the strategy is still going strong because sustainability *is* good for business.

'If anything we've accelerated,' says Richard Gillies, director of Plan A. 'The first year was about doing some obvious stuff; making some mistakes and doing trial stores and factories. The second year has been about learning, understanding and evaluating what works.

'Going into the third year, it's about leveraging that scale. We've got five, six, seven eco factories. How are we going to get to 2000? Now we've learned all this stuff about saving energy, how are we going to get it into stores? How do we get all of our colleagues to respond to these new systems? Now we've got all these fantastic tools, how do we now sweat these assets to get them to deliver those savings?

'We have been through a lot of business restructures/renegotiations and changes in contracts. We've done work with waste going to landfill in the first year. So this year its going to be a bit flat but we've identified what's important to us and created a new plan, put that plan out for tender, been through the tender process, and got a new contractor. Now, we have an aim to send zero waste to landfill in the first three years from their appointment.'

'Although Plan A is less than two years old, it is already becoming ingrained into the way we do business,' said chairman Sir Stuart Rose, on Plan A's 22 month anniversary. 'Conditions may be challenging on the high street but Plan A has made us think of new ways of working. This has helped to deliver not only benefits to the environment and people across our supply chain, but also savings to our customers and our business. Progress made on energy saving, reducing waste and increasing efficiency means that, 22 months in, Plan A is cost neutral. We know our customers expect us to take a lead on ethical and environmental issues and we will continue to deliver.' 🌿

Watch out for greenwash

From cars that spew flowers to washing powders that will save the world, putting a green spin on something that doesn't deserve it is greenwash. Greenwash is dangerous because it stops people trusting your commitment to sustainability and makes employees jaded and cynical. It's also bad for business because, once spotted, it destroys credibility and can dent sales.

One of the most common traps is to make empty generalisations, such as when a story or initiative that applies to a small part of a company is presented in a way that makes it appear typical of the whole business. It is worthwhile to talk about the good things that the business does, even if these are only small steps, but be careful not to overstate or generalise.

'The safest way to avoid greenwash is to maintain an appropriate degree of humility,' says Roger East, the consultant editor of environmental magazine *Green Futures*. 'People understand that moving towards being more sustainable is a process, not an instant switch where you go from being perfectly brown to perfectly green. There is always going to be room for improvement but, if you talk honestly about what you have achieved as well as the challenges you face, your messages will be more widely accepted.

'To give an old example, when Shell really started to address how it was perceived in the 90s, it produced a report that included forthright criticisms of what the company was doing. This gave the report, and by extension, the company, a degree of credibility and did an awful lot to improve their image. There are lots of examples of companies who have been heavily criticized during particular periods, but who, by being open and honest, have gone through transitions to make them more favourably regarded.'

For top tips on avoiding greenwash, see Figure 7.1.

10. LOOK TO THE FUTURE

Smart businesses and smart people within them are looking to the future and working out how the company can contribute to a brighter future – and how they can position themselves strongly in that future.

10 signs of greenwash

1.
Fluffy language

Words or terms with no clear meaning,
e.g. 'eco-friendly'

2.
Green products v
dirty company

Such as efficient light bulbs made in a factory
which pollutes rivers

3.
Suggestive pictures

Green images that indicate a (un-justified) green
impact e.g. flowers blooming from exhaust pipes

4.
Irrelevant claims

Emphasising one tiny green attribute when
everything else is un-green

5.
Best in class?

Declaring you are slightly greener than the rest,
even if the rest are pretty terrible

6.
Just not credible

'Eco friendly' cigarettes anyone? 'Greening'
a dangerous product doesn't make it safe

7.
Gobbledygook

Jargon and information that
only a scientist could check or understand

8.
Imaginary friends

A 'label' that looks like third party endorsement ...
except it's made up

9.
No proof

It could be right, but where's the
evidence?

10.
Out-right lying

Totally fabricated claims or data

Cut out and keep

Figure 7.1. Futerra's ten signs of greenwash, which are drawn from their definitive *Greenwash Guide*. The full version of the report may be downloaded from their website at www.futerra.co.uk/services/greenwash-guide

'One of the things which can be helpful,' says Sara Parkin at Forum for the Future, 'is to encourage colleagues to envisage what a good or bad sustainable future would look like in 10, 20 or 50 years time. What are the different scenarios? Take cuttings from the newspaper to promote discussions and ask: "What will life be like in a resource-constrained world with tough regulations? What would business success, a good company and good life look like in this environment?"

'Anybody who wants to change their workplace needs to get that future thinking. It could be an extremely hard and difficult future. The people who have already thought about solutions are going to be the ones who are successful.

'These are the people who don't just think, "We need to get people recycling," but the innovators who ask, "How can I move back up the consumption chain and eliminate waste in the first place?" These initiatives should help save money now because the solutions are likely to use less energy and resources, so giving cost gains right the way up the supply chain. Developing this type of thinking is also beneficial when the future is likely to be defined by scarce resources.'

Major organisations, from GE and Google to PepsiCo, Tesco, HP and the British Government, take these types of visioning exercises very seriously. Often in partnership with NGOs and nonprofit groups, they investigate ways to develop and provide products, services and infrastructure that contribute a sustainable future.

For example, in a bid to find out how IT can contribute to a more sustainable future, Hewlett Packard commissioned Forum for the Future to research and write the *Climate Futures* report.[5] This vast visioning exercise explored four alternative futures to help stimulate discussion on how businesses, government and society needs to adapt in the face of environmental challenges such as climate change. The idea is that this type of research can be used to ensure the right sustainable infrastructure, products and services can be put in place to ensure the brightest future.

'People can describe success,' says Jeff Melnyk, head of engage at Futerra, 'but, when you ask what they personally want out of it, that's when it becomes real to them. Visioning helps you work out ways to align sustainability with your colleague's business plan, as well as revealing what they're passionate about. Creative people are motivated by the idea of being a leader or an innovator and they love trying or testing new things. And structured thinkers like engineers may be motivated by a new way that is easier or more efficient.'

11. CHECK IT'S WORKING

Once you've got your strategy in place, check how it's doing. Measurements matter – with 82% of employees feeling they are important to making sustainability strategies a success.[6] This step is often overlooked as people feel that once the strategy has been implemented, it can be forgotten. However, like all business changes, there are likely to be areas that work well and areas that need improvement.

Monitoring can bring to light all sorts of beneficial knock-on effects that you didn't anticipate or expect, but more importantly, it demonstrates the strategy's success. Valuable feedback will inspire and motivate your colleagues, ensuring their continued support.

'A lot of research shows that while programmes can get people engaged, they may revert afterwards if the message isn't reinforced,' says Scott Davidson, behaviour change researcher at Global Action Plan, UK. 'However, if you measure what they did and feed this back to them, it makes people think, "Wow, I can actually make a difference, so I'll continue that behaviour." Often this will lead to bigger behaviour change.

'Look at water usage, electricity meters, do spot checks on bins, monitor the tonnage of recycling and get all those measurements as best and robustly as you can. It's usually quite simple to do and it makes a huge difference.'

Many companies have introduced quantifiable targets for reductions in electricity, water and fuel, and methodologies exist for carbon footprinting, such as one developed by the Carbon Trust.

'Once you start monitoring things like energy use, you can start asking questions,' says Professor Martin Fry of the Royal Academy of Engineering and visiting professor at City University in London. 'You can ask things like: "Why do we always use more energy on a Monday?" You can draw a table with energy used on one axis and other relevant variables such as temperature, meals served, production lines open or whatever on the other. This often helps you pinpoint easy ways to cut energy use; perhaps by identifying when something is being left on or used inefficiently.'

Once you put in an installation, keep an eye on what it's doing. Make sure that you're getting the information quickly because you won't be able to remember what happened if you see the figures a month later. This is why it's helpful to use devices that allow people to see their energy usage in real time, such as the Owl, Efergy, Eco-eye or Wattson 01.

'It's also worth checking how things are being used,' says Martin. 'You can have efficient equipment such as boilers, chillers, air handling units, lighting and controls, but if these things aren't being used properly – for example, by having the air conditioner on in winter which is incredibly common – they are useless! So, compare actual consumption patterns for your building to typical consumption for a building of the same type. This happened with a client of mine. They had a water leak for 10 years but, as the unit was just taking readings, it didn't show up, because the water use was constant. But when we compared it with typical usage readings, we realised there must be a leak and fixed it. And water use, and the bills, went down dramatically!'

Measurements are also often necessary to get support and funding for your initiative, for example by demonstrating to a local authority how much waste your initiative is diverting from landfill.

12. ACCEPT IT WILL BE A JOURNEY

Sustainability can be like a game of whack-a-mole. You may think you have one area effectively accounted for, when another area pops its head up and has to be addressed. This may be frustrating, but keep at it, because the results are immensely rewarding.

'Sustainability is not something you achieve,' says Veena Ramani, from Ceres. 'It's not a number you reach and say, "Aha – I am done!" As with so much of business, it's a journey of continuous improvement.'

Integrating sustainability does take time. However, unlike more standard business changes – such as the introduction of a new budgeting or compliance system – sustainability inspires and motivates people, giving the process energy and a sense of reward.

Richard Gillies, at Marks & Spencer, has seen this first hand:

'In a previous incarnation, I was the head of change. For me, Plan A is simply another change programme. It requires people to do something different tomorrow than they do today, so you need to apply the normal rules of change management.

'Creating a compelling vision for this subject is much easier than if it was a simple process change involved with normal business. People are much more engaged and motivated. It's easier to get people to commit, as it doesn't take long for them to engage with the rationale behind it. For example, if you remove bottled water because you're cost cutting, that doesn't go down well. But if you are reducing your carbon footprint while providing other water vending facilities, to reduce waste and carbon, people are much more engaged. We have found that, across the vast majority of activity involved in Plan A, people have been very positive.

'The normal barriers exist – the interrelationship with other parts of the business, the unintentional consequences, the normal change timetable capacity the business can cope with, from IT infrastructure to where to spend money. But none of the barriers are different to any other change programme. The big difference is that it's easier to engage people.

'We've had to go through the breaking down of pre-conceived ideas such as, "It's got to be expensive" or "It's a distraction from the core business". It's got to be economically sustainable, otherwise you're unlikely to survive. Handled in the right way, it can be of enormous business benefit.'

'Changing structures that are bureaucratic and blocked can be difficult,' agrees Freya Williams from Ogilvy & Mather, 'but when you realise that these structures were put in place years ago, before we realised the implications of our actions, you have more patience. They were developed before we knew a carbon-based economy is a major cause of climate change. Recognising that times and people were different may help you start to see new ways to move your workplace forward. Change is inevitable. It may not be easy, but you'll get there in the end.'

◗ Souped up influence

'If you want to lead CSR at a major corporation,' says Dave Stangis from Campbell Soup Company, 'you need influence and persistence. When I was at Intel, it took a while to get things going. I listened to people's needs and concerns and I found a way to align sustainability with their goals. It took several years but, when it finally got going, it was rolling like a flywheel.

'Early on, I felt, if I left, the CSR efforts would stop. But when the flywheel took off, everyone was on board from the CEO to the marketing folks. It wasn't a grassroots effort by a dedicated few, but a business opportunity.

'We called it the Intel Employee Sustainability Network; a social network of employees who were passionate about it. They were doing everything from marketing to finance – everything but "sustainability" as their day job. The network could tap and channel their passion. When I left we were the "best corporate citizen" in the Russell 1000, and the only US Supersector Leader in the Dow Jones Sustainability Index.

'It's a sign that you've successfully managed to embed sustainability when it's bigger than one or two people. You can leave, and the programme continues to grow and live on.' ◗

Aim high

The message from those who have helped embed sustainability into their culture is 'aim high'. Once your target is in place, the energy and the creativity will come to find a way to get there.

'If you want to get somewhere,' says Dr Paul Toyne at Bovis Lend Lease, 'do you always know how you will get there? Probably not! So don't be inhibited by where you are now. Work your way backwards from your target or goal, and identify what needs to happen. If you're developing a campaign, a strategy and a goal, then work out who needs to be involved and what you need to do to get there. Then you can set your journey, your route map and your milestones.'

Jo Confino at *The Guardian* is certain that strategic thinking helped the UK media group transform:

'We've been known for 20 years as the newspaper for the environment – we should be building on it. We realised embracing sustainability could be the key to the long-term success of *The Guardian*, so our strategy is to be the world-leading environmental site. This will be good for our brand, and our business, and it is already providing commercial opportunities. The holy grail is getting an integrated strategy.

'We set out an exciting vision: imagine a world in which we can go to work and feel proud, not guilty, about our contribution to society from our editorial, to our offices and our production and distribution processes. We set ourselves the goal of being environmentally regenerative. We will investigate how we can become carbon positive – to go beyond carbon neutral to positively affect climate change.

'We created a vision which we don't know if we are going to be able to achieve. But we thought it was worth aiming for the ideal, and that it would set a much more challenging agenda.'

Ask searching questions

As you embed sustainability into your organisation, there are three questions you should ask to check whether your strategy is working.

Is it genuinely working?

Is your strategy reducing your impact on the environment and improving the wellbeing of people and the environment? Critically appraise your contribution to sustainability and ask: 'Is it genuine?' and 'Could I make it better?'

For example, it seems positive to buy fair trade products from one rural village, but if the whole village is now dependent on your order, what would happen if the expected sales don't materialise? In this instance, encouraging the production of a more diverse range could help.

Is it everywhere?

Check to see that understanding and activity isn't trapped in one department, or limited to one active green team, but that it has genuinely spread throughout the company.

Is it influencing others?

Have you managed to influence your customers or your industry? Remember, you do not need to have all the answers; you just have to know how to ask questions so that the people you influence can think about solutions.

Feeling the shift

Businesses take time and effort to change direction. Changing the culture can feel frustrating and exhausting, and the journey to become sustainable is sometimes through uncharted territory. However, if you keep at it, the shift will bring satisfaction and reward. It will also mean you become someone whose influence is respected and felt throughout your organisation.

You will have helped your organisation take a leadership role, a role that will benefit society while bolstering your brand. Your influence will have helped the business spot opportunities and gain competitive advantage. You will have been responsible for engaging and motivating staff, and attracting the best talent. You will have helped to insulate your company against risks and inefficiency, to become a stronger and more sustainable business. You will also ensure your company is ahead of the curve on compliance, which will help you avoid having to catch up at short notice and great expense. You will be noticed as a forward thinking force-for-change who can future-proof the business, thus bolstering and improving your own career.

By shifting your organisation's direction by helping sustainability to become part of its DNA, you will be a leader – a leader who joins others all over the world to play your own unique part in ensuring a successful, sustainable future for us all.

Chapter 8
CONCLUSION: CLIMB THAT LADDER

❛Business cannot thrive in a community if profit is its only objective. A healthy society is essential as a framework for growth and stability.❜ James Wolfensohn, 9th President of the World Bank[1]

Sustainability makes sense – it is good for people, planet and profits. Society thrives from healthy business, and business needs a healthy society in which to operate to survive. The research and examples presented throughout *Climb the Green Ladder* demonstrate *why* an understanding of the principles of sustainability is important and *how* they are integral to business success, as well as your own personal, professional success.

This research and examples have shown how switched-on, innovative thinkers – people like yourself – have been able to convince colleagues and management to embrace sustainability, and how their companies and careers have reaped the benefits – people like Freya Williams, Victoria Hands, Ken Bosley, Kristen Thomas, Jo Confino, Keith Pitcher, Coral Rose and many more. These inspiring individuals represent just a fraction of the millions around the world who are working to create a better, more sustainable world. By distilling their knowledge into a comprehensive toolkit, *Climb the Green Ladder* gives you the skills to ensure your efforts to improve your company (and career) are successful. Each chapter provides another rung; another set of approaches you can use to make your ideas fly.

Climbing the green ladder doesn't simply mean painting the corporate ladder green. It represents a new way of thinking and achieving – one that takes into account the social, environmental *and* economic impact of your actions, and one that engages your colleagues, that takes a long-term view and that isn't afraid to question the status quo to find a new way of doing things better. It's about finding genuine success – success that doesn't come at the expense of people, planet or profit.

To help you on your journey, this chapter is a quick reference guide. It is a summary of the main strategies described in this book in checklist form. Think of it as a 'crib sheet to sustainability' which you can stick up on your wall. It's designed to give you the key facts at your fingertips so you have instant inspiration whenever you need it.

CHAPTER 1: WHY WE NEED THAT GREEN LADDER
Climate change and the global financial crisis have shown we need to find a new way to do business. We *need* to think differently to survive. Corporations and governments are made up of individuals – and that gives

us the power to change those organisations from within. One individual *can* make a difference!

The need for action

The planet is in crisis because we're living beyond its ecological limits. Climate change is happening, and the more the temperature increases, the greater the impacts on the planet. These pose a severe threat to water, food and land. The effect on humans will include the increased frequency and severity of extreme weather, drought, desertification and crop failure, while there will be significant species loss.

Resources at risk

The Earth's resources are finite. To survive, we need to start using what we have more responsibly.

People in peril

Access to the Earth's resources and wealth is not equally distributed between people and nations – 20% of the population consume 86% of the world's resources, while half of the world's population lives on less than $2 a day. These injustices could be alleviated by more socially and environmentally responsible business.

Sustainability as a solution

Sustainability addresses these challenges by considering the social, environmental and economic dimension of each action to ensure they can continue indefinitely.

Climb the green ladder

These issues can be tackled by adopting a 'sustainability mindset'. This means taking your values to work and automatically incorporating sustainability concerns into your everyday thinking.

Doing well while doing good

Major businesses have realised that embracing sustainability makes excellent business sense. Incorporating sustainability into business thinking:

- strengthens business and brand;
- provides opportunities;
- reduces costs and provides revenue streams;
- offers competitive advantages;
- keeps pace with increasing environmental regulation;
- meets or exceeds customer expectations;
- reduces risk;
- motivates staff;
- helps to attract and retain talent.

Future-proof your career

Helping your company strengthen its business and brand will help you meet targets and get promoted, while marking you out as a dynamic, creative achiever. Living your values at work is also immensely rewarding, and increases your enjoyment and motivation for work.

Taking care of business

Business needs to transform. You can help shape a more sustainable future using the six approaches that underpin successful sustainability initiatives:

- Get the mindset
- Make the business case
- Get your colleagues on side
- Have two-way conversations
- Work together
- Make it part of the culture.

CHAPTER 2: GET THE MINDSET

People can be the solution, and one person can make a difference. You just need to 'get the mindset'.

1. **Think sustainably.** If you train your brain to think about the environmental, social and economic impact of every decision, you will make business decisions that don't compromise people, profits or planet.

2. **Believe in your own power.** Small changes can have big impacts. With the right attitude, and the right approach, you can create a ripple effect that transforms your work place for the better.

3. **Live your values at work.** It's one of the simplest ways to feel satisfied, and if you lead by example, others will follow.

4. **Think positive.** Success will come more easily if you think positive, see yourself succeeding and see challenges, instead of obstacles.

5. **Don't be overwhelmed.** You don't have to save the world single-handed – focus on the areas you can influence. It *is* okay to start small – small changes *can* lead to quantum leaps.

6. **Be determined and tenacious.** The road may be bumpy at times, so be ready to take setbacks in your stride. Keep at it and success *will* come.

7. **Question the system.** Companies and people become accustomed to systems but that doesn't mean they are the best way to do it. Question everything and challenge the status quo to find ways to do things better.

8. **Be creative in looking for solutions.** Don't be hampered by protocol or the same old way of doing things; when you hit a brick wall, think of creative ways to find a solution.

9. **Plan for a sustainable future.** Imagine what the future will be like 20, 50 or 100 years from now. Now work out what you need to do to make it the brightest future possible – for yourself, your business and your planet.

CHAPTER 3: MAKE THE BUSINESS CASE

Being sustainable can generate income. Being unsustainable costs money. The ability to present a strong business case will help you win over colleagues and management. First, decide what issues you want to address; then make the business case to make your idea a reality.

Making your workplace more sustainable

1. **Work out where to start.** Look around your workplace to assess what are the most significant impacts of your operations, and where they occur.

2. **Understand your impacts.** From the way you get to work to your treatment of suppliers, start with your day-to-day and work outwards.

3. **Take measurements – then act on them.** Measure your impacts so you can assess what they are, find ways to address them and track your progress.

Presenting the business case

1. **Keep pace with new market realities.** In a volatile marketplace, you must think strategically to survive. Consider what environmental or social pressures could disrupt your business. Use peer pressure to show how sustainability can help you keep up, and how understanding your social, environmental and economic impacts will help you make better business decisions.

2. **Show them the money.** Inaction on climate change will cost more than dealing with the aftereffects later. Investing in sustainability will make you a stronger, more efficient, more desirable company – the sums will speak for themselves.

3. **Gain competitive advantage.** From demonstrating leadership to developing new products and being a differentiator, sustainable business thinking brings competitive advantages.

4. **Minimise compliance risks.** If you keep pace or ahead on compliance, you won't be caught off guard and have to scramble to comply.

5. **Reduce business risk.** Being socially or environmentally responsible can cost money. Look closely to see where you might be exposed to potential issues. This will allow you to show that your initiative will cost less than damaging press or dented sales.

6. **Social conscience matters.** The moral case can be a powerful persuader so appeal to people's human side. Show them how negative relationships with stakeholders damage business, and how sustainability goals are aligned with their public, corporate agenda.

7. **Keep with your customer and keep up.** Consumer concern is driving a whole new marketplace of greener products, while

business customers are increasingly implementing green procurement policies. You can either keep with your customer or be left behind.

8. **Enhance your brand reputation.** As social concerns move up the public agenda, investors and customers want businesses to use their power to set the world on a better path. Negative exposure *does* damage sales.

9. **All stakeholders count.** All stakeholders, from customers, employees, suppliers, board members, investors and the local communities in which you operate, can have an effect on your business. Look after them and you'll strengthen your business on all levels.

10. **Attract, retain and motivate skilled employees.** Employees want to bring their values to the office, and it will motivate and inspire them if they can do so. You can use the evidence to prove it.

CHAPTER 4: GET YOUR COLLEAGUES ON SIDE

Use the six tricks to successful engagement to make people feel interested, involved and influential, and your initiative will be a success.

1. **Stop, look and listen.** Take stock of the existing situation to understand the culture of your workplace so you can decide on the best approach.

2. **Find allies.** Teaming up with others who share your views will give you inspiration and support, and the more people you have behind you, the more seriously your idea will be taken.

3. **Harness the power of peers.** Nothing beats the influence of peer pressure to make a powerful force for change. Creating peer-to-peer and support groups are effective ways to shift attitudes, create new behaviours and build momentum.

4. **Make it the norm.** Make people feel that unsustainable behaviour, like only printing on one side of a sheet of paper, is abnormal, and you will create change on a much larger scale.

5. **Give people the freedom to develop their own solutions.** Setting colleagues the task of solving challenges gives them ownership and means they'll buy in, while their expertise will help create better solutions.

6. **Set up green champions and teams.** Creating teams and champions gives people an outlet and a focus, and can help to coordinate company-wide efforts.

CHAPTER 5: HAVE TWO-WAY CONVERSATIONS

Finding engaging, interesting and eye-catching ways to communicate will help ensure your success. The key is to listen and understand your audience, and then make your messages real, relevant, fun and feel good.

1. **Remember, positive messages work.** Help people feel good about themselves, and they'll get involved – and love you for it.

2. **Understand where they are.** Get to know the person you want to reach and find out what makes them tick so you can present your case in a way that make sense to them.

3. **Information isn't enough.** Information is valuable, but on its own, it's not effective at motivating people to act. To make it effective, put it in context, give them the tools to act *and* emphasise the positive impact that their actions will have.

4. **Beware: people are not logical.** Humans rarely make the rational choice – people respond best to personal stories or the promise of feeling good.

5. **Make it fun and catch their attention.** Be creative and use your imagination to draw people in. Generate a buzz with events, games and competitions to get people enthused and engaged.

6. **Make it relevant and real.** Tailor the message to the function, role and mission that connects to the real business case. Choose the angle that matters to your colleagues and remember to use language they'll identify with.

7. **Use a variety of different messages.** People respond to different approaches so target your messages to different groups and use a wide range of mediums to deliver them.

8. **Keep up the momentum.** Feedback and show progress to stop people reverting back to their old habits. Praise and reward are particularly effective.

CHAPTER 6: WORK TOGETHER

Joining forces to work in partnership with others can cause a multiplier effect that will maximise your impact. There are five key areas of collaboration you should explore:

1. **Work with your colleagues.** Working as a team across the company helps prevent efforts being duplicated, while pooling efforts, collaborating across departments and working towards a shared goal produces better results.
2. **Co-create with your customers or clients.** Understand your customers' values and concerns and where they overlap with your brand's values. Invite customers to co-create solutions and they'll be happier and more loyal.
3. **Practice co-opetition with your competitors.** Working with competitors to find shared solutions can benefit both parties – such as improving industry standards or sharing knowledge, technology or, even, deliveries!
4. **Work with your supply chain.** Your supply chain can account for a large part of your impact, so work with suppliers as they'll be keen to keep you, their customer, happy.
5. **Engage with NGOs, nonprofits and social partners.** There is so much knowledge and expertise out there – and you can harness it to make better decisions, while earning kudos too.

CHAPTER 7: MAKE IT PART OF THE CULTURE

Integrating sustainability into your company's thinking and operations is the definition of success: it will mean a sustainable approach becomes second-nature to your company and colleagues. The twelve steps to taking sustainability up-the-spine are:

1. **Win over management (again and again!).** Getting management on your side is one of the quickest ways to change the

culture, and the tools outlined in this book should make converting them easy.

2. **Think strategically.** Working out how social and environmental impacts will effect you now and in the future, and then adapting your company strategy to suit, will ensure sustainability is at the heart of your company thinking.

3. **Make an action plan.** Setting out your plan, with targets, goals and assigning responsibilities, is one of the best ways to make sure pledges translate into *action*.

4. **Work together and engage the entire company.** This will stop the duplication of efforts and ensures integrated efforts and thinking.

5. **Make it personal and part of everyone's job.** Show people how sustainability relates to their job role, their targets and their day-to-day, and you'll make sustainability an everyday part of the process.

6. **Give people the skills.** Give people the knowledge and training they need to understand sustainability and how to apply it in the context of your business. This gives them the skills to design and implement truly effective solutions.

7. **Innovate and use your imagination.** Take a fresh look at what you're trying to achieve to see if there is a better way to achieve the same results while maximising your positive impacts.

8. **Tell people the plan.** Having a clear plan and being able to articulate it helps to raise the profile of your efforts, and gives people the information they need to embrace it.

9. **Create a culture of openness.** Celebrate successes and see failures as a valuable learning exercise because you won't find the solutions if you aren't able to make mistakes. Being open and honest will also ensure staff, the media and the wider community sees your efforts as genuine and authentic – not greenwash.

10. **Look to the future.** Imagine the future and work out the most effective and efficient way to ensure your company positively influences it while being ready to adapt to its challenges.

11. **Check it's working.** Evaluate your progress so that you know what's working and what's not; then you can fine-tune perform-ance and feedback to re-motivate staff.
12. **Accept it will be a journey.** Changing organisations and behaviour can be demanding, but taking on the challenge is immensely rewarding. Celebrate victories and don't let setbacks make you give up. You will get there in the end.

CLIMBING THE LADDER

These tools will help you to help your organisation stay strong in an uncertain tomorrow. As you *Climb the Green Ladder* and start bringing sustainability into your workplace, your company or organisation will come to appreciate the valuable and essential role you have played.

They will understand how your knowledge and understanding of the new rules of business have helped to bolster the brand and the bottom line and how your creativity has helped align day-to-day operations to eliminate inefficiencies and waste – both in terms of resources and people. They will notice how you have quantified corporate values in ways that they can use to publicly demonstrate their commitment. They will appre-ciate your influence in identifying opportunities, gaining competitive advantage, engaging and motivating staff, and attracting and keeping top talent.

Being marked out as an innovative thinker will lead to rewards. From promotion to personal fulfilment and recognition, thinking sustainably should protect your business today and into the future. It should also future-proof your career.

Your workplace is waiting for you to bring it on a new course. We wish you an inspiring and successful journey as you *Climb the Green Ladder*. We can't guarantee the length of the journey or predict the particular challenges you will face, but we can guarantee you this: you *can* make a difference. Together, we *can* conquer the challenges ahead. Taking the decision to *Climb the Green Ladder* will be an adventure, and it could be one of the most rewarding and fulfilling journeys of your life.

Let's hope we meet some day on the way up.

WHO CAN HELP

Below is a list of resources and organisations that may be able to help you with advice, information or sustainable services. The list is by no means exhaustive – it represents many of the resources and organisations we used during our research or who we have come across over the years.

Even if you aren't in the same country as many of these organisations, the majority of their websites have incredible resources. These resources can be accessed and applied in your own workplace, wherever you are in the world, and should help to get you started on your journey. For a more extensive list of resources, visit our website: **www.climbthegreenladder. com** for the latest, and do drop us a line if you know of a good resource or organisation that should be included!

Thanks,

Amy Fetzer and Shari Aaron

NGOS, ADVISORY GROUPS, THINKTANKS AND CONSULTANTS

Amnesty International
www.amnesty.org
+44 (0) 207 413 5500
A charity/nonprofit organisation dedicated to protecting human rights around the world. They conduct research and generate action to prevent and end abuses of human rights and to demand justice for those whose rights have been violated. Many resources are on their website, including facts, reports and news.

As You Sow
www.asyousow.org
+1 415 391 3212
An organisation that works to increase corporate accountability by engaging and challenging corporations through dialogue and shareholder advocacy, and who works to refine economic arguments to move corporations and financial markets towards environmentally and socially responsible practices. Their website provides information on toxic reduction, environmental education and environmental justice.

Beyond Grey Pinstripes
www.beyondgreypinstripes.org
+1 212 895 8000
An organisation that carries out research to construct a ranking of business schools and highlights innovative MBA programmes worldwide that integrate environmental and social issues into their curricula.

BRE Trust Companies
www.bre.co.uk
+44 (0) 1923 664 000
A consultancy organisation focused on building better communities and environments. They offer a range of services including energy audits, energy certification, auditor training and certification in codes for sustainable homes.

Business in the Community
www.bitc.org.uk
+44 (0) 207 566 8650
A membership organisation that mobilises business for good with a focus on the workplace, the marketplace, the environment and the community. They advertise related events and a number of their publications are available free online. See also CommunityMark.

Business Link
www.businesslink.gov.uk
0845 600 9 006 (UK only)

An organisation that provides information to businesses to help improve their performance and comply with regulations. They provide advice on business startup and sources of grants and support. Extensive resources online include a database of business and government contacts, publications from government departments and a selection of case studies. Phone support is available. They also provide guides on making business more sustainable.

Carbon Trust
www.carbontrust.co.uk
0800 085 2005 (UK only)
+44 (0) 207 170 7000
Highly respected organisation, set up by the UK Government in 2001, focused on helping reduce carbon emissions, saving money and developing commercial low-carbon technologies. They provide the business (and public sector) with expert advice, finance and accreditation. Their site offers a large amount of information as well as grant and loan opportunities.

Carbon Disclosure Project
www.cdproject.net
+44 (0) 207 970 5660
+1 212 378 2086
A nonprofit organisation that holds the largest database of corporate climate change information in the world. This organisation requests climate change information from 475 institutional investors, 35 purchasing organisations and UK government bodies and 3700 corporations to help organisations measure, manage and reduce emissions and climate change impacts.

Ceres
www.ceres.org
+1 617 247 0700
A US-based, national network of investors, environmental organisations and other public interest groups who work with companies and investors

to address sustainability challenges. They bring stakeholders together to encourage companies and capital markets to incorporate environmental and social challenges into their day-to-day decision making. They launched the Global Reporting Initiative (GRI).

Climate Counts
www.climatecounts.org
+1 603 216 3788
A US-based nonprofit organisation that provides rigorous tools and reliable information to help companies and consumers make informed decisions on climate change. They provide scorecards and an engaging, simple rating system on the environmental merits of companies across a range of industries.

Climb the Green Ladder
www.climbthegreenladder.com
+ 44 (0) 7747 11 4452
+1 914 879 5326
A consultancy with offices in the US and UK set up by the authors of *Climb the Green Ladder: Make Your Company and Career More Sustainable.* Climb the Green Ladder's work ensures that more companies and organisations can embrace sustainability on a business-wide scale. It provides the tools and motivation employees need to embed sustainability into company thinking. Services include motivational workshops, training, research reports, CSR literature, editorial support, communications, market research and branding. The website also has an online resource guide and blog.

CommunityMark
www.bitc.org.uk/community/communitymark
+44 (0) 207 566 8650
Developed by Business in the Community and open to companies in the UK of all sizes and sectors, this national mark is rigorous. It provides an independent assessment of how a business invests in and works with its local communities, including scrutiny by its employees and community partners.

Compassion in World Farming

www.ciwf.org.uk

+ 44 (0) 1483 521 950

A UK-based charity that campaigns on issues related to farming and animal welfare. The website contains a range of information and advice on the most environmentally and ethically sensitive food types and processes.

Ecology and Environment

www.ene.com

+1 716 684 8060

A global company with 1000 specialists with expertise in sustainability and energy efficiency, environmental planning and assessment, compliance support, construction monitoring, environmental oversight, air/noise monitoring and mitigation, hazardous waste investigation and emergency management and training. They have completed 45,000 projects in 83 countries.

Energy Saving Trust

www.energysavingtrust.org.uk

0800 512 012 (UK only)

+44 (0) 207 222 0101

An organisation that provides advice on how to reduce energy consumption through energy checks, travel arrangements, employee engagement and the use of energy-efficient appliances. The Trust offers advice to UK based organisations on relevant grants and loans; many of the services are free of charge.

Environmental Defense Fund

www.edf.org

+1 800 684 3322

A leading US-based, national nonprofit organisation that partners with business, governments and communities to work towards sustainable solutions. They link science, economics and law to create innovative, equitable and cost-effective solutions. They work with companies on partnerships that deliver environmental results, benefit businesses and change industries.

Envirowise
www.envirowise.gov.uk
0800 585794 (UK only)
Public company that provides UK businesses with practical free advice and support to improve resources and efficiency, and to reduce their environmental impacts. Their website provides extensive resources, tools, news and event information.

Environment Resource Management (ERM)
www.erm.com
+44 (0) 203 206 5200
+61 2 8584 8804
A company that assists businesses and public authorities in managing their environmental risks. They specialise in environmental, health and safety, and social consultancy and have offices in 40 countries. They provide technical and innovative solutions to help respond to the challenges of sustainable development.

Fair Trade Foundation
www.fairtrade.net
+ 44 (0) 207 405 5942
A charity/nonprofit organisation that includes 24 global organisations working towards improving the welfare of producers in the developing world through a certification programme. Fair Trade certification acts as a guarantee that producers are getting a fair deal on their goods. Many resources are available online including details of their Fair Trade certification programme.

Forestry Stewardship Council (FSC)
www.fsc.org
+44 (0) 1686 413916 (UK)
+1 612 353 4511 (US)

An organisation that aims to encourage the responsible management of forests through a certification programme. The website offers information on companies that hold certification and free online resources on FSC certification and forestry, including publications, presentations and facts.

Forum for the Future
www.forumforthefuture.org
+44 (0) 207 324 3630
A UK-based sustainable development organisation that offers practical, solutions-based advice to businesses and local authorities on how to improve sustainability performance. They publish a monthly environmental issues magazine called *Green Futures*, with several articles available for free online.

Friends of the Earth International
www.foei.org
+31 20 622 1369
A charity/nonprofit and international organisation that operates in 77 countries and is dedicated to protecting the environment and engendering higher environmental awareness. Grassroots oriented, they campaign on today's most urgent environmental and social issues and promote solutions that will help to create environmentally sustainable and socially just societies.

Futerra
www.futerra.co.uk
+44 (0) 207 549 4700
A communications agency focused on sustainability and corporate responsibility. Their areas of expertise include business ethics, social marketing, environment and climate change and behaviour change. Their website has many helpful reports and advice guides, including the *Guide to Greenwash* referenced in **Chapter 7** of *Climb the Green Ladder*.

Global Action Plan
www.globalactionplan.org.uk
+44 (0) 207 405 5633
An environmental organisation that works with businesses to make employee working practices more sustainable. Their services include energy performance certificates, environment champions toolkit, greening the supply chain and guidance on policy direction.

Global EcoLabelling Network (GEN)
www.globalecolabelling.net
+1 613 247 1900
A nonprofit association of third-party, environmental performance labelling organisations that aims to improve, promote and develop the 'ecolabelling' of products and services.

Global Organic Textile
www.global-standard.org
The organisation creates standards for certifying that textiles have been produced in an organic manner. Information includes sourcing organic cloth to meet the Global Organic Textile Standard.

Global Reporting Initiative (GRI)
www.globalreporting.org
+31 (0) 20 531 00 00
A large multistakeholder network of thousands of experts, in dozens of countries worldwide, who participate in GRI's working groups and governance bodies. The GRI is the most widely used sustainability reporting framework. The GRI provides principles and indicators that organisations use to measure and report on their economic, environmental and social performance. Extensive online information regarding the framework, events, news and resources.

Green Alliance
www.green-alliance.org.uk
+44 (0) 207 233 7433

A charity organisation that works with businesses, government, parliament and NGOs to integrate the environment into decision making and to stimulate research and new thinking. Their reports are available free online.

Greenpeace
www.greenpeace.org
+44 (0) 207 865 8100
+ 1 415 255 9221
An international nongovernment organisation (NGO) that campaigns on environmental issues and works to change attitudes and behaviour to protect and conserve the environment. Their website includes news as well as position and research papers.

Green Seal
www.greenseal.org
+1 202 872 6400
A US-based nonprofit organisation, Green Seal provides environmental certification standards to help manufacturers, retailers and consumers make responsible choices that positively impact business behaviour and improve quality of life.

Human Rights Watch
www.hrw.org
+1 212 290 4700
One of the world's leading independent organisations dedicated to defending and protecting human rights. They conduct rigorous, objective investigations and strategic, targeted advocacy that increases action against human rights abuses. Their publications are available on their website alongside a range of multimedia articles.

Institute for Sustainable Communication
www.sustainablecommunication.org
A US-based nonprofit organisation that works with public and private sector organisations to increase eco-efficient collaboration and communi-

cation work flows. They offer outreach and education, research and analysis, and a mentoring programme, to help organisations tackle sustainability issues that relate to the sustainability and carbon footprint of marketing campaigns and communication processes. Online resources include articles, reports, factoids, blogs on sustainability issues, event listings and a social network for youths.

Investor Environmental Health Network (IEHN)
www.iehn.org/home.php
+1 703 970 4790

A collaborative partnership of investment managers advised by non-governmental organisations that serve as an information source for companies. Through dialogue and shareholder resolutions, they encourage companies to adopt policies that reduce or eliminate toxic chemicals in their products. Online resources include information on government policies, case studies and podcasts.

Live Earth
www.liveearth.org
+1 310 550 3888

Founded by former US Vice President, Al Gore, Live Earth communicates environmental issues through live events and media and was built upon the belief that entertainment has the power to transcend social and cultural barriers to move the world community to action. Online resources include a range of articles on environmental issues and guidelines for green events.

Marine Stewardship Council (MSC)
www.msc.org
+ 44 (0) 207 811 3300
+ 1 206 691 0188

An international nonprofit organisation that focuses on marine issues and acts as a certifying body to encourage sustainable fishing practices. MSC also works with food suppliers to help gain accreditation or to ensure a sustainable seafood supply.

National Industrial Symbiosis Programme
www.nisp.org.uk
+44 (0)845 094 9501
NISP is a business opportunity programme that helps businesses to achieve their triple bottom line of social, economic and environmental objectives. NISP brings companies of all sizes together so they can work to create commercial opportunities through the exchange of resources, including materials, energy and water and sharing assets, logistics and expertise.

Natural Logic
www.natlogic.com
+1 877 628 5644
A highly regarded company that provides sustainability consulting to companies and communities, with integrated, results-focused programmes that build profit and competitive advantage while reducing an organisation's environmental footprint, waste and risk.

OgilvyEarth
www.ogilvyearth.com
+ 44 (0) 207 345 3000
+ 1 415 782 4700
A global sustainability practice within the Ogilvy & Mather network that provides tools and thought-leadership to help companies capture the opportunity in the new sustainability economy. They offer highly experienced teams and access to a global panel of sustainability experts that span six continents.

Organic Trade Association
www.ota.com
+1 413 774 7511
A membership-based business association concerned with the organic industry in North America. The website contains an extensive directory of organic products, producers, supplies and services, as well as information on organic certification. News articles and information are available online.

Oxfam International
www.oxfam.org
+44 (0) 1865 473 727
+1 617 482 1211 (toll-free 1 800 77 OXFAM)
A confederate of 13 organisations that work towards improving people's lives and livelihoods. Their work is worldwide and their projects concentrate on development, disaster relief, campaigning, advocacy and policy research.

Rainforest Alliance
www.rainforest-alliance.org
+1 212 677 1900
A nonprofit organisation that works towards conserving biodiversity and supporting sustainable livelihoods. They act as a certifying body ensuring that products with Rainforest Alliance approval are produced sustainably.

Resource Recovery Forum
www.resourcesnotwaste.org
+ 44 (0) 1756 711 363
An international nonprofit network set up to research and promote the recovery of natural resources from waste. A range of materials are available online concerning their current projects as well as a list of links on waste-related topics from bio-waste to waste minimisation and tradeable permits.

Sierra Club
www.sierraclub.org
+1 415 977 5500
A US-based charity/nonprofit organisation that works throughout the US and Canada to protect the environment. Focus areas include green energy solutions, green transportation and methods to protect habitats and safeguard communities. They offer extensive online resources including news, reports, podcasts, radio links and information on student chapters.

Social Accountability International
www.sa-intl.org
+1 212 684 1414
A nonprofit organisation dedicated to the ethical treatment of workers worldwide. They offer a certification programme called SAI8000, an international standard for improving working conditions. The website contains resources on related research, a list of relevant articles and reading, and a list of useful links to websites focused on sustainable and responsible employment and investment.

Soil Association
www.soilassociation.org
+44 (0) 117 314 5001
A UK charity focused on promoting organic, sustainable farming and raising awareness of their implications for human health. The certification programme ensures that produce that carries the seal is produced to high organic standards. This organisation also certifies and labels timber and wood products from well-managed forests.

Strategic Sustainability Consulting
www.sustainabilityconsulting.com
+1 202 470 3248
A sustainability consultancy that works with smaller, under-resourced businesses and nonprofits to develop a sustainability plan, calculate their carbon footprint, identify ways to go carbon neutral, manage supply chains and develop a communications strategy. They offer green audits and also provide training programmes that certify green auditors.

SustainAbility
www.sustainability.com
+44 (0) 207 269 6900
A hybrid strategic consultancy and independent think-tank working globally to provide counsel and practical support on all aspects of corporate sustainability strategy and implementation. This includes risk management, innovation, reporting, accountability and engagement. The website

has in-depth information, reports and news on sustainability and business.

Tyndall Centre for Climate Change Research
www.tyndall.ac.uk
+44 (0) 1603 593900
A research group that brings together scientists, economists, engineers and social scientists that focus on climate change issues. A variety of published documents and working papers are available on their website.

UK Green Building Council
www.ukgbc.co.uk
+44 (0) 207 580 0623
An organisation that brings together different areas of industry and government to help tackle sustainability issues in the building sector. A variety of reports, articles and audio files are available on their website.

UN Global Compact
www.unglobalcompact.org
A United Nations voluntary initiative to encourage businesses worldwide to adopt sustainable and socially responsible policies, and to report on their implementation. This principles-based framework helps companies align to ten principles concerned with human rights, labour, the environment and anticorruption. Free online publications are available, including annual reviews, implementation guides and summit meeting reports.

US Green Building Council
www.usgbc.org
1800 795 1747 (US only)
+1 202 742 3792
A nonprofit organisation dedicated to sustainable build, design and practice. Having developed the Leadership in Energy and Environmental Design (LEED), they provide information on the steps towards achieving green buildings as well as a green building certification programme. Green building research is available on their website, alongside case studies and relevant government resources.

World Business Council for Sustainable Development
www.wbcsd.org
+41 (22) 839 3100
+1 202 420 7745
An association of approximately 200 companies focusing on business and sustainable development. Publications on a range of issues are available free online as well as annual reviews, case studies and a calendar of sustainability events.

WWF
www.wwf.org
+44 (0) 1483 426 444
+1 202 293 4800
A campaigning organisation focused on safeguarding the natural world by encouraging people to change how they live so that their activities are in harmony with nature. They work with local authorities, schools and businesses and provide a range of free publications on their site on a variety of environmental and social issues.

POLICY, REGULATION AND COMPLIANCE

Department for Environment, Food and Rural Affairs (DEFRA)
www.defra.gov.uk
+44 (0) 8459 33 55 77
A UK government department that is concerned with ensuring a healthy environment for UK residents, now and in the future. Information on legislation, health and safety, and policy issues is available on their website along with contact details for various departments. Free publications are also available online.

Environment Agency
www.environment-agency.gov.uk
+44 (0) 8708 506 506
A public body that works to protect and improve the environment in England and Wales. They provide advice and information on a wide range of environmental regulations.

European Commission
ec.europa.eu/environment/index_en.htm

The European Commission is the executive branch of the European Union. They are responsible for proposing legislation, implementing decisions, upholding the Union's treaties and the general day-to-day running of the Union, and are a source of news on the latest legislation on environmental policy in the EU member states. Many businesses are adopting standards for sustainability set by the Commission. Online resources include press releases and coverage of EU events, with links to policies implemented by the Commission.

(IPCC) Intergovernmental Panel on Climate Change
www.ipcc.ch

+41 22 730 8208/84

The IPCC independently assesses the latest scientific, technical and socio-economic literature produced worldwide relating to climate change and its observed and projected impacts and options for adaptation and mitigation. This website offers a source of impartial, independent information on the science of climate change.

Reach
ec.europa.eu/environment/chemicals/reach/reach_intro.htm

REACH is a European Community Regulation on chemicals and their safe use. The website details the associated legislation on Registration, Evaluation, Authorisation and Restriction of Chemical substances (REACH), which went into effect in June 2007.

Scottish Environmental Protection Agency
www.sepa.org.uk

0800 80 70 60 (UK only)

+44 1786 457 700

A national body responsible for environmental regulation in Scotland. They provide advice to business and industry on environmental responsibilities, and produce publications on a wide range of topics, from air, water and soil quality to climate change and corporate responsibility.

The Stern Review
www.occ.gov.uk/activities/stern.htm
The Stern Review on the Economics of Climate Change is a 700 page report released on 30 October 2006 by economist Lord Stern of Brentford for the British government. The report discusses the effect of climate change and global warming on the world economy. Although not the first economic report on climate change, it is significant as the largest and most widely known and discussed report of its kind.

(EPA) United States Environmental Protection Agency
www.epa.gov/climatechange
An agency of the US federal government whose mission is to protect human health and the environment. The EPA is charged to regulate chemicals and protect human health by safeguarding the natural environment (air, water and land) and is chiefly responsible for the environmental policy of the United States. Online resources include up-to-date information on laws and regulations, news on green living, energy efficiency, pollution, health and air quality.

SOCIALLY RESPONSIBLE FINANCE

Co-operative Bank
www.co-operativebank.co.uk
An ethical bank concerned with the social and environmental impacts of its investments and loans, but offering all the financial services of a normal financial institution.

Dow Jones Sustainability Index
www.sustainability-index.com
Launched in 1999, the Dow Jones Sustainability Indexes are the first global indexes tracking the financial performance of the leading sustainability-driven companies worldwide. Based on the cooperation of Dow Jones Indexes, STOXX Limited and SAM, they provide asset managers with reliable and objective benchmarks to manage sustainability portfolios.

EIRIS (Ethical Investment Research Service)
www.eiris.org
+44 (0) 207 840 5700
+1 (617) 428-0540
EIRIS is a global provider of independent research which provides information on the social, environmental and ethical performance of companies.

FTSE4Good
www.ftse.com/Indices/FTSE4Good_Index_Series/index.jsp
The FTSE4Good Index Series measures the performance of companies that meet globally recognised corporate responsibility standards and facilitates investment in those companies. It is useful as a basis for responsible investment, financial instruments and fund products.

Innovest Strategic Value Advisors
www.innovestgroup.com
+44 (0) 207 063 5600
+1 617 768 3000
+86 10 6629 0686
Innovest specialises in analysing companies' performance on environmental, social and strategic governance issues, with a particular focus on their impact on competitiveness, profitability and share price performance.

Principles for Responsible Investment
www.unpri.org
+44 (0) 207 749 5106
+1 347 551 02 73
The principles are a set of global best practices for responsible investment allowing users to incorporate environmental, social and governance criteria into investment decision making and ownership practices.

Social Funds
www.socialfunds.com
Personal finance site devoted to socially responsible investing. Features over 10,000 pages of information on SRI mutual funds, community investments, corporate research, shareowner actions and daily social investment news.

Triodos Bank
www.triodos.co.uk
+44 (0) 117 973 9339
Triodos Bank is one of Europe's leading ethical banks. Established in 1980 in the Netherlands, with a UK office following in 1995, Triodos Bank enables money to work for positive social, environmental and cultural change.

LOW CARBON TRAVEL

Cycle Scheme
www.cyclescheme.co.uk
+ 44 (0) 1225 448 933
Company that provides tax-free bikes in the UK for work through a variety of schemes under the UK Government's Cycle to Work initiative.

Green Globe
www.greenglobe.org
+61 7 3238 1900
Green Globe helps companies and communities monitor performance and identify areas that need attention. Members are continually challenged to improve their environmental performance over time, with the annual benchmark report a useful tool for pursuing best practice.

Green Hotel Initiative
www.ceres.org/hotel
+1 617 247 0700
Initiative launched by CERES in order to raise awareness about environmental and social concerns in the hospitality industry and to encourage

meeting planners and travel buyers to demand green services. Provides an easy-to-use list of criteria that helps a purchaser to assess a hotel's environmental commitment and performance.

International Rail
www.international-rail.com
+44 (0) 8700 84 14 10
Website contains information on rail timetables in Europe, Australia and North America. It also contains information on passes and special offers.

No Fly Travel
www.noflytravel.com
Website that provides information on ways to travel around America, Europe, Australia and Asia without using a plane. Train and cruise timetables are available on the website.

Rail Europe
www.raileurope.co.uk
+44 (0) 8448 484 046
Website offers information on rail travel throughout Europe. Tickets for rail travel can be booked on the website.

Sustrans
www.sustrans.org.uk
+44 (0) 845 113 00 65
Sustainable transport charity that communicates the benefits of more sustainable modes of transport through a variety of projects. The National Cycle network map illustrating walking and cycling routes in the UK is available on the website.

The Man in Seat Sixty One
www.seat61.com
Information on how to travel around the UK, Europe, Middle East, Africa, East Asia and Australia without flying. Information on routes, fares and timetables is displayed on the website.

Travelling Light

www.wwf.org.uk/travellinglight

WWF report discussing expected reduced levels of business flights and the role video conferencing can have in this process.

MEDIA – MAGAZINES, BLOGS, OPINION LEADERS AND OTHER GOOD READS

Ecologist

www.theecologist.org

+44 (0) 207 422 8100

The Ecologist is an environmental affairs magazine with a myriad of articles and features on subjects ranging from food and politics to farming and mass media. It is a useful reference tool for current affairs and innovative emerging research.

Ethical Consumer

www.ethicalconsumer.org

+44 (0) 161 226 2929

An organisation that researches the social and environmental records of companies. Their website provides information on a range of goods and services, and ranks companies according to their environmental and social performance.

George Monbiot

www.monbiot.com

An author, journalist and activist who writes on a wide range of environmental and social issues. His website contains a backlog of the many articles he has authored and a link to his blog.

Green Fiscal Commission Blog

www.gfcblog.wordpress.com

A resource for policy makers and all those with an interest in the green fiscal reform agenda. The blog carries news on environmental tax developments from around the world and provides expert commentary on them from the Commission. Issues covered include all aspects of green fiscal reform and the implications of environmental taxes.

GreenBiz
www.greenbiz.com
+1 510 550 8285
This website provides resources on environmental responsibility in business. Resources include electronic newsletters, briefing papers, podcasts and webcasts, many of which are available free of charge.

Green Futures
www.forumforthefuture.org/greenfutures
+44 (0) 207 324 3660
A magazine centred on green issues with articles, debates and interviews on the latest news in sustainability. The magazine is largely directed at decision makers and opinion formers in business, government, education and the campaigning world.

London School of Economics and Political Science (LSE) Lectures
www.lse.ac.uk/collections/LSEPublicLecturesAndEvents
This website offers information on lectures that are open to the public (booking often necessary) on a range of topics that include economic and environmental issues. Podcasts of previous lectures are available online.

Mark Lynas
www.marklynas.org
An author, journalist and activist who focuses on climate change, his website offers discussions on climate change, an extensive list of articles and a link to his blog.

Ode Magazine
www.odemagazine.com
Ode Magazine is both a print and online publication about positive news and about the people and ideas that are changing our world for the better – an interesting read and also an online community.

Stanford Social Innovation Review
www.ssireview.org
+1 888 488 6596
This magazine, based at Stanford's graduate school of business, concentrates on issues affecting society and discusses research findings on how to address social issues. The website offers numerous resources including articles, event information, blogs and podcasts.

Sustainable Life Media
www.sustainablelifemedia.com
+1 650 344 9693
This organisation produces sustainable business conferences and events and offers online resources that include news, case studies, events and resources for sustainability.

TED Talks
www.ted.com
+1 212 346 9333
Annual series of lectures from thought leaders on a variety of topics including technology, the environment, art, economics, education and science. Over 300 talks are available free online.

Triple Pundit
www.triplepundit.com
This website focuses on responsible business, with a range of articles on the creation and development of sustainable organisations.

World Changing
www.worldchanging.com
A media organisation working on a range of issues on how to build a sustainable future with topics such as business, community, politics and the planet discussed in detail in a range of articles, webcasts and features, many of which are available free online.

NETWORKING AND COMMUNITIES

There are so many networks out there and it can be immensely helpful to link up with others to share ideas, solutions and support. Listed below are a few of the networks we have found helpful. Please share your favourites via our website: **www.climbthegreenladder.com**.

CSR Asia
www.csr-asia.com
+852 3579 8079
Organisation that provides information, training, research and consultancy services on business practices in Asia. A range of their published reports are available free online.

CSR Blokes Yahoo Group
finance.groups.yahoo.com/group/csrblokes/
A group of (mainly) men concerned about Corporate Social Responsibility. Members can post up CSR-related queries for other members to answer.

CSR Chicks Yahoo Group
www.groups.yahoo.com/group/csr-chicks
A group of (mainly) women concerned about Corporate Social Responsibility. Members can post up CSR-related queries for other members to answer.

CSR Europe
www.csreurope.org
+32 2 541 1610
Business-oriented membership network. A toolbox is available online that provides resources on communications and transparency, sustainable production and consumption, business models, human capital and workplace integration.

Echoing Green
www.echoinggreen.org
+1 212 689 1165

A nonprofit organisation that provides funds for social entrepreneurs in the form of competitive fellowships. To be eligible for a fellowship you must have a powerful and compelling idea that is original and innovative.

JustMeans
www.justmeans.com
+44 (0) 207 953 0542
+1 917 326 8944
A media company and online network that specialises in sustainability communication and building a network of CSR and sustainability practitioners. The website displays job vacancies in related fields, event listings and editorials on a variety of CSR issues.

Net Impact
www.netimpact.org
+1 415 495 4230
A nonprofit organisation that acts as a consultancy to students, universities and organisations on how to improve the social, economic and environmental impacts of their activities. Website resources include guides on how to instigate change, newsletters and a variety of publications.

Skoll Foundation and Social Edge
www.socialedge.org
Social Edge is a programme by the Skoll Foundation; it is an online networking site for social entrepreneurs and people working in the social benefit sector providing access to a range of blogs, interviews and discussion forums. It has an advice feature that enables you to submit questions to their experts on issues relating to social entrepreneurship.

Wiser Earth
www.wiserearth.org
WiserEarth is an online community space connecting the people, nonprofits and businesses working towards a just and sustainable world. The

website includes an international directory of NGOs and socially responsible organisations and online groups and communities to share resources, tools and ideas.

Wise Women
www.wisewomen.me.uk
A global network of women interested in sustainability and environmental protection. The website provides information on events and a Yahoo group to share advice.

(YWSE) Young Women Social Entrepreneurs
www.ywse.org
+1 415 378 4417
An organisation that supports female social entrepreneurs with information on related events, funding opportunities, career counselling and advice on how to start up a business.

BOOKS
Listed below are a few books that we have found useful and informative. There are obviously many more. Please check our website, **www.climbthe-greenladder.com**, for a more complete listing and be sure to send us your favourites.

Blessed Unrest: How the Largest Movement in the World Came into Being and Why No One Saw It Coming by Paul Hawken

Capitalism As If the World Matters by Jonathan Porritt

Cradle to Cradle: Remaking the Way We Make Things by William A. McDonough

Creating a World Without Poverty by Muhammed Yunus

Green to Gold by Daniel Esty and Andrew Winston

Heat by George Monbiot

Hot, Flat and Crowded by Thomas Friedman

Necessary Revolution: How Individuals and Organisations Are Working Together to Create a Sustainable World by Peter M. Senge, Bryan Smith, Sara Schley, Joe Laur and Nina Kruschwitz

Strategies for a Green Economy by Joel Makower

The Triple Bottom Line by Andrew Savitz

The High Price of Materialism by Tim Kasser

Appendix 2
CLIMB THE GREEN LADDER RESEARCH

ABOUT THE RESEARCH

Between November 2008 and June 2009, the authors began a two-phase research programme to provide insights and case studies for *Climb the Green Ladder*. More than 500 individuals participated in this research. Participants were drawn mainly from the US and the UK, as well as from countries including Italy, Germany, Canada, China, Australia and India.

The research included both a qualitative and a quantitative phase:

Qualitative: 80+ participants from business, education, government and nonprofit organisations participated in in-depth interviews. Respondents were roughly split between the UK and the US. They came from a range of industries and job functions. They all shared some expertise in implementing sustainability strategies in the workplace. They had taken on the challenge of focusing their time and effort on fostering more sustainable approaches in business practices.

Quantitative: 430 respondents, from a range of industries, countries and job functions completed a seven-minute online survey. These respondents expressed varying levels of interest in sustainability at their workplaces – from moderate interest with no action to high interest and high action.

MORE ABOUT THE RESEARCH

The research covered a wide variety of voices and viewpoints. Opinions came from all levels of employees or founders/owners from many sectors including business, NGOs, government, media and academia. The respondent base ranged from junior-level employees to senior management, the self-employed and expert consultants.

The primary focus of the research was to understand what the impacts are of making a business/workplace more sustainable. It also strove to understand how employees feel about sustainability in the workplace, what makes them engage and how individuals can increase the level of sustainable practice in their workplaces.

Respondents shared their views on what makes sustainability initiatives successful, discussed challenges and shared success stories. They provided important insights into how to achieve positive outcomes. These included:

- motivating co-workers;
- delivering cost savings;
- developing stronger revenue streams;
- improving competitive advantage;
- reducing risk;
- fostering innovation;
- identifying opportunities;
- cultivating stronger employee and customer loyalty;
- elevating brand reputation.

This detailed research ensures readers of *Climb the Green Ladder* receive effective, proven advice, actionable tools and inspiration to take decisive, immediate action to bring sustainability to their workplace.

QUALITATIVE RESEARCH DETAILS

Interviews were conducted with over 80 sustainability experts, or those who had successfully implemented sustainability strategies in their workplace. These took the form of telephone, in-person or video interviews, lasting up to three hours. The people who participated include:

Camilla Flatt	Africapractice
Ian Barnes	Alliance Boots
Richard Ellis	Alliance Boots
Michael Passoff	As You Sow
Gwyn Jones	Association of Sustainability Professionals
Mark Parker	Aztec
Peggy Connolly	Boston Center for Corporate Citizenship
Dr Paul Toyne	Bovis Lend Lease
Maria Figueroa Kupcu	Brunswick Group
David Stangis	Campbell Soup Company
David Vincent	The Carbon Trust
Matthew Hawtin	Careers Development Services
Veena Ramani	Ceres
Erika Vandenbrande	City of Redmond
Wood Turner	Climate Counts
Alastair Fuad-Luke	Co-design Services for Sustainability Transition
J. B. Schramm	College Summit
Simon Graham	Commercial
Ryan Mickle	Companiesandme.com
Sara Ellis Conant	Deloitte Consulting, LLP
Tom Fogden	Deloitte Consulting, LLP
Coral Rose	Eco Innovations
Julie Chang	Ecology and Environment
Tony Gale	Ecology and Environment
Amy Hall	Eileen Fisher
Sophie Hanim	Energy Saving Trust
Sara Parkin, OBE	Forum for the Future
Kathee Rebernak	Framework:CR
Ed Gillespie	Futerra
Jeff Melnyk	Futerra
Jo Confino	*The Guardian*
Scott Davidson	Global Action Plan
Trewin Restorick	Global Action Plan
Frank Dixon	Global Systems Change

Roger East	Green Futures Magazine
Michael Dupee	Green Mountain Coffee Roasters
Sandy Yusen	Green Mountain Coffee Roasters
Helen Trevorrow	Green Row PR
Joel Makower	GreenBiz.com
Sarah Daly	Heath Avery Architects
Randy Boeller	Hewlett Packard (HP)
Ken Bosley	Hewlett Packard (HP)
Debbie Ledbetter	Hewlett Packard (HP)
Bonnie Nixon	Hewlett Packard (HP)
Charlie Browne	IKEA
Don Carli	Institute for Sustainable Communication
Rich Liroff	Investor Environmental Health Network (IEHN)
Martin Smith	JustMeans
Martin Horwood, MP	Liberal Democrats
Dr Victoria Hands	London School of Economics and Political Science
Birgitte Rasine	Lucita
Richard Gillies	Marks & Spencer
Lynn Frosch	Microsoft
Will Rowberry	Monitor
Gil Friend	Natural Logic
Natalia Oberti Noguera	New York Social Women Entrepreneurs
Melissa Perlman	Office Depot
Yalmaz Siddiqui	Office Depot
Freya Williams	Ogilvy & Mather, OgilvyEarth
Mike Jones	Open Minds Consulting
Chantal Cooke	Passion for the Planet Radio
Kristen Thomas	The Phelps Group
Abby Ray	Rainforest Alliance
Tensie Whelan	Rainforest Alliance
Mark Gough	Reed Elsevier
Neil Turner	RES
Guy Watson	Riverford Organic Vegetables

Dr Martin Blake	Royal Mail
Vicky Forster	Sherborne School for Girls
Bruce Lowry	Skoll Foundation
Jennifer Schramm	Society of Human Resource Management
Holly Fowler	Sodexo
Thomas Jelley	Sodexo
Shelley Rowley	Speechly Bircham, LLP
Jennifer Woofter	Strategic Sustainability Consulting
KoAnn Skrzyniarz	Sustainable Life Media
Sofia Bustamante	Turn up the Courage
Lisa Landone	United States Postal Service
Ian Christie	University of Surrey
Tim Jackson	University of Surrey
Yacob Mulugetta	University of Surrey
Alex Salzman	VizCapital
Perry Abbenante	Whole Foods
Libba Letton	Whole Foods
Anthony Kleanthous	WWF

Question areas included:

- Is sustainability important to business?
- What are the benefits and drawbacks of making an organisation more sustainable?
- What are the personal benefits and drawbacks of making your workplace more sustainable?
- What are the most effective ways for an employee to make their workplace more sustainable?
- What strategies have the most effective outcomes?
- What is the key to making sustainability initiatives a success?
- What is a 'sustainability mindset' and how do you help others to adopt one?
- What are the most effective ways to present a strong business case for sustainability to management and colleagues?

- How does incorporating the social and environmental impacts into business thinking impact brand and the bottom line?
- What are the most effective ways to get others interested and engaged in sustainability?
- How do you facilitate behaviour change?
- What are the most effective ways to communicate sustainability messages to co-workers?
- What are the most effective ways to convey environmental messages?
- How do you embed sustainability into organisational culture?

QUANTITATIVE RESEARCH DETAILS
2009 Sustainability in the Workplace Study

From January 2009 through April 2009, a quantitative survey was conducted online, where 430 individuals completed the survey.

As with the qualitative interviews, respondents represented a wide spectrum of industries, sectors and job roles. Participants were drawn mainly from the US and the UK, as well as from countries including Italy, Germany, Canada, China, Australia and India. Respondent identities remain confidential, unless the respondent granted authority to use their information in a public forum.

The survey was publicised through an extensive database of employees and employers around the world, as well as through postings on relevant social network groups. The survey was also spread virally, through email newsgroups, group postings, email forwarding, Twitter and blogs.

The social networks on which the survey was published included JustMeans, CSRChicks (Yahoo Group), CSRwire, Net Impact as well as subgroups on Twitter, Facebook and LinkedIn.

The survey was self-selecting and, based in part on the forums it was posted to, respondents are assumed to have had some interest in sustainability. Of those who completed the survey, 32% had sustainability in their job title/role. The majority indicated they worked in other job functions but that they were working to help their workplaces become more sustainable or were trying to work out how to get started.

Questions included:

- What is your personal level of commitment to 'being sustainable'?
- Do your job role and responsibilities include sustainability?
- What tactics, actions or communications make you more likely to participate in sustainability strategies/programmes?
- In your opinion, has the financial crisis of 2008–2009 had an impact on sustainability activities or programmes at your workplace?
- How interested and invested do you feel management is in helping you obtain the knowledge and tools you need to address sustainability?
- How does it feel to bring up sustainability issues at your workplace?
- If you have done something to help move sustainability forward at your workplace, has it impacted your career?
- How prepared do you feel to help your workplace address social and environmental impacts?

A few key findings are summarised below:

- Of those who took the survey, 80% say they are willing to take actions that support sustainability at work:
  - 66% of respondents chose 'I try to be as sustainable as possible both at home and at work';
  - 14% chose 'I do what I can, when it's easy'.
- Respondents were not afraid to discuss sustainability in their workplace:
  - 89% said they bring up sustainability when it feels relevant or that they are working with others to discuss solutions or ideas.
- We asked respondents what was more likely to motivate them to participate in sustainability programmes at their workplaces. The most popular options included:
  - When it makes me feel my actions can make a difference (71%).

- ○ When it is part of the organisation's culture so it's an every-day part of the process (71%).
- ○ When I am shown how it will reduce waste (69%).
- ○ When I am shown how it will reduce emissions (62%).

The least motivating were:

- ○ When I am shown how it will help my employer meet its targets or goals (33%).
- ○ When I hear about my employer's efforts in the press or news (31%).
- ○ When I am rewarded for sustainable behaviour (28%).
- ● Respondents rank the following actions as important to the success of sustainability initiatives:
  - ○ My employer has coordinated efforts across the business (87%).
  - ○ My employer openly discusses values and concerns of staff and management (86%).
  - ○ My employer takes time to explain the issues and solutions (86%).
  - ○ My employer takes measurements to show improvements and results (82%).

Findings from the survey and interviews have been used throughout *Climb the Green Ladder*. A more detailed research report with results from the quantitative study can be found by visiting: **www.climbthegreenladder.com**.

NOTES

CHAPTER I   WHY WE NEED THAT GREEN LADDER

1 Shari Aaron and Amy Fetzer, '2008 Corporate Employee Sustainability Study', Fresh Marketing, May 2008, Climb the Green Ladder, http://www.justmeans.com/showreportdetails?reportid=153&iscompany=1, accessed June 2009.

2 FMSP Policy Brief 1 MRAG and DFID, 'Fisheries and Poverty Reduction', Marine Resources Assessment Group and UK Department for International Development, http://www.mrag.info/Documents/PolicyBrief1_Poverty_ Reduction.pdf, accessed 30 June 2009.

3 Intergovernmental Panel on Climate Change (IPCC), 'Climate Change 2007: Synthesis Report', IPCC (2007), http://www.ipcc.ch/pdf/assessment-report/ ar4/syr/ar4_syr.pdf, accessed 29 June 2009.

4 Intergovernmental Panel on Climate Change (IPCC), 'Climate Change 2007: Synthesis Report', IPCC (2007), http://www.ipcc.ch/pdf/assessment-report/ ar4/syr/ar4_syr.pdf, accessed 29 June 2009.

5 United Nations Development Programme (UNDP) Human Development, 'Consumption for Human Development Report', UNDP (1998), http://hdr. undp.org/en/media/hdr_1998_en_overview.pdf, accessed 30 June 2009.

6 Duncan McLaren, Simon Bullock and Nusrat Yousuf, *Tomorrow's World: Britain's Share in a Sustainable Future, Friends of the Earth*, 1997 (UK: Earthscan Ltd A), cited in Adisa Azapagic, Alan Emsley and Ian Hamerton, *Polymers: The Environment and Sustainable Development*, 2003 (New York: John Wiley and Sons. Inc.), p. 3.

7 United Nations Development Programme (UNDP) Human Development, 'International Cooperation at a Crossroads: Air, Trade and Security in an Unequal World Report', UNDP (2005), http://hdr.undp.org/en/media/ HDR05_complete.pdf, p. 36, accessed July 2009.

8 United National Development Programme (UNDP) Human Development, 'Beyond Scarcity: Power, Poverty and the Global Water Crises Report', UNDP (2006), http://hdr.undp.org/en/media/Human_development_indicators.pdf, p. 269, accessed July 2009.

9 United National Development Programme (UNDP) Human Development, 'Beyond Scarcity: Power, Poverty and the Global Water Crises Report', UNDP (2006), http://hdr.undp.org/en/media/Human_development_indicators.pdf, accessed July 2009.

10 United Nations Development Programme (UNDP) Human Development, 'International Cooperation at a Crossroads: Air, Trade and Security in an Unequal World Report', UNDP (2005), http://hdr.undp.org/en/media/HDR05_complete.pdf, p. 37, accessed July 2009.

11 United Nations Development Programme (UNDP) Human Development, 'International Cooperation at a Crossroads: Air, Trade and Security in an Unequal World Report', UNDP (2005), http://hdr.undp.org/en/media/HDR05_complete.pdf, p. 24, accessed July 2009.

12 'Green is the new gold', Aberdeen Group Press Release, March 6, 2008. http://www.reuters.com/article/pressrelease/idUS168003+06-Mar-2008+RNS20080306, accessed June 2009.

13 Debby Beilak, Shelia M.J. Bonini and Jeremy Oppenheim, 'CEOs on Strategy and Social Issues', *The McKinsey Quarterly*, October 2007.

14 Shari Aaron and Amy Fetzer, '2008 Corporate Employee Sustainability Study', Fresh Marketing, May 2008, Climb the Green Ladder, http://www.justmeans.com/showreportdetails?reportid=153&iscompany=1, accessed June 2009.

15 Sian Harrington, 'CSR Research: Make a Difference', *HR Magazine*, 4 January 2008, http://www.humanresourcesmagazine.com/news/774913, accessed June 2009.

CHAPTER 2 GET THE MINDSET

1 American psychologist, philosopher and doctor, 1842–1910.

2 Transcript of President Barack Obama's Inauguration Speech, *The New York Times*, 20 January 2009, http://www.nytimes.com/2009/01/20/us/politics/20text-obama.html, accessed March 2009.

3 Paul Hawken, *Blessed Unrest: How the Largest Movement in the World Came into Being and Why No One Saw It Coming*, 2007 (New York: Penguin Group).

4 Paul Hawken, 'Healing or Stealing?', Speech given 3 May 2009, at University of Portland, Commencement Address, http://www.paulhawken.com/paulhawken_frameset.html, accessed 2 June 2009.

5 Norman Vincent Peale, *Power of Positive Thinking*, 1952 (New York: Fireside), p. 11.

6 Examples can be found in Tim Kasser, *The High Price of Materialism*, 2002 (Cambridge, Massachusetts: MIT Press) and Tim Jackson, 'Prosperity Without Growth – The Transition to a Sustainable Economy', SDC Report (March 2009), Sustainable Development Commission, http://www.sd-commission.org.uk/publications.php?id=914, accessed July 2009.

CHAPTER 3   MAKE THE BUSINESS CASE

1 Rainforest Alliance, 'Greening for Growth, Why Investing in Sustainability Still Makes Good Business Sense', Rainforest Alliance website, http://www.rainforest-alliance.org/about.cfm?id=greening4growth, accessed June 2009.

2 Jonathan Watts, 'South Korea Lights the Way on Carbon Emissions with Its £23bn Green Deal', *The Guardian*, 21 April 2009, http://www.guardian.co.uk/environment/2009/apr/21/south-korea-enviroment-carbon-emissions, accessed 10 June 2009.

3 National Environmental Education Foundation, 'The Engaged Organisation Report' (March 2009), National Environmental Education Foundation, http://www.neefusa.org/business/es_2009.htm, accessed 8 June 2009.

4 Carbon Trust, http://www.carbontrust.co.uk.

5 Climate Counts, climatecounts.org and their new Industry Innovators Program, http://www.climatecounts.org/industry_innovators.php.

6 Carbon Disclosure Project, http://www.cdproject.net/index.asp.

7 The Global Reporting Initiative, http://www.globalreporting.org/Home.

8 KPI for environmental performance, http://www.businesslink.gov.uk/bdotg/action/detail?type=RESOURCES&itemId=1079404154; for more about reporting and the Balanced Scorecard: http://www.greenbiz.com/feature/2005/10/24/the-balanced-scorecard-and-corporate-social-responsibility-aligning-values-profit.

9 CommunityMark, developed by Business in the Community (BITC), http://www.bitc.org.uk/community/communitymark/about_the_communitymark/about_the.html.

10 McKinsey, 'How Companies Think About Climate Change: A McKinsey Global Survey', *The McKinsey Quarterly*, February 2008, http://www.

mckinseyquarterly.com/Energy_Resources_Materials/Environment/ How_companies_think_about_climate_change_A_McKinsey_Global_ Survey_2099, accessed 10 June 2009.

11 Sir Nicholas Stern, 'The Stern Report', HM Treasury (30 October 2006), http://www.hm-treasury.gov.uk/sternreview_index.htm, accessed June 2009.

12 Carbon Trust, 'Climate Change – A Business Revolution? How Tackling Climate Change Could Create or Destroy Company Value' (2008), http:// www.carbontrust.com/publications/CTC740_business_rev%20v5.pdf, accessed June 2009.

13 Lindsey Morse, 'Sustainability, Is It the Economy's Only Hope?', g-Think paper, Issue 19 (March 2009), Green Team, http://www.g-think.com/ keepout/articles/175/article_175.pdf, accessed 8 June 2009.

14 KPMG, 'Climate Changes Your Business. KPMG's Review of the Business Risks and Economic Impacts at Sector Level', KPMG (2008), http://www. kpmg.com.cn/redirect.asp?id=8776, accessed 8 June 2009.

15 Bill Baue, 'Got Water? Report Recommends Solutions for Businesses to Address Water Scarcity', *Institutional Investor*, 24 August 2004, http://www.institutionalshareowner.com/article.mpl?sfArticleId=1503, accessed July 2009.

16 *The Corporation*, directed by Mark Archbar and Jennifer Abbott, 2004 (Big Picture Media Corporation in association with TV Ontario, Vision TV, Knowledge Network, Saskatchewan Communications Network and ACCESS: The Education Station), http://www.thecorporation.com.

17 Interface, 'Toward a More Sustainable Way of Business', Interface Company website, http://www.interfaceglobal.com/Sustainability.aspx, accessed 10 June 2009.

18 Havas, Sustainable Futures 09, Havas Media (2009), http://www.havasmedia. com/#/en/SustainableFutures/Introduction/, accessed June 2009.

19 Carbon Trust, 'Green Expectations: Consumers Still Want to Buy Green, but Expect Evidence of Action', Carbon Trust press release, 13 March 2009, on Carbon Trust website, http://www.carbontrust.co.uk/News/presscentre/ green-expectations.htm, accessed 8 June 2009.

20 Rainforest Alliance, 'Greening for Growth, Why Investing in Sustainability Still Makes Good Business Sense', Rainforest Alliance website, http://www.rainforest-alliance.org/about.cfm?id=greening4growth, accessed June 2009.

21 Dov Seidman, *How: Why How We Do Anything Means Everything...In Business (and in Life)*, 2007 (New York: John Wiley & Sons, Inc.).

22 Joel Makower, 'Taking Care of Business', *Greenbiz.com*, 8 June 2009, http://www.greenbiz.com/enewsletter, accessed 20 June 2009.

23 Rainforest Alliance, 'Greening for Growth, Why Investing in Sustainability Still Makes Good Business Sense', Rainforest Alliance website, http://www.rainforest-alliance.org/about.cfm?id=greening4growth, accessed June 2009.

24 Society of Human Resource Managers, 'Executive Roundtable Symposium on Sustainability and Human Resource Management Strategy', 29 May 2008, Society of Human Resource Managers, http://www.shrm.org/Research/.../08-0632SustainSymp_FNL_lorez.pdf, accessed June 2009.

25 Hill & Knowlton, 'Reputation and the War for Talent', Hill & Knowlton Corporate Reputation Watch Study (2008), http://www2.hillandknowlton.com/crw/, accessed June 2009.

26 'MonsterTRAK Joins Forces with ecoAmerica to Launch GreenCareers by MonsterTRAK', MonsterTRAK press release, 3 October 2007, on Enhanced Online News website, http://eon.businesswire.com/portal/site/eon/permalink/?ndmViewId=news_view&newsId=20071003105337&newsLang=en, accessed July 2009.

27 GlobeScan 2009 study.

28 'U.S. Workers Favor Green Companies', National Geographic press release, 19 February 2008, on Reuters website, http://www.reuters.com/article/pressRelease/idUS115891+19-Feb-2008+BW20080219, accessed June 2009.

CHAPTER 4   GET YOUR COLLEAGUES ON SIDE

1 Shari Aaron and Amy Fetzer, '2009 Sustainability in the Workplace Study', *Climb the Green Ladder*, August 2009, http//www.climbthegreenladder.com/research, accessed September 2009.

2 Tandberg/Ipsos MORI, 'Corporate Environmental Behaviour and the Impact on Brand Values', Tandberg/Ipsos MORI (October 2007), www.ivci.com/.../corporate-environmental-behaviour-and-the-impact-on-brand-values.pdf, accessed June 2009.

3 J. Nolan, P. W. Schultz, R. B. Cialdini, N. J. Goldstein and V. Griskevicius, 'Normative Social Influence Is Underdetected', *Personality and Social Psychology Bulletin* (2008), **34**: 913–923.

4 Some good examples include N. A. Christakis and J. A. Fowler, 'The Collective Dynamics of Smoking in a Large Social Network', *The New England Journal of Medicine* (2008), **358**(21): 2249–2258.

5 H. Tajfel and J. C. Turner, in *An Integrative Theory of Intergroup Conflict in the Social Psychology of Intergroup Relations*, eds W. G. Austin and S. Worchel, 1979 (Monterey, California: Brooks/Cole).

6 Morton Deutsch and H. B. Gerard, 'A Study of Normative and Informational Social Influences upon Individual Judgment', *Journal of Abnormal and Social Psychology* (1955), **51**: 629–636.

7 Solomon Asch, 'Effects of Group Pressure upon the Modification and Distortion of Judgments', in *Groups, Leadership, and Men*, ed. H. Guetzkow, 1951 (Pittsburgh, Pennsylvania: Carnegie Press), pp. 177–190.

8 V. Griskevicius, R. B. Cialdini and N. J. Goldstein, 'An Underestimated and Underemployed Lever for Managing Climate Change', *International Journal of Sustainability Communication* (2008), **3**: 5–13.

9 For more information on LEED certification, see US Green Building Council in **Appendix 1**: **Who can help** or go to http://www.usgbc.org/DisplayPage. aspx?CMSPageID=147.

CHAPTER 5 HAVE TWO-WAY CONVERSATIONS

1 For a good discussion of this phenomenon, see Professor Tim Jackson, 'Motivating Sustainable Consumption, A Review of Evidence on Consumer Behaviour and Behavioural Change. A Report to the Sustainable Development Research Network' (2004) (London: Policy Studies Institute), University of Surrey, http://portal.surrey.ac.uk/portal/page?_pageid= 822,512810&_dad=portal&_schema=PORTAL, accessed June 2009.

2 Muhammed Yunus, *Creating a World Without Poverty: Social Business and the Future of Capitalism*, 2007 (USA: Perseus Books), p. 60.

3 Edward T. D. Chambers and Michael A. Cowan, *Roots for Radicals: Organizing for Power, Action and Justice*, 2003 (London, Continuum).

4 Roger Brown, *Social Psychology*, 2nd edn, 1986 (New York: Free Press).

5 Ipsos Global @dvisors study conducted online November 2008 among 23,000 consumers in 23 countries around the world.

6 Doug McKenzie-Mohr, 'Promoting Sustainable Behaviour: An Introduction to Community Based Social Marketing', *Journal of Social Issues*, Fall 2000.

7 Professor Tim Jackson, 'Motivating Sustainable Consumption, A Review of Evidence on Consumer Behaviour and Behavioural Change. A Report to the Sustainable Development Research Network' (2004) (London: Policy Studies Institute), University of Surrey, p. 101.

8 Michelle Shipworth, *Motivating Home Energy Action – A Handbook of What Works* (2000) (Australian Greenhouse Office), http://www.environment.gov.au/settlements/publications/government/pubs/water-efficiency-guide.pdf, accessed June 2009.

9 See also Leon Festinger, *A Theory of Cognitive Dissonance*, 1957 (Stanford, California: Stanford University Press).

10 Futerra, 'The Rules of the Game: Principles of Climate Change Communications', Futerra (2000), http://www.defra.gov.uk/environment/climatechange/uk/individual/pdf/ccc-rulesofthegame.pdf, p. 18, accessed June 2009.

11 For example, D. Halpern and C. Bates, 'Personal Responsibility and Changing Behaviour: The State of Knowledge and Its Implications for Public Policy' (February 2004) (London: Prime Minister's Strategy Unit).

12 Richard Gross, *Psychology: The Science of Mind and Behaviour*, 2nd edn, 1995 (London: Hodder and Stoughton).

13 Susan Fiske and Shelley Taylor, *Social Cognition*, 1984 (Wokingham: Addison-Wesley).

14 Richard Gross, *Psychology: The Science of Mind and Behaviour*, 2nd edn, 1995 (London: Hodder and Stoughton).

15 Futerra, 'Words That Sell: How the Public Talks about Sustainability', Futerra (2007), http://www.futerra.co.uk/downloads/Words-That-Sell.pdf, accessed June 2009.

16 Futerra, 'The Rules of the Game: Principles of Climate Change Communications', Futerra (2000), http://www.defra.gov.uk/environment/climatechange/uk/individual/pdf/ccc-rulesofthegame.pdf, p. 18, accessed June 2009.

17 'Light's Labour's Lost – Policies for Energy-Efficient Lighting', International Energy Agency press release, 29 June 2006, on IEA website, http://www.iea.org/Textbase/press/pressdetail.asp?PRESS_REL_ID=182, accessed June 2009.

18 'Change a Light, Change the World', US Department of Energy press release, on DOE website, http://www.energystar.gov/index.cfm?fuseaction=globalwarming.showPledgeHome, accessed June 2009.

19 Malcolm Gladwell, *The Tipping Point: How Little Things Can Make a Big Difference*, 2000 (New York, Little Brown and Company).

20 For more on the power of role models, see Professor Tim Jackson, 'Motivating Sustainable Consumption, A Review of Evidence on Consumer Behaviour and Behavioural Change. A Report to the Sustainable Development Research Network' (2004) (London: Policy Studies Institute), University of Surrey.

21 For more on the power of role models, see Professor Tim Jackson, 'Motivating Sustainable Consumption, a Review of Evidence on Consumer Behaviour and Behavioural Change. A Report to the Sustainable Development Research Network' (2004) (London: Policy Studies Institute), University of Surrey.

22 J. Nemes, 'Leading from the Middle, The Power of the Green Champions', *GreenBiz*, 13 October 2008, www.greenbiz.com/feature/2008/10/13/leading-from-middle-the-power-green-champions, accessed June 2009.

23 Tim Kasser, *The High Price of Materialism*, 2003 (London: MIT Press).

CHAPTER 6   WORK TOGETHER

1 Justmeans.com, 'Green Mountain and JustMeans Announce New Green House Gas (GHG) Reduction Contest', 16 February 2009, http://www.justmeans.com/challenge/climate, accessed 17 February 2009.

2 Shari Aaron and Amy Fetzer, '2009 Corporate Employee Sustainability Study', August 2009, Climb the Green Ladder, http//www.climbthegreenladder.com/research, accessed September 2009.

3 IBM, 'Value of Relationships in a Networked World – Business Issues', IBM Company website, http://www-935.ibm.com/services/uk/index.wss/multipage/igs/ibvstudy/a1008082?cntxt=a1006870, accessed June 2009.

4 Waste Electrical and Electronic Equipment Directive (WEEE), European Union Directive, http://ec.europa.eu/environment/waste/weee/index_en.htm.

5 Erica L. Plambeck and Lyn Denend, 'The Greening of Wal-Mart', *Stanford Social Innovation Review*, Spring 2008, http://www.ssireview.org/articles/entry/the_greening_of_wal_mart/, accessed April 2009.

6 Erica L. Plambeck and Lyn Denend, 'The Greening of Wal-Mart', *Stanford Social Innovation Review*, Spring 2008, http://www.ssireview.org/articles/entry/the_greening_of_wal_mart/, accessed April 2009.

7 'Nike Sets Business Targets to Achieve Ambitious Corporate Responsibility Goals', CSRwire press release, 31 May 2007, http://www.csrwire.com/press/press_release/24976-Nike-Sets-Business-Targets-To-Achieve-Ambitious-Corporate-Responsibility-Goals, accessed March 2009.

8 Daniel Esty and Andrew Winston, *Green to Gold: How Smart Companies Use Environmental Strategy to Innovate, Create Value, and Build Competitive Advantage*, 2006 (New Haven, Connecticut: Yale University Press), p. 1.

CHAPTER 7   MAKE IT PART OF THE CULTURE

1 2008 Executive Roundtable Symposium on *Sustainability and Human Resource Management Strategy*, Executive Summary of the Conference, Alexandra, Virginia, 29 May 2008, p. 4, available on SHRM website, http://www.shrm.org/Research/Articles/Articles/Documents/08-0632SustainSymp_FNL_lorez.pdf, accessed May 2009.

2 Shari Aaron and Amy Fetzer, '2009 Sustainability in the Workplace Study', August 2009, Climb the Green Ladder, http//www.climbthegreenladder.com/research, accessed September 2009.

3 Shari Aaron and Amy Fetzer, '2009 Sustainability in the Workplace Study', August 2009, Climb the Green Ladder, http//www.climbthegreenladder.com/research, accessed September 2009.

4 Shari Aaron and Amy Fetzer, '2009 Sustainability in the Workplace Study', August 2009, Climb the Green Ladder, http//www.climbthegreenladder.com/research, accessed September 2009.

5 Forum for the Future, 'Climate Futures Report', released by Forum for the Future, in collaboration with researchers from HP, http://www.forumforthefuture.org/node/9177, accessed 7 June 2009.

6 Shari Aaron and Amy Fetzer, '2009 Sustainability in the Workplace Study', August 2009, Climb the Green Ladder, http//www.climbthegreenladder.com/research, accessed September 2009.

CHAPTER 8   CONCLUSION: CLIMB THAT LADDER

1 James Wolfensohn, 9th President of the World Bank, http://www.leadersindubai.com/speakers1/james_wolfensohn.html.

INDEX

Compiled by INDEXING SPECIALISTS (UK) Ltd
Indexing House, 306A Portland Road
Hove, East Sussex BN3 5LP, UK
Tel: +44(0)1273 416777
email: indexers@indexing.co.uk
Website: www.indexing.co.uk